"*Tom Chesshyre's new book trundles gently through Spain much like the trains he so loves. By turns humorous and sharply insightful, he affectionately paints a vivid portrait of a deeply divided and contrasting country, bringing to life its characters and landscapes like few other travel writers can. Always curious, witty and intelligent, his writing style and subject matter are deeply rewarding – even cathartic. This is armchair travel at its satisfying best.*"

Francisca Kellett, travel writer

PRAISE FOR *SLOW TRAINS TO VENICE*

"*He casually, and beautifully, bats away the earnestness of travel literature.*"
Caroline Eden, *The Times Literary Supplement*

"*There is something nostalgic about the clatter of wheels and sleeper trains… by the end, the reader will struggle to resist the urge to follow his lead.*"
The Economist

"*Bristling with vitality, Chesshyre's new tome is a joyfully rudderless romp through Europe's railway system… It's a work of brilliant geekery, but for the most part it's a love letter to the continent, a Eurocentric work for our Brexit-beleaguered times.*"
National Geographic, Top Ten Travel Books for Summer 2019

"*Like the trains he travels on, Tom Chesshyre meanders through Europe and the result is entertaining and enjoyable.*"
Christian Wolmar, author of *Blood, Iron and Gold: How the Railways Transformed the World*

"*At a time when European unity is fraying at an alarming rate, here comes Tom Chesshyre's travelogue to remind us of the virtues of connectedness. Better still, his explorations are made by train, and use the Continent's historic, unpredictable routes from the era before high-speed rail. A diverting and thought-provoking read.*"
Simon Bradley, author of *The Railways: Nation, Network and People*

"*An engaging picaresque series of encounters and reflections on Europe as many of its countries struggle to find common ground amid the populist reaction to its dilemmas.*"
Anthony Lambert, author of *Lost Railway Journeys from Around the World*

"Beethoven with attitude, masochism in Lviv, the smell of cigarettes in the corridor, adventurous great-aunts who travelled on the roofs of crowded trains, Carniolan pork-garlic sausage, Jimi Hendrix in the Slovene Ethnographic Museum and, of course, the 13:49 from Wrocław. Tom Chesshyre pays homage to a Europe that we are leaving behind and perhaps never understood. Che bella corsa! He is the master of slow locomotion."

Roger Boyes, *The Times*

"Meander through Europe in the excellent company of Tom Chesshyre, who relishes the joys of slow travel and seizes every opportunity that a journey presents: drifting as a flâneur in Lille, following in the tracks of James Joyce in a literary exploration of Ljubljana, cosseted in luxury on a trans-Ukrainian express, all decorated with a wealth of detail and intrigue. As Tom discovers, it's not just Brexit Britain – the whole Continent is in disarray. But at least Europe's railways still bind us together."

Simon Calder, *The Independent*

"One of the most engaging and enterprising of today's travel writers, Chesshyre has an eye ever-alert for telling detail and balances the romance of train travel with its sometimes-challenging realities... but for all its good humour, the book impresses as a poignant elegy for the Europe which Britain once embraced."

Stephen McClarence, travel writer

"We love reading about train travel... Pick up Slow Trains to Venice by Tom Chesshyre."

The Sunday Times Travel Magazine

PRAISE FOR *FROM SOURCE TO SEA*

"Chesshyre's book stands out from other accounts of walking the Thames Path in its contemporary (post-Brexit, pre-Trump) immediacy. A portrait of England and the English in our time, it is peppered with fascinating historical and literary markers. It's also a usefully opinionated guide to watering-holes and B & Bs from the sleepy Cotswold villages to the dystopian edgelands of the estuary."

Christina Hardyment, author of *Writing the Thames*

"Chesshyre cuts an engaging figure... He has a true journalist's instinct for conversational encounters – Kurdistani picnickers in the river meadows upstream of London, pub thugs in the badlands of the lower Thames, other Thames Path pilgrims he rubs up against along the way. He also demonstrates a nose for a juicy tale, from a Pre-Raphaelite ménage à trois at Kelmscott Manor to the discreet nookie column in the Marlow Free Press. Chesshyre's journey is rich in history and thick with characters, fables and happenstance – a highly readable and entertaining saunter along England's iconic river."

Christopher Somerville, author of *Britain's Best Walks*

"An enjoyable refuge from everyday life."

Clive Aslet, *The Times*

"I found myself quickly falling into step beside Tom Chesshyre, charmed by his amiable meanderings, pointed observations and meetings with strangers along the way... but most of all Chesshyre champions the joys of a good walk through fascinating surroundings – with beer and blisters at the end of the day."

Fergus Collins, *BBC Countryfile Magazine*

"Readers should perhaps prepare themselves for a whole new wave of Whither England? type books in the months and years ahead, and Chesshyre's is a not unwelcome early attempt to answer that seemingly urgent question."

Ian Sansom, *The Times Literary Supplement*

PRAISE FOR *TICKET TO RIDE*

"Trains, dry wit, evocative descriptions, fascinating people and more trains – what's not to like?"

Christian Wolmar, author of *Blood, Iron and Gold: How the Railways Transformed the World*

"This is an engaging, enjoyable and warm-hearted book that will appeal as much to general readers as to lovers of trains."

Simon Bradley, author of *The Railways: Nation, Network and People*

TOM CHESSHYRE

SLOW TRAINS AROUND SPAIN

A 3,000-Mile
Adventure on 52 Rides

summersdale

SLOW TRAINS AROUND SPAIN

We are grateful for permissions to reproduce the following material in this volume:
Homage to Catalonia by George Orwell (Copyright © George Orwell, 1938)
Reproduced by permission of Bill Hamilton as the Literary Executor of the Estate of the Late Sonia Brownell Orwell.

An Hachette UK Company
www.hachette.co.uk

Summersdale Publishers Ltd
Part of Octopus Publishing Group Limited
Carmelite House
50 Victoria Embankment
LONDON
EC4Y 0DZ
UK

www.summersdale.com

Printed and bound in the UK

ISBN: 978-1-80007-263-3

Substantial discounts on bulk quantities of Summersdale books are available to corporations, professional associations and other organizations. For details contact general enquiries: telephone: +44 (0) 1243 771107 or email: enquiries@summersdale.com.

For Spain lovers

ABOUT THE AUTHOR

Tom Chesshyre is the author of eight previous travel books and worked for the travel desk of *The Times* for 21 years. He has contributed to the *Daily Mail* and *The Mail on Sunday*. He has also written for *Condé Nast Traveller*, *National Geographic*, *Monocle* and *Geographical*, the magazine of the Royal Geographical Society. He is the author of *How Low Can You Go?: Round Europe for 1p Each Way (Plus Tax)*, *To Hull and Back: On Holiday in Unsung Britain*, *Tales from the Fast Trains: Europe at 186 MPH*, *A Tourist in the Arab Spring*, *Gatecrashing Paradise: Misadventures in the Real Maldives*, *Ticket to Ride: Around the World on 49 Unusual Train Journeys*, *From Source to Sea: Notes from a 215-mile Walk along the River Thames* and *Slow Trains to Venice: A 4,000-mile Adventure across Europe*. He went to comprehensive school and studied politics at Bristol University and newspaper journalism at City University in London. He lives in Mortlake in London.

CONTENTS

Don Quixote continued on his chosen way, which in reality was none other than the way his horse chose to follow, for he believed that in this consisted the essence of adventure.

Miguel de Cervantes, *Don Quixote*

For "horse", substitute "train"
(subject to rail replacement buses)

PREFACE

George Orwell did not much like Spanish trains. Travelling between Barcelona and the front during the Spanish Civil War, he commented drily: "In theory I rather admire the Spaniards for not sharing our Northern time-neurosis; but unfortunately I share it myself." The spirit of *mañana* – putting off business until tomorrow – got up the nose of the author of *Nineteen Eighty-Four*, *Animal Farm* and, in this quotation, *Homage to Catalonia*.

Spain and trains have not always gone together – far from it. Hard times in the nineteenth century, too many mountains and fear of the French (Napoleon still fresh in minds) meant slow early progress. In 1837, the first "Spanish" line was in Cuba, then part of the empire. It was only in 1848 that a home track, of about 20 miles, was laid along Barcelona's coast.

This was way behind much of Europe. Britain (the pioneer), Belgium, Germany and France were well advanced by the late 1830s.

Then Spain's trains faced another problem. Not only was the country a late starter, but a choice from the beginning was made to go for a wide gauge of five feet and six inches (wider than the "standard" of most of Europe). This was for national security reasons, although the result was loss of trade via France.

Stagnation set in. By the time of Franco's death in 1975, the country's railways were second-rate. Some steam trains still chugged, quite prettily admittedly, across the plains.

Skip forward to 1992, however, when a Madrid–Seville high-speed line opened (in time for Expo '92), and onward to the bright, shiny stations of today, and the country has one of Europe's very best railways. Spain now has excellent trains. Some fast, some slow and all usually on time (of which Orwell would surely have approved).

With a few weeks free, I decided to hit the tracks. Spain is Britain's number one holiday destination, almost twice as popular as France. Yet beyond beach breaks to the costas, weekends in Barcelona and Madrid, and sunny trips to the Balearic Islands or the Canaries, what do we know of the country?

The answer for me was: *muy poco* (very little).

A journey along the slow lines – the way I prefer to go – seemed in order.

¡Viva España!

¡Trenes todo el camino! (Trains all the way!)

NOTE: This journey took place in the summer before the COVID-19 pandemic and was written before then, too.

CHAPTER ONE

MORTLAKE IN LONDON TO FIGUERES IN SPAIN, VIA PARIS AND TOULOUSE IN FRANCE

EIGHT HUNDRED MILES SOUTH

It is pouring down at the 209 bus stop in Mortlake. Murky grey water runs in a stream along the gutter. Thuds and clanks emanate from a building site across the busy road. A procession of white vans and SUVs growls past, windscreen wipers flapping manically. This feels a long way from sunny Spain.

After some time, a grimy red bus arrives to take us to Hammersmith Bridge. We roll along in a crawling traffic jam to the bridge, whereupon the driver announces matter-of-factly that the back door is "broken". So we, the passengers, shuffle out of the front door and across the Thames on a narrow pedestrian path in a slow-moving line. The bridge is closed to traffic for repairs. It has been so for a while. Men in fluorescent jackets handling mobile devices rule the roost, *doing something*.

At Hammersmith, a curly-haired woman wearing headphones pushes by at the Tube station's ticket barrier, before doing precisely the same as the Piccadilly Line train arrives. Just bad luck, I suppose. I find a corner away from the woman with headphones and begin to read a front-page newspaper article headlined: *SHAMED OXFAM GIVEN THREE WEEKS TO REFORM*, about sex scandals at the charity.

Shortly after I do so, an arm shoots across the page blocking the words. This arm belongs to a dandyish yet dead-eyed man clutching a lime-green bag. I regard him for a moment; there are plenty of other places to cling on in the carriage. The man returns my gaze as though monitoring whether I am about to "take issue".

I am not. What's the point? What does the dandyish yet dead-eyed man clutching a lime-green bag want? To avoid confrontation on the first day on the way to Spain, I stare at a greasy section of Piccadilly Line Tube window, holding the paper by my side before closing my eyes.

The train rattles onward beneath London, humming and rumbling – heavy with passengers squashed close together, counting down stations and listening to the squeal of the tracks.

In this manner, we arrive at King's Cross St Pancras, where many of us disembark.

SLOW TRAINS AROUND SPAIN

After the barriers above the platforms, I step forward, unsure of which exit to take. At precisely this moment, a tall bald man in a hurry crosses my path so closely my foot nips his heel. He spins round and snarls.

"Look what you ****ing just did," he says, examining his shoe.

I do as he says. I appear to have done nothing whatsoever.

"You cut across me," I reply. "I'm sorry, it was an accident. What was I supposed to do?"

"Move out of my ****ing way," he says.

With that, he departs.

In this manner, somewhat nonplussed, (and, to be frank, not a little bit annoyed) I arrive at the Eurostar terminal at St Pancras International.

Trains, I do love them, but not always office-day trains in London. They do tend to chew you up and spit you out.

Before passing through immigration, to get my bearings and calm down, I look about the famous old station. It has been a while since I was last here and things are even more upmarket – or just plain posher – than I recall. Fancy clothes shops lead to expensive chocolatiers, French perfumeries, sushi bars, delis selling elaborate food hampers favoured by royals including many an old king and queen (and Prince Harry and Meghan Markle), underwear boutiques and booths offering cucumber, mint and cayenne "pick-me-up" sodas.

A suited man strides by speaking loudly into a phone. "Are any big changes or hot fixes required?" he asks, his voice trailing off in the direction of a champagne bar and a hotel with a cocktail lounge.

It is busy in the concourse and around the scented-candle and caviar shops in the heart of the station. To escape the crowds, I retreat to the top of an escalator by the statue of the poet and broadcaster John Betjeman, who famously campaigned to prevent the elegant Victorian buildings at St Pancras being pulled down in the 1960s... and who so loved trains himself.

This statue feels like an old friend. On each trip I took during a series of pleasurable high-speed train adventures across Europe for a train book entitled *Tales from the Fast Trains* I would make a pilgrimage here before setting off. Gazing upward from this spot, the arched roof of the station is revealed in its full glorious bloom of sky-blue beams. Sleek Eurostar trains purr gently at platforms behind glass panels. The air is still. Engines rumble. A faint smell of oil wafts across the tranquil, wide-open space. If you are a train lover, "enthusiast", "trainspotter" – or call it what you will – this is an almost heavenly spot.

What a peaceful place to consider a journey ahead and purge thoughts of broken buses and bridges, sardine-can carriages and irrationally irate commuters. This time tomorrow I will be in the birthplace of Salvador Dalí in a little town in Catalonia in northern Spain, about 800 miles due south, without having left the ground.

There is something marvellous about the prospect of travelling a long distance without taking to the sky; something to do with a feeling of connection, an attachment to the landscape as you move onward. To arrive in Spain by train to explore its vast, mysterious (to me) interior from its tracks just seems somehow right.

To have flown into Barcelona or Madrid and headed for the station would have been a false start, a kind of magician's trick of arrival. Suddenly, hey presto, Spain's trains would have been at my disposal. But I want to enter via the railway line. To roll in by train is the way to go, and St Pancras is the place to start. After Paris, an overnight connection on a sleeper service to Toulouse awaits, followed by another train, in the morning, across the Pyrenees into the wilds of the Iberian Peninsula.

With these thoughts percolating, I pass security – no queues, pleasingly – and enter the busy Eurostar lounge.

At the Station Pantry, I buy an Estrella Damm lager, appropriately brewed in Barcelona, and raise a glass to the journey ahead: why not? Others with backpacks like me seem to be doing the same. It is easy – a glance is all that's required – to single out the *travellers* from the weekend breakers with their roll-along Samsonites and business folk, eyes glued to smartphones (as ever).

Now that I can, I peruse the day's paper.

The Oxfam story makes grim reading. An inquiry has uncovered "a culture of poor behaviour" in which donations matter more than what staff get up to in the Third World. Another article reveals that one in five children in the UK lives in poverty. Yet another reports on a "vicious cycle" of extreme weather patterns in Britain that is "only likely to worsen" due to global warming.

This is aside from all the usual bitter wranglings over Brexit, of course: the accusations and "facts" tossed this way and that.

Elsewhere in Europe, neo-Nazis have been charged over a terror plot in France. Seven migrants have died after a boat sank near Lesbos in Greece. A man has been beaten at a rally held by an anti-migrant party in Italy after yelling "love thy neighbour". And the German government is considering banning electric shock treatments recently developed at private clinics to "cure" homosexuality.

Spain has made headlines too. A far-right party, Vox, has formed a coalition to govern Madrid. This is the first time the far right has held power in Spain since Franco's death. So: quite big news. Meanwhile, a middle-aged man from Colombia has been arrested at Barcelona Airport after 500 grams of cocaine were found beneath his toupee. A picture is shown of this "disproportionately large hairpiece", which looks like a small furry animal clinging to his head. So: not such big news (but quite amusing).

I mention all of this here, putting aside turbulent times beyond European shores in the Middle East, Asia and elsewhere, simply to point out that things are *not exactly great* in the world right now. All of this has happened in the course of a *single day* in mid June. Multiply goings-on by 365 and the sheer scale of the general mayhem of the average year of the early twenty-first century becomes apparent.

What better moment to take to the tracks on a long train journey in a hot country to get away from it all for a while?

"Let the train take the strain," as the wise old British Rail adverts used to say.

"Première classe *is only for* première classe"
St Pancras to Paris

My Eurostar is called and the passengers of the 17:01 to Paris Gare du Nord slide up escalators to the purring platform above.

On board my seat is by the aisle, facing backward. The large man beside me, who neither utters a single word nor rises once during the entire journey, fiddles with his phone. Across the aisle, a woman sprays herself with a haze of lavender and fixes her hair. I take her to be French, although she says absolutely nothing either.

We depart on the stroke of 17:01 and soon afterward a female announcer with a cut-glass accent – as though we are being welcomed on the grand staircase of an English country manor for a society event – explains where the food kiosk/bar is to be found, tells us phones should be kept on silent, notes that smoke detectors in the loos are "very sensitive" and warns that "*première classe* is only for *première classe*". No trying to sneak in to see how the other half lives.

Going backward is vaguely unnerving – I always prefer forward – and being in the aisle means there is not much of a view, just a blur of grey sky. Library-like silence descends, aside from the rustle and crunch of crisps somewhere close by. This soon ceases. An advert highlighting the attractions of Aix-en-Provence flashes on a screen depicting magnificent gardens, pretty little squares, fountains and impressionist paintings hung in ornate museums; exotic eye candy for this section of M25-land Kent with its lorry-laden carriageways and football-pitch-sized warehouses. Then we slow down and pass a long train laden with wagons bearing FedEx containers. High metal fences appear, the train dips and, at 17:36, we slip effortlessly into the Channel Tunnel.

As we do so, a comforting humming sound takes over and no one in the carriage moves or says a word. This may just be my imagination, but I get a strong collective sense of *thank God for that*. In little more than half an hour we are well away from the madness of one of the busiest cities in the world, listening to gentle train noises with a whole load of seawater and fish up above. Admittedly, another pretty busy city awaits – but London, even on a short journey to St Pancras, seems to presents another level of daily chaos these days.

It is both strange and frankly terrifying at this point, with all that water and all those fish up above, to think of those who may at this very moment be risking their lives travelling in the opposite direction on flimsy boats on the surface of the Channel.

Just about every day such journeys are of course attempted, and although most boats are intercepted safely by coastguards, not all are. One vessel has just capsized, resulting in the tragic death of an Iranian woman, a thirty-one-year-old PhD student named Mitra Mehrad. Her boat ran into difficulty in poor weather not so far away from where we are now. Before departing Mehrad had stayed for several days at a makeshift migrant camp in Dunkirk. The price of such a crossing, with no assurance of safety and gangs running the racket, can be as much as ten thousand pounds.

Première classe in the depths; desperation on the waves above.

The Eurostar rises into Coquelles in Pas-de-Calais in France, where the hole on the other side of the Channel was dug, allowing the two tunnels to meet in October 1990. With this act, some believe, Britain effectively gave up its island status.

It took a while for the 31-mile tunnel to be readied for commercial use, though. It was in May 1994 that the Queen eventually travelled across on Eurostar for the official inauguration. On the way back from Coquelles, President Mitterrand of France joined Her Majesty in her Rolls-Royce Phantom VI, which had been placed on a car-carrying train. "I've had a very comfortable journey in a very comfortable car, and it just happened to be yours, Ma'am," the president gushed afterward. The Duke of Edinburgh and Mrs Mitterrand were in the French state Citroën travelling behind on the same shuttle. So began what was believed at the time to be an inevitable process of bringing Britain and Europe together, solidifying the peace and togetherness achieved in the aftermath of the Second World War.

I stroll along to the food kiosk/bar.

A group of tall men in charcoal-grey suits – they seem to be on a corporate outing – has commandeered the centre of an area with high tables for consuming food and drink. They are clasping little cans of Heineken that seem almost too small for their large hands, looking faintly ridiculous with all their swagger as they take dainty sips. As I queue for a can of my own, I listen to one of them.

"I think ideally I'd like a house in Europe," he says. Dainty sip.

"Really, not in Britain?" asks one of the others.

He ignores this, as he seems in a dreamy mood.

"Yes, a house in Europe. Or perhaps Asia," he continues. Dainty sip.

"Asia?" asks his companion. He takes a dainty sip too.

"Yes, Asia or Europe, ideally. A house in Britain too," says the first guy, who notices his little Heineken is finished and clicks out of his state of reverie. "Whose round is it anyway?"

I return to my seat with my own dainty can.

Rain streams down the windows, but after a while the outburst ceases and streaks of ethereal blue sky emerge amid bomb-like dark grey clouds.

Going backward like this, at such a high speed, feels constantly as though the train is about to fly off the edge of a cliff. I do realize that some people prefer going backward (apparently for reasons to do with safety in the event of a crash) and others believe such seats allow more time to stare at views. But really, how likely is a disaster? And, frankly, isn't facing backward as you go forward just a little bit odd?

From my reverse-aisle vantage point, flashes of electricity pylons and swathes of olive-green countryside sweep by. Rows of tall, thin trees materialize every now and then, looking like the teeth of giant upturned combs. And that's about it.

The "French" woman on the seat across the aisle turns in my direction momentarily, shocking me. In my absence she has plastered on a glue-like face mask, a beauty product of some sort. At first glance, though, she appears to have been treated for terrible burns or is trying out some ghoulish Halloween costume.

I turn away, drink my Heineken and watch more bomb-like clouds on the horizon. An American mother on the seat behind attempts to cajole her daughter into reading a book, but after a while gives up and I hear her say: "Wow, it's so green." She is referring to the countryside, and indeed it is, with oak and beech trees and flickering sunlight. Not long afterward, however, tower-block estates arise in sprawling suburbs and the train rumbles into Paris.

We disembark. From Gare du Nord I board a bouncy Line 5 Métro train with hard multicoloured seats, sitting next to a woman watching a video of herself dancing at a party. Her phone, I cannot help noticing, is adorned with pink bunny ears. The woman seems quite enrapt by her energetic performance, regularly pressing play for another viewing.

As I ponder quite what this might say about the future of humanity, the train crosses the River Seine and pulls into Gare d'Austerlitz.

"Have a nice... life"
Paris to Figueres, via Toulouse

Gare d'Austerlitz is right by the river. Notre-Dame Cathedral, which only recently lost its roof and spire in the devastating blaze that so shocked France, is about a mile to the north-west. Down by the water's edge, a brass band practises as the last of the day's sun fades above the silvery water. Métro trains on Line 5 rattle across the metal-framed bridge. There is something truly wonderful about arriving in Paris so quickly beneath the Channel by trains. Maybe I will just never get over this, no matter how many times I take the ride.

Inside a modern annex of Gare d'Austerlitz, workers in red uniforms move about on Segways looking like robots in a science fiction film. In a corner near the platform for Toulouse, a lounge with faux leather chairs and power points seems to be popular both with passengers and various Parisian drifters. Idle characters with possessions in plastic bags rest by the power points, appearing perfectly content in the faux leather seats. A man wearing both cargo trousers and tracksuit bottoms, one *on top of the other*, sits next to me, listening to music and tapping his feet. A woman with a bottle of cider places it on a side table and mumbles to herself happily as though greatly amused by some notion or other. Whether the designers of this IKEA-style lounge had all this in mind when plans were drawn up is perhaps unlikely, but at least it is getting good use and proving popular (possibly for the night).

The train is called. In the queue, a middle-aged British man travelling with an elderly couple begins whistling an annoying tune repeatedly, quite loudly. He has a crew cut and a pot belly. He informs his grandparents, whom I gather he is accompanying on their summer holiday, that this is the melody from "Ring of Fire" by Johnny Cash and he likes to whistle the song as he supports Liverpool Football Club. Apparently, his grandparents and I learn, two famous Liverpool players were once filmed singing this song. So he, and some other Liverpool fans, whistle the tune loudly in public places.

"If anyone else 'Liverpool' is about, they whistle back," he says.

His grandparents say absolutely nothing and just watch him as he continues to whistle. It is as though he is a (big fat) bird that has lost its way and is trying to find the others. No one at Gare d'Austerlitz returns his "call".

The man stops whistling. There are a couple of young backpackers ahead of us – possibly Scandinavian. They are within earshot. They seem nervous about their tickets and are asking the guard some questions.

"Probably on *gap years*," he says to his grandparents, in a sneering tone. "On *gap years*. Taking *time off*." He imitates a gap year student's voice, as he imagines one to be: *"I'm going to take time off to find myself."* His grandparents look as though they do not have the first clue what he is talking about. Then he says: "**** off!" And begins whistling again.

The fresh-faced Scandinavians almost certainly understand him. For that matter, I understand him. I have a backpack and could well be trying to find myself too. I may even be taking time off on a gap year too, though perhaps not one between A levels and university.

I really do not like the Whistler.

We all board the long, dirty, grey-blue Société Nationale des Chemins de Fer (SNCF) Intercités service to Toulouse.

The Whistler and his grandparents are not in my compartment on coach eleven. Inside are two bunks, each with three berths. Mine is the lower berth on the right. A Chinese woman with an absolutely enormous metal suitcase somehow manoeuvres her luggage behind the ladder.

"OK perfect," she says. "Too big," she apologises, before flapping her T-shirt. "Hot! Hot!"

She climbs the steps and asks a neighbour: "Where you come from?"

A voice says: "French." End of conversation.

She asks another neighbour up above the same question. "Spain" is the reply. End of conversation.

At least she's trying.

A man above and opposite me has his skateboard propped beneath his pillow and is wearing his shoes (which he never takes off). The Chinese woman has left pink flip-flops with *Sweet Years* written within a heart shape at the foot of the ladder.

We roll away at 22:08, not long after passing the cooling towers of a power station. Then, an arm shoots out from above, the blind is pulled down and darkness descends in our sleeper to the south. We clatter along. A conductor wearing a beret glances in before scurrying down the long, narrow corridor, a little like the White Rabbit from *Alice in Wonderland*. Wondering if the 22:08 to Toulouse has a public area, I hop off my bunk and take chase, catching him to ask if there is a buffet carriage.

He swivels his eyes momentarily, as though suggesting "if only", and shakes his head.

"My colleague. Black girl," he says in English. He points at his face, seemingly to convey his message, although he is pale-skinned. "Glasses." Points at his face again. "White jacket." Points at his chest. "Tea and coffee only."

She will come round with a trolley. He points at his face once more to make sure I know who to look out for.

I return to my bunk berth and listen to the rumble of wheels and electric buzz of the train to Toulouse. The Chinese woman, having given up meeting anyone new, is chattering to a travelling companion I had not previously noticed on a high-up bunk. After a while, a dramatic Chinese soap opera plays (no headphones used, so the compartment can hear all). A man and a woman seem locked in the throes of a life-changing exchange, with truths finally being told and emotions on the line. Then this cuts off and for a while all that can be heard is a gentle clickety-clack of the track.

* * *

This does not last long.

Mysterious clanks, bangs, creaks and muffled coughs mark the passage of the night.

At six o'clock, the skateboarder rises, sliding open our compartment door to reveal a pink dawn sky.

We are moving alongside a canal flanked by cream-coloured houses with green shutters. There is almost total silence now – no voices, just the rattle of the track – and I realize I have slept quite well despite the earlier noise. Phones charging in sockets dangle in the hall, where a few of us lean against a railing staring out. Apartment blocks, football pitches and sidings come and go. An office with mirrored windows lights up in a bizarre blaze of orange, catching the sun's reflection. The passengers in the hall *oh* and *ah* about this for a while, pointing at the building.

We arrive at Toulouse Matabiau Station 19 minutes late at 06:20.

This is a pit stop. I go outside to check out the station's grand stone facade with the coats of arms lined above arched windows. The station dates from the early nineteenth century and from the outside looks as though little has changed since then apart from the addition of a sign advertising a "QUICK" burger restaurant. Inside, I sit at a table near the Whistler (no longer whistling) and his grandparents, as well as a man wearing a baseball cap adorned with *RULES ARE FOR SUCKERS*. A team of four burly soldiers carrying machine guns patrols the station concourse, keeping an eye on us all.

The next train is a combined SNCF and Red Nacional de los Ferrocarriles Españoles (Renfe) service – my first Spanish train.

This turns out to be a bullet-nosed, although it never seems to go that fast. A convoluted announcement in English says that the train manager "remains your preferential contact person throughout your journey" and we depart at 08:07 in smart double-decker carriages with lilac carpets and powder-blue seats. Mine is on the top deck with clear views of custard-yellow wheat fields lined by streaks of red poppies, hawks wheeling above. The sky is perfect blue with the majestic snow-capped peaks of the Pyrenees rising to the south-west. Tan-coloured cattle huddle in the shade of trees. Grain silos cast long shadows. A Citroën 2CV putters and bumps down a potholed lane. Husks of corn billow in a swirling wind, as though forming the surface of a strange yellow sea.

A tractor sprays fertilizer, leaving a ghostly trail of haze. The impenetrable-looking fortifications of Carcassonne arise majestically beyond the high arched windows of the ancient city's station. We traverse the bend of a river and enter hills clad with dark-green forest interspersed with ragged granite ridges. Wispy clouds cling to hilltops as though afraid to break free and evaporate in the rising heat of the day. Bushes thick with yellow flowers grow by cypress trees that fan out across a plain. Vineyards appear with emerald vines and twisty trunks that look like snakes charmed out of the soil. The landscape is rich and fertile and splendid. From the cramped confines of the

London Tube to a comfortable seat with a soul-lifting view: *this is why I bought my ticket south.*

I start talking to my neighbour, Frank.

He is wearing a blue sleeveless jacket and has a tattoo of a bear on one arm. Bedding is attached to his backpack and he is in his fifties with gimlet eyes, a black nose ring and a ginger beard. He looks careworn. First impressions are that he could be homeless. He is not. He is a social worker from the German village of Schluchsee in the Black Forest. He has bought tickets to visit his soon-to-be eighteen-year-old daughter, who is on a holiday with friends in Perpignan. He wants to surprise her by turning up for her eighteenth birthday so he can give her a present and take her out.

"She don't know about it," he says.

How pleased he imagines she will be to have her father turn up unannounced for her party, I do not ask.

Frank has travelled by train from Basel – "that's in Switzerland" – after crossing the border from Schluchsee. "It is very small. It is very nice there," he says of Schluchsee. "Just mountains and black trees."

Frank has opinions about trains.

He likes French trains. "The TGV is better than the InterCity in Germany," he says. "More comfort on TGV and the signs in France are so easy you can't go wrong. There is always someone to help you."

He does not like German trains. "Trains in Germany always delayed, big problems, crowded," he says, looking at me for a moment, perhaps to judge whether I will be offended by what comes next.

"It is not as bad as British railways," he says. "Not as bad as *that*. But it's getting that way."

He looks out of the carriage window. We are passing a wide expanse of water. Perpignan is coming up. Frank has to go. He shakes my hand. "Have a nice..." he pauses as though wondering what to say next, "life".

He heads down to the lower deck.

The train crosses marshland with pools of copper-coloured water beside the tracks.

Then the land turns arid and becomes rockier and rockier. More snowy mountains arise. A red-brick castle appears on the right-hand side, dome-topped turrets shooting up like missiles. A Ryanair plane soars above an emerald valley of vines. Four Spanish police officers, who must have boarded at Perpignan, enter the carriage wearing bulletproof vests and revolvers in holsters. They ask to see other passengers' documents, but not mine. My guidebook and my backpack seem good enough for Spanish immigration requirements.

"Buenos días," says a female officer.

And with that, they depart.

We enter a long pitch-black tunnel before emerging amid undulating green hills lit by long streaks of golden sunlight.

My train is in Spain. Sunny Spain indeed.

CHAPTER TWO

FIGUERES TO VILANOVA I LA GELTRÚ, VIA BLANES AND BARCELONA

"VAGABOND DAYS"

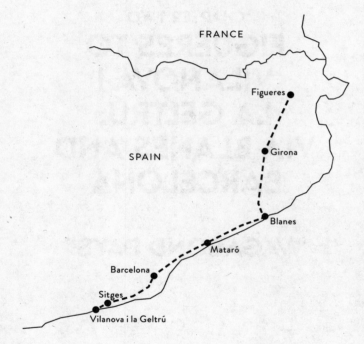

So here is the plan: to travel in a big, wobbly "S" by slow trains around Spain. From the north-east corner the tracks will lead onward, I hope, along the north coast using narrow-gauge railways for some of the way to Santiago de Compostela, the ancient pilgrimage city, before looping south via Madrid to the remote region of Extremadura near the Portuguese border. From there, the idea is to weave across to València, Spain's third largest city, then down to the south coast and westward once again via a beach or two to Seville, the flamenco-dancing capital of Andalusía.

Spanish trains seem easy to book via the website of Renfe, the state-owned rail operator, nationalized by Franco in 1941 and pronounced *ren-fay*. My intention is to make it up as I go along, following the vague route described above. Each day I will look at tomorrow's departures and book another ride, taking the slowest trains possible to the next destination. In this manner I hope to: 1) Lose myself for a while in a large intriguing country. 2) Dip into matters of interest at my destinations, particularly those train related. 3) Let whatever happens, happen. 4) Perhaps most importantly, break free and *enjoy the ride*.

When Laurie Lee came to Spain in July 1935, he was equipped with a violin for busking and a single phrase in Spanish: "Will you please give me a glass of water?" In his delightful memoir, *As I Walked Out One Midsummer Morning*, his follow-up to the childhood memoir *Cider with Rosie*, Lee describes tramping across the country, occasionally hitching lifts on mule wagons. Well, it is in the spirit of Lee that I set forth, with only a little more Spanish and minus a fiddle. For a few weeks *los trenes* will lead the way and I will be a mere *pasajero*, with a smartphone to check Renfe timetables.

Places to stay? Apart from the first night, nowhere is booked. This is, of course, one of the wonderful things about travel these days: with a few simple clicks it is possible to fix what might in the past have required phone calls, faxes, or even "snail-mail" letters. There is no pretending otherwise: our ways of getting about have been transformed by the internet and I intend to make the most of them. Train journeys like this one, and those I describe in *Slow Trains to Venice*, a book about a meandering European train journey, do not always necessitate slumming it. Yes, the popular image of train travel around Europe is of cheap hostels and rough going, but the popular image is wrong.

It is very simple indeed to have a very nice time without a trip costing an arm and a leg.

There is another consideration here, which I will touch upon and move on.

I do not profess to be an evangelical eco-traveller. Greta Thunberg, the Swedish wonder teenager of All Things Green and many others have the sermons of eco-travel done and dusted. All I will say is this: trains are obviously greener than planes. From Paris to Barcelona travelling by train releases 12.48 kilograms of carbon per passenger. To fly this route, however, would release 78.37 kilograms. On this basis, on an average-length journey in Europe, planes are six times dirtier than trains. With stories about "extreme weather" and climate change not about to go away, *these things matter*.

As I left St Pancras, Britain was drizzling, dripping, thundering and splashing (almost drowning) in the second wettest June on record. Floods and treacherous weather warnings were reported daily; dams at bursting point. If we are going to be greener in the future and enjoy a more stable climate – check the weather records for almost any recent year and it is abundantly clear that weather patterns are far from regular – we are going to have to change our old travel habits.

But not if you love trains already, though. No need to alter a thing. Feel very smug and step on board.

World-famous Swedish teenagers with good social media and intentions, eat your hearts out.

Sentimientos *in Catalonia*
Figueres

On the platform at Figueres Station eight police officers have cornered a man who has just disembarked. He appears bewildered and scared, as though he would dearly like to make a dash for it. As I take the steps down into a tunnel to the exit, he is shakily holding forth flimsy pieces of paper as proof of identification. His back is to the train and he cuts a tragic figure, a picture of desolation and fear. What are his circumstances? Has he been collared? It certainly looks like it. Borders in Europe seem not to be as free and easy as they once were (for some).

Within the station, a corridor is decorated with images of Salvador Dalí, the surrealist local hero (1904–1989). Dalí is buried in a crypt beneath the stage at the Dalí Theatre-Museum, the big attraction in Figueres, which Dalí himself built. I chose Figueres for the first Spanish stop to come and see this extraordinary, fantastical castle-like structure topped with giant golden eggs and with walls studded with golden loaves of bread.

No other tourist has disembarked at Figueres. The little tourist office by the concourse is empty save for an assistant with round-rimmed glasses who initially, whenever I ask anything about Figueres (which translates in Catalan as "fig trees"), hands me a new map.

"I am a tourist and I am staying here tonight…" I begin, triggering a blur of hand movement behind the counter as the assistant with round-rimmed glasses cuts me short by presenting a map.

I look at the map and say: "Oh, thank you, thank you, that's really great" or something along those lines. It is a lovely, useful local map.

I ask about what there is to see aside from the Dalí Theatre-Museum, but before this is fully expressed, another map of Figueres – a slightly different lovely, useful local map – is passed across, stopping me in my tracks.

"Oh, thank you, thank you," I say, examining the new, almost identical but subtly different map.

I ask about where I might go next in Catalonia, beginning to mention that I would prefer to miss Barcelona, and the assistant puts a hand up as if to say *No more please – I have the answer!* – before flamboyantly passing across two further lovely, useful maps of Figueres, these ones with a wider perspective showing the region.

Looking at the four maps laid out on the table before me, I have no excuse if I get lost in Dalí's birthplace and resting place or anywhere nearby.

I enquire about the length of the walk from the station to the centre.

No further maps are proffered (as I seem to have them all already) and the assistant with round-rimmed glasses replies casually: "Forty-five minutes, perhaps an hour."

This seems like a lot, I suggest, judging by the various maps.

"*Sí,*" he concedes, equally casually. "Maybe fifteen, twenty minutes is more like it."

Perhaps time itself has a surreal quality in the home of the world's most famous surrealist.

Looking at one of the regional maps, I point to a place called Malgrat de Mar. Maybe that would be a good place to stop after Figueres?

"Oh no," replies the assistant. "Blanes: better, better, better."

Blanes is a town slightly before Malgrat de Mar on the Costa Brava. The tourist official does not elaborate on why Blanes is better, but seems absolutely certain on the point, telling me I must catch a train from another station in Figueres: "A very slow train – it stop at every station". I am currently at Figueres-Vilafant Station, which is just for international or long-distance trains; the station for local trains is on the other side of town. He gives me the train time for tomorrow, 09:52, and bows slightly.

Muy buen (very good) service at Figueres-Vilafant Station.

As for the poor soul detained on the platform, he does not pass by the tourist office during this exchange. I have an eye out for him. As this is the only exit, for now at least the border guards seem to have him. Perhaps France will again, quite soon.

* * *

Hotel Los Angeles is down an alley, a stone's throw from the Dalí Theatre-Museum.

Figueres, I gather during the walk over, is a provincial town with a market selling famous-brand clothing at remarkably cheap prices, knick-knacks, knickers, leather belts and a wide selection of five-euro straw hats. *"Bonjour, monsieur. Bon soir, monsieur. Tourist, monsieur?"* asks a Del Boy trader as I pass, taking me for a French backpacker.

The market is at the foot of a hill by a park not so far from Figueres-Vilafant Station. In the spirit of *qué demonios* (what the hell) I buy a polo shirt from the Spanish Del Boy, who tells me he was born in Morocco but brought up in Girona – an early reminder of the close ties between Spain and North Africa. No other part of Europe is, of course, so close to the African continent. The Strait of Gibraltar is 9 miles wide at its narrowest point.

The market stalls lead onward to labyrinthine lanes connecting to little tucked-away squares with cafés and twisting alleys snaking off at corners. Lizards bask in the sun on the steps of houses. Elderly men sip coffees beneath drumstick trees. Some of the restaurants, I notice, offer *tastets surrealistes* menus. A popular one has oysters with caviar and cava, "gratinated prawns and octopus" and "pork fillet with ice cream of mustard and brioche". Dalí-friendly diners: dig in! Local restaurant owners seem to have gone for a Dalí slant. And who, I suppose, could blame them?

It does not take long to reach the hotel, past a series of pro Catalonia independence signs that have been sprayed on walls beside yellow and tomato-red Catalonian flags; Figueres appears to be a hotbed of the separatist movement. *NO REMORSE, NO FREEDOM!* says one piece of graffiti, written in English close to the hotel entrance. In the little lobby Dalí pictures are plastered on the wall and copies of his works are for sale in a cabinet. Unusual purple lights emanate from a reception desk by a rubber-tree plant. Surreal, indeed.

The owner's name is Angel. He has grey hair and glasses and sits on a low swivel chair behind a marble counter, his head just popping up. He is mild-mannered... until the subject turns to Catalonian independence, that is.

"Did you ever lay eyes on Dalí?" I ask at check-in. Given the artist died in 1989, I suppose there is a possibility.

"I am not that old. I did not see him. I am very young," he replies.

What age was he during Dalí's last days?

"School age," he replies. "I am very young: just forty-nine now."

I like this definition of *very young*.

"Dalí, for the last ten years of his life, did not go out much," says Angel. Hence the rare sightings of him during that period. Dalí's health went into rapid decline in later years after the death of his wife Gala in 1982.

I ask about the pro Catalonian independence graffiti on the street outside.

"Ah!" he says, standing for the first time. "Ah!"

I am holding my *Rail Map Europe*, produced by the compilers of the *European Rail Timetable*, the train map version of the holy grail. Angel eyes it and indicates he wants a look. He takes the map and lays a pencil down on it to mark a line from a point south-west of Barcelona to the middle of the Pyrenees.

"This is Catalonia!" he says, indicating the space to the right of the pencil, where we now are. "This is Spain!" He points to the much larger area to the left. "We hope for independence. Catalonia wants independence but Spain says 'no'. It's just like Scotland. It's the same, I think. In ten or twenty years' time maybe. Maybe!"

He thumps the reception desk and pauses. "The *sentimientos*! The *sentimientos*!" Angel says. He places his hand on his heart; *sentimientos* translates as "feelings".

"The young people have the *sentimientos* in Catalonia. There are many people who in the last seventy years came to work in Catalonia from other parts of Spain. My father is from Granada. My mother is from Cáceres." Granada is in Andalucía in the far south while Cáceres is in Extremadura in the remote south-west. "Cáceres is very poor. My mother, she came with her parents when she was ten."

Now that there is a generation one step removed from this exodus, the sense of Catalonian identity has strengthened among the young, Angel says.

"The culture and the language are different. Democracy!" Angel looks squarely at me. "Simple! If people want independence, they vote for independence! Then normally there will be independence!"

Such a referendum was held in the region of Catalonia in 2017, when ninety-two per cent of voters – more than two million people – opted to break free from Spain, although the Constitutional Court of Spain refuses to recognize the result. Catalonia is an historical principality, which was ruled as such from the twelfth century to the early eighteenth century.

Angel is on a roll. "But another country! Another country! Spain! Another country thinks it is impossible to split." He widens his arms as though to suggest *I rest my case*. "I don't know why another country can say that."

He hands me my key.

The Spanish, I am noticing already, can be quite talkative.

Upstairs via hallways festooned with pictures by Dalí, I drop my backpack in a spotlessly clean little room with a Buddhist image fixed above a desk, a double bed and shutters opening on to a view of a wall. Decent enough for a night – plus a good location, an impassioned owner and, I noticed on the way up, a small cosy-looking lobby bar with *Las Aventuras de Sherlock Holmes* and *Otelo* on a shelf.

On the advice of Angel, I walk up the hill above the centre of town to go and see Sant Ferran Castle.

Even though this adventure is all about trains in Spain, I do intend to see at least a few of the sights.

Sant Ferran Castle turns out to be an enormous star-shaped fortress on a prominent hilltop facing the Pyrenees. The entrance is beyond a ramp above a deep, dried-out moat. Afterward, a gateway leads to a huge yard surrounded by crumbling stone barracks and stables with weeds and cacti growing in gutters. Extraordinarily, no one else is about. I say *extraordinarily* as this really is quite a fortress. Built in the eighteenth century, Sant Ferran Castle is, according to the leaflet from the ticket office, the largest "bastion fort" in Europe – this is a type of fort with cannon defences and barracks for garrisons. In the past more than four thousand troops were billeted here complete with a year's worth of supplies in the event of a siege; this was a key defensive position against attack from the north.

At the beginning of the Peninsular War with France (1808–1814), however, no such siege was required. Napoleon's troops occupied the fort "under the guise of being allies," says the leaflet – which sounds pretty sneaky and might explain Spain's decision to use their own broad gauge of railway rather than the "standard gauge" of northern countries. Who knew what the French, so soon after conning their way into Sant Ferran Castle, might get up to if they could simply roll all the way on trains to Madrid?

In more recent history, Sant Ferran Castle was the setting of the final meeting of the Republican parliament on Spanish soil, on 1 February 1939, before the surrender to Franco's Nationalist forces. On their departure, the Republican Army blew up ammunition stores, causing major damage to some of the fortifications. Many battles were fought in Catalonia during the Spanish Civil War and Sant Ferran Castle, like Figueres as a whole and Barcelona, was a Republican stronghold, where members of the International Brigades of overseas volunteers gathered.

Purple wild flowers sprout amid the battlements now. There is birdsong and calm and splendid isolation, all alone on the fort. Staring out across the mountains here is a perfect starting point for a journey round Spain. Ahead lies the jagged lilac outline of the Pyrenees, the dividing line between the Iberian Peninsula and the rest of Europe, and the sense of Spain being in some way cut off and removed is strong here. Yes, Spain is part of mainland Europe, but it feels quite apart too. You get that straight away after crossing the Pyrenees.

You get something quite different from the Dalí Theatre-Museum.

It is just about impossible to visit Figueres without poking your nose about in the Dalí Theatre-Museum. It is, without any doubt, impossible to miss the building. Down the hill from Sant Ferran Castle, there it is, straight ahead in pride of place in the town centre, golden eggs and loaves of bread gleaming.

The museum is on the site of the town's old theatre (destroyed in the Spanish Civil War). In its place is a shrine, almost a mausoleum, to Salvador Dalí, who oversaw construction of one of the most pleasingly odd museums anywhere.

It is hard to convey the sheer peculiarity of the Dalí Theatre-Museum. Upon entering, a circular courtyard opens up with classical music playing and a bronze of a naked woman with chains around her neck and snakes crawling down her arms, positioned on the bonnet of a shiny old black Cadillac. In recesses in the walls above, golden naked figurines gaze down, striking various poses and looking like a welcoming committee of aliens, harmless and benevolent in nature but high, so it would appear, on psychedelic drugs.

Inside a glass-domed chamber beyond the courtyard, a huge mural at first looks like an abstract work depicting yet another nude woman; step back a few paces, however, stare at the painting for a while, and the visage of Abraham Lincoln miraculously appears. Very Unusual Indeed. Cast your eyes down at the terracotta floor here and in the centre is a rectangular slab of marble, beneath which Dalí lies. Even More Unusual, If Not Simply Strange.

In another room, visitors are encouraged to climb steps on one side and stare across through a magnifying glass pointed at a giant wig beyond which a sofa shaped like ruby red lips is placed beside a sculpture of a nose attached to a purple wall. Through the nostrils of this nose, golden light emanates as though from fireplaces. Above the nose are two gilt-framed black-and-white pictures of the River Seine. Gaze at these pictures of Paris for a while and a pair of eyes emerges. Suddenly, the image of a glamorous platinum-blonde woman is revealed – the combined effect of the wig, sofa, weird nose and River Seine scenes seen through the magnifying glass – and you understand why this is called the Mae West Room.

In galleries leading from the Mae West Room, expect paintings of headless torsos with doorways opening into tunnels through their chests, beds on desolate beaches, clocks hanging like rags from trees, and red ribbons dangling from clouds. The walls of the corkscrew staircase in a tower are decorated with cobs of corn. A chamber in a side room off the staircase is home to a bed with a frame shaped like the bodies of fish topped with dragon heads. Next to the bed is a "skeleton" of a large caveman-like creature. Meanwhile, a ceiling mural in this room depicts Dalí, complete with his trademark moustache, next to his wife Gala. The pair tilt their heads toward an ethereal light and appear to be drifting like ghosts toward the heavens.

Even though I have visited the Dalí Theatre-Museum once before, the images seem to mutate and take on an entirely new life; some springing out that I never noticed before, others seeming to develop a new interpretation. Dalí said he wanted the museum to induce the "sensation of a theatrical dream". Well, he achieved just that.

Then there is the Dalí Theatre-Museum gift shop, which is surreal in its very own way. Socks, mugs, ties, T-shirts, trays, notebooks, cushion covers, tea towels, wooden spoons, espresso cups, toiletry bags, jigsaws, coasters, fans, magnets, eye masks, laptop covers, earrings, necklaces, reading glasses, bags, shawls, calendars, stress-relief balls, key rings, bookmarks, rulers, pens, pencils, pencil sharpeners, cards, brushes, stickers, thimbles, posters, postcards, books, tank tops, piggy banks, perfumes, bracelets, clocks, salt-and-pepper shakers, spoons, water bottles and bed headboard decorations are on offer. All with a Dalí theme. Just about every practicality required for going about daily life is covered, Dalí-wise.

The people of Figueres know they are on to a good thing with their most famous son and are clearly not ashamed to milk him for all he's worth.

After dinner at Bar Cèntric restaurant, I head back to the hotel for a drink at the little bar. No sign of Angel and I am the only customer; the receptionist doubles as the bartender, scooting round to take my order after a late check-in. A self-portrait of Dalí hangs on a wall, the artist keeping his startled egg-like eyes on me as though shocked to have some company. The Daft Punk song "Get Lucky" plays. I flick through *Otelo*. James Brown sings "Get Up Offa That Thing". Dalí seems to wink at me.

Surreal, yes… Figueres is like that.

"Holiday people"
Figueres to Blanes

In, out – and move onward. This is how I want Spain by train to be. And so, in this spirit of moving along (albeit slowly), I turn up dutifully the next morning at Figueres Station for the 09:52 to Blanes.

Figueres Station is a functional-looking place with limestone columns, orange and green decor, Dalí posters (of course), and a fountain outside the entrance with fish-shaped spouts and a pair of men on benches smoking cigars without using their hands – quite a talented achievement and, like most things in Figueres, a little odd.

If a centenary plaque on the platform is anything to go by, there has been a station here since 1877, although not the current rather ugly one. Also of note is that the station is 29.7 metres, precisely, above sea level as measured in Alicante on the Costa Blanca. How do I know this? Another little plaque imparts the information, provided by the Instituto Geográfico y Estadístico. Every station in Spain is said to have such a plaque hidden somewhere or other.

Taking the advice of the man with the round-rimmed frames from the tourist office, I board the 09:52 to Blanes from Figueres Station, due to arrive at 11.17, and we are off on time from platform two.

We are soon travelling beneath an overcast sky on this Rodalies de Catalunya train service, rolling past allotments and then along a raised track with bamboo thickets immediately on each side and olive trees and umbrella palms beyond.

We are on a rattling orange-coloured train with purple seats. The horn toots a few times as we cross a bridge over a river. More bamboo thickets arise by the tracks and we pass a station splattered with pro Catalonian independence slogans. A door between the carriages becomes jammed after teenagers bang it shut, and a security team discovers the problem near Celrà Station. The guard is called, but she cannot open the door either. The train keeps moving past an ochre-coloured settlement with a bell tower and a disused red-brick factory on the outskirts. The team of security guards and the ticket inspector somehow manage to open the door by bashing it with a spanner – seeming quite surprised at their success.

This is as much excitement as there is to report until the train arrives at Girona, with its glorious fifteenth-century cathedral rising beyond the platforms. A painting of a crocodile and an upside-down horse feature on the side of an apartment block near Girona Station. Dalí's local influence? Red and yellow Catalan flags hang from the apartment windows alongside drying underpants and jeans. Then, as we move on, a skinny young man sitting opposite, whom I take to be Muslim, looks at his watch, closes his eyes and begins silently mouthing prayers into his hands.

Giving him some space, I cross to seats on the other side and get talking to a couple sitting there. They had been amused by the spanner-bashing antics of the security team and we had exchanged a few comments earlier.

What do they think of Catalan independence, I ask.

"Whoa!" says the woman – pink cardigan, green trousers and a pleasant smile. "A big question! Big!" She pauses and then says: "Sure, yes, I want independence. I think I have sentimental emotions about this."

She does not appear, for now, to want to say any more on the subject, but I soon learn that Mariona is an architect and her husband Eduard – bald, stubbly and does not say much at all – is a policeman. They live in Barcelona and are in their early thirties. They have been visiting family in Figueres and Mariona says that the trains on this line are "not good – every day having problem: broken electric cables".

I mention enjoying the Dalí Theatre-Museum. Mariona loves Dalí: "Exceptional art. He was a surreal deity."

I mention Blanes. They both think I would be better off going to Calella Station as they prefer the beach there to the one at Blanes (though I'm sticking to my plans).

After a while, Mariona returns to the subject of politics – in particular the subject of Vox, the far-right party that has just gained power in Madrid and holds a strong anti-Catalonia-independence position.

"We respect Vox," she says. "But we don't have the same opinions. Extremism. Radicalism. We don't believe in either. Some people have bad opinions of Catalonia, elsewhere in Spain."

She pauses as the horn of the train hoots once again. "The social situation is not good in Spain," she whispers as though we might be overheard. "We have a tense situation in general in Spain right now. The governance of our country is not good."

We clatter over a railway crossing and sit in silence, watching a man in ragged trousers tending a herd of goats in a wasteland on the edge of town. Then the train pulls into Blanes Station and I say goodbye to Mariona and Eduard, who merely nods *adiós*.

Which is how I find myself at Blanes Station, precisely 12.5 metres above the sea at Alicante, slightly wondering: *¿Qué sigue?* (What next?)

* * *

Blanes is not in my guidebook. Its station is burgundy coloured and distinguished-looking, standing on the edge of town near a factory, a police station and a Mercedes showroom. The walk down a hill into town is about 2 miles past a roundabout with a green steam locomotive mounted in the middle. Out of curiosity – and in the spirit of rail enthusiasm, or perhaps just solidarity with *railway stuff* on a long train journey – I cross to the roundabout and check out the old loco.

A little brass panel by the driver's door is inscribed with: *ORENSTEIN Y KOPPEL, ARTHUR KOPPEL, SA, MADRID, BARCELONA, BILBAO.* It does not take much digging to discover that the locomotive was the work of a collaboration between the German industrialists Arthur Koppel and Benno Orenstein, who formed a company selling and later producing locomotives in the late nineteenth century that was soon to have offices as far away as South Africa, Mexico, the United States, Argentina, Egypt, Russia, Indonesia and China. Locos are known to have been delivered to the Yucatán railway and the Swakopmund–Tsumeb railway, while orders were made by the German Imperial Army during the rule of Kaiser Wilhelm II. At its peak in the early 1930s, the company employed more than eight thousand people. Later, in 1935, the company was seized by the Nazis under Hitler's policy of Aryanization. Orenstein was from a Jewish family.

Trains often have stories – and this one is no exception.

Further on via narrow streets with Catalonian flags and independence slogans hanging from buildings – *¡Sí! ¡Sí!* (*Yes! Yes!* to independence) – is Blanes beach. A rocky headland connected by a short, narrow causeway is to the right, beyond which is a more developed area of beach that I never get round to visiting. A jumble of concrete apartment blocks lines the promenade, but there are no hotels or tacky souvenir shops; Blanes seems to be mainly for Spaniards, not marauding northern Europeans. Although tourism is here in the form of a squadron of pedalos lying unused on the beach (as the sea is too rough) and seafood restaurants (packed), so is a small self-contained town with a café culture for locals, medieval fountains, Roman remains and lanes with churches with glittering chapels dedicated to sailors. Like so many parts of the Spanish costas, fishing was once the mainstay.

In Blanes I learn something about Spanish accommodation categories. Using my phone on the way in, I have booked a *hostal* just off the beach in the old town: Hostal Regina. On the website, it looks as though this *hostal* mainly comprises smart little wine-red rooms, each with a corresponding smart little wine-red bathroom. This is the closest place to the centre in my price bracket – no more than forty euros a night if I can possibly help it, preferably less, although as I have mentioned, I am hoping not to slum it too much.

This *hostal* has me curious. Is Hostal Regina really a hostel? If so, the Spaniards appear to do very smart little hostels.

At Hostal Regina, Josep is sitting at one end of a small bar with wine-red walls and pictures of a local fireworks festival held in July. This acts as the reception as well as a kind of forum for neighbourhood affairs. Josep asks and answers his own question – "You have city map? I give you one" – in a single breath. The northern Spanish appear to be hot on the distribution of local maps. Josep then explains that Hostal Regina has been in his family since 1960 and has twenty-five rooms. He runs the *hostal* with his brother and their wives. *Hostals*, I soon learn, are a category of accommodation that is above a mere youth hostel but below a full-blown hotel: small, individually-run places that act like efficient B & Bs, usually with a bar offering snacks. They are inexpensive and rather perfect for this type of train trip.

Josep wears a pale-blue checked shirt and has long straight features that seem to hint at Blanes's Roman past. It is a busy week as there is a motorbike competition in Barcelona and many guests are staying to make the 40-mile journey south-west each day. He makes revving motions with his hand to indicate that they ride there and back on motorbikes. He tells me that Blanes (population: 38,000) has a "nice beach and nice garden"; he points on the map at the Marimurtra Botanical Garden, which is very close by. He also tells me that there is a strong local Cuban connection as many from these parts emigrated to the Spanish colony (which lasted from the early sixteenth century until 1898) and returned wealthy; hence the odd Mexican flag hanging on facades of buildings.

Regarding Catalonian independence, Josep replies with a raised Romanesque eyebrow: "This is politic. This is another problem. I don't speak politic." He waves his hand to dismiss the subject.

* * *

Along a path winding upward above a marina I reach the Marimurtra Botanical Garden, where I am soon meeting another Josep.

This Josep is the manager of the garden, who happens to be by the entrance and who is soon explaining all about Carl Faust, a successful "piping systems" businessman, who decided in 1924 at the age of fifty to escape the piping systems rat race, retire and indulge in his love of plants. The gardens are run by a charity and spread over 4.5 hectares by dramatic sea cliffs. They now contain more than four thousand species from Europe, America, Africa, Australia and Asia divided into subtropical, temperate and Mediterranean zones. A total of 120,000 tourists visit each year. "He never opened the garden to the public," says Josep, referring to Faust, who died in 1952. "He described it as an *epicurean republic for botanists* – that was his exact phrase. He wanted botanists from across Europe to come." The gardens were originally for visiting plant specialists only.

Josep is super laid-back in a yellow polo shirt and jeans, looking like a tourist himself. For a moment or two he reflects on Faust's decision to pack in the piping business and retire aged fifty. "Ah, yes – oh, yes," he says, his eyes taking on a faraway look about the thought of retiring at fifty. "I would like to do this too – truly."

We talk about George Orwell. Orwell served for the Republicans during the Spanish Civil War, fighting in trenches close to the city of Zaragoza. They seem to be conveniently on my way to the north coast. So, after this detour south from Figueres, I have a vague idea of stopping off along the way to see where one of my favourite writers took up arms.

"Orwell! Orwell!" Josep exclaims upon noticing I am carrying *Homage to Catalonia*. "I like Orwell! It is not bad, that book he wrote about Paris and London."

He is referring to *Down and Out in Paris and London*.

"Ah yes, not bad. I would love to do that."

"What do you mean?" I ask.

"I would like to recreate that book," he says.

"As a tramp?" I ask.

"Yes, ideally as a homeless person," he says.

"Why?" I ask.

"Because I'm sure it hasn't changed much at all," Josep says with a shrug, as though this is as good a reason as any. "I have read many of his books. I'd like also to go to the island where he wrote *Nineteen Eighty-Four*: Jura. I'd like to see the cottage where he wrote *Nineteen Eighty-Four*. I may be a manager here but I studied philosophy at Girona University. *Nineteen Eighty-Four* – it is crucial! We're walking into *Nineteen Eighty-Four*, if not already in it!"

Josep pauses to ponder this point – he seems to be warming to his theme. "What Orwell never imagined, of course, was social media," he says. "I think he never imagined we'd have Big Brother in our pockets. I like the way he foresaw the future. He lived in a technological age of advancement and he pushed it forward. People must have thought he was crazy. But the difference between crazy and not crazy is small."

"Like Dalí?"

"Yes, yes," says Josep, beaming. He's another local fan of the artist (I do not meet anyone who isn't).

We talk about Orwell for quite some time. Then we exchange emails and Josep suggests meeting for a *cerveza* (beer) to discuss our mutual hero some more, but he cannot make this evening and the trains are taking me onward tomorrow. So we shake hands and promise to keep in touch. Yes, I know it is probably an unpardonable travel cliché to say that Spain is a nation of chatterboxes, to which I have already alluded, but early indications seem to be: *yes, they are – the Spanish like to talk very much indeed*. Which is good news for me as it's preferable to have some company on a long train journey.

The Marimurtra Botanical Garden is magnificent. The subtropical zone is alive with fragrance and oxygenated air. Bees buzz beneath pergolas draped in Japanese vines. Delicate flowers from South Africa bloom in little orange explosions of petals. Creepers tumble from exotic South American trees, casting eerie shadows on paths winding by purple lily ponds and banks of twisted cacti from Lanzarote. It is easy to lose track of the zones, finding yourself carried along as though lost in a dream induced by the sublime surroundings.

Down to the cliff's edge, waves crash, thunder and dissolve in great pools of fizz. Parakeets yak and squeak above. Wafts of lavender, rosemary, lemons, oranges and roses blend in perfumed passages leading to gardeners in pith helmets attending immaculate beds. A quote from William Wordsworth on a wall here seems to be a good motto for Marimurtra: "Nature never did betray the heart that loved her."

Just how it feels in Blanes. Thank you, tourist office man back in Figueres-Vilafant Station.

From the gardens it is a short stroll down steep steps to Cala Sant Francesc, a suntrap beach with a sandwich bar and restaurant and glamorous sunbathers – apparently it is a popular spot for people from Barcelona. Middle-aged bathers, it is hard not to notice, seem to have an ambivalent attitude to the need to wear clothing, occasionally stripping off either to put on swimsuits or resume 'dry clothes. I read *Homage to Catalonia* and eat a baguette before walking back via flags on an apartment calling for ¡LLIBERTAT, PRESOS, POLÍTICA! (*FREEDOM, PRISONERS, POLITICS!*). This is referring to Catalonian separatist leaders who have been jailed. Judging by the many banners with such slogans, Blanes seems to be another centre of separatist feeling.

At Hostal Regina, motorbike tourists are chatting to Josep, while elderly women whom I take to be locals play cards in a corner. The motorcycle tourists are tucking away *sangria* and encouraging Josep to have a glass or two. A woman with shopping bags enters and Jordi, Josep's brother, pours her a shot of some kind before she has sat down or said a word. They begin to discuss matters animatedly but are out of earshot.

Jordi is the younger brother by ten years, aged forty-eight, but unmistakably related with strong Roman features too. When the woman with the shopping has left, he helpfully prints out the rail timetable to my next destination: Vilanova i la Geltrú. This is where the Catalonia Railway Museum is to be found. I need to catch the 09:33 train to Barcelona tomorrow morning, taking another to arrive in Vilanova at 11:44. Solidarity with railway stuff has me interested in this museum; I want to visit to find out about the first trains in Spain, which rolled along this very coast.

Jordi pours me a glass of *grappa* – I offer to buy him a drink and he opts for a *cerveza* – and he explains his family's switch to tourism half a century ago.

"In 1960 we have one house here with no floors above. It was small, so small." Now the building is four storeys. "Then my grandparents buy next door's house. Then they add some more rooms. Then slowly, slowly, in the 1970s we build up and have more. At this time my grandfather still worked at the factory making nylon. That was my father's job too. In the seventies and eighties that factory employed three thousand. Now there are just fifty people. Now it is finished. When I was a boy, many of my friends' parents worked there. But there is no future in nylon. Nylon is no more. The factory got bought by one investment management company and then another."

"Is the economy better now with tourism?" I ask.

"No," Jordi replies quickly. "The factory days were good. Then in the sixties, Europe opened up to tourism. The holiday people came from Sweden and Denmark one year. There was a bar for these holiday people. Then next year German and Belgian holiday people came. Then many people who were working in the factory thought: *I think I could have an extra business here.* One room, then two, three. Bigger places for the holiday people. Buy next house, and next house!"

"Is this what your grandparents did?"

"Yes. Two rooms, then more. Two more rooms, then more again. In those days the wife would say to the husband: 'It is better in hotels.'

In the eighties that was the peak: there were twenty-three hotels along the beach here. That was the boom. Now it is all apartments. Now we are the only one with rooms like this. In 1980, the city was happier than now. There were jobs! Not now. Not so happy now. That is my impression. Now there are only apartments. Rich people from Barcelona, they have a little house here. In winter it is dead. It is nothing, nothing."

Jordi spreads his arms to indicate nothing and looks beyond the counter. The trio of motorcycle tourists has gone upstairs, Josep has vanished and the card players have returned home.

At nine in the evening the bar is deserted; chairs empty, waiting for holiday people who may never come.

"Loco *for locos*"
Blanes to Vilanova i la Geltrú

The 09:33 to Barcelona departs on time. Past a factory, possibly the old nylon factory, patchwork farmland with plots of low green crops spread out before the train hugs the coast. This is a very slow train. We potter along a sunny beach with volleyball games already in progress, joggers, lifeguards and bars shaded by umbrella palms. Big ugly concrete hotels shoot up here and there. A holiday park emerges with long rows of identikit huts that at first glance look like chicken farms.

A ferry churns along the coast. A solitary figure buzzes across choppy waves on a jet ski. Musclebound athletes perform pull-ups in exercise yards. Our packed train creaks forward – the Mediterranean Sea dazzling in a blinding gleam toward the horizon – before slipping in and out of tunnels. Coves with red cliffs and pink sands appear and disappear as we dive through the rocky landscape. It is great simply to be on the move. I am already used to the pattern (and pleasure) of the get-up-and-go of a train adventure. This is like no other kind of escape:

no itinerary, no tickets booked, no commitments… no limits – other than where the tracks are laid, that is. Let the random enjoyments of lazy days take over for a while. Let the trains lead the way, wherever they may go. That's what I'm after right now.

The American adventurer Richard Halliburton, who swam the length of the Panama Canal and who died crossing the Pacific Ocean in a Chinese junk in 1939, aged thirty-nine, once said: "A vagabond life is the logical life to lead if one seeks the intimate knowledge of the world we were seeking." I do not intend to die trying but there is something in what he says. To be a vagabond for a month or so: why not? Cut loose! Let it go! Forget things are perhaps not so wonderful back home – the dodgy politics, name-calling, divided nation, "them and us", all that jazz. *¡Ovídalo todo!* (Forget it all!) Take a few rides in a big hot country: *As I Rolled Out One Midsummer Morning*, if you like, *And Wondered Where Next*.

These thoughts are interrupted by a German couple with a child and a Barcelona guidebook who occupy the three seats of my set of four. I put my backpack on the rack above for extra room.

The German woman thanks me in English and asks if I am going to see the sights in Barcelona – so I explain my mission to visit Vilanova i la Geltrú. They are staying at one of the big hotels and are on a day trip to "see what she likes", she says, eyeing her daughter. "The chocolate museum may come into it."

They are on a nine-day holiday and have got to grips with train timetables, having organized airport transfers and various rides such as this one. Jutta and Joe are secondary-school geography teachers from Villingen-Schwenningen in the Black Forest. German tourists from the Black Forest seem to be everywhere. All three wear silver wristbands to indicate which hotel meal plan they are on as well as matching pale-blue tops. They are very orderly German tourists from the Black Forest.

"It is our passion and our profession," Jutta says.

"What is?" I ask.

"Travel. Tourism. Geography," she says, folding her hands neatly and turning to me. "For example, overtourism. Barcelona has too many tourists."

So begins my *geographie klasse mit Frau Jutta*.

"Tourism preserves certain traditional customs: costumes, old ways of communities, the cultural identity. But it changes things. The infrastructure! The prices!" Jutta says, regarding me closely. I nod to show I am paying attention.

"Overtourism in Barcelona: so many people are around and about. The infrastructure must cope! Airbnb! Apartments become expensive for locals, so they have to find alternatives. Prices rise! And people are really bothered by the party people." She says this last bit almost as an aside.

I ask Jutta what she means.

Jutta shifts geography for a moment. "In Munich during the beer festival, really big problem. Party people! And in Venice! In Ibiza! Party people! Locals must work eighteen hours a day just to rent an apartment next to party people! Prices have gone crazy!"

I nod to show I am paying attention.

"The shopping changes, the infrastructure!" she says. Jutta is keen on infrastructure. "For the people who live there it's bad: only sandwiches and takeaway food. For tourists it's convenient to find exactly what you need. Cruise-ship places are especially affected: Venice, Dubrovnik, Barcelona. Berlin has changed a lot. The number of flights to Berlin has tripled. It is now a party city!" Jutta is not so keen on parties. "Berlin, it is suffering from Airbnb and gentrification! In the Black Forest we are quite touristy too, but in a different way. People tend to come but then travel on. A friend who visits each year asked me the other day if anything has changed recently, and suddenly I realized so much has. You don't appreciate it, what's happening. But you have to appreciate it as it's part of your identity."

Jutta pauses and exhales. She has become quite animated. "I just can't stand it!" she says, shifting tourism problems this time. "We have really discussed whether we will ever fly again. We are very concerned about the environment."

Her husband Joe, who has been listening to us, nods. I nod too. Jutta nods back. We seem to have all started nodding.

"In lessons we have to care about the environment and care about what we do. We teach this. It's the first time our daughter has flown." Her daughter, who understands English, nods. "She always wanted to fly. She is aged ten now."

Totally shifting subject, Jutta tells me she cannot bear the German habit of putting towels out early to reserve sunloungers at hotels – and neither can her uncle, who once "sneaked out like a little boy while everyone was at breakfast and threw all the towels in the pool". She chuckles at the thought of this.

Then Jutta rummages in her bag and pulls out a tablet for playing an electronic game, which she gives to her daughter. Her husband helps her daughter play the game and Jutta comments: "A friend of mine once said: 'Happy wife, happy life.' She needs things to do – this is good. It makes me have a relaxing time. Hungry or annoyed children can ruin a holiday."

I nod. We all nod. And we pull into the depths of Barcelona-Sants Station, nodding.

I say goodbye and rush to catch the 11:06 to Vilanova i la Geltrú.

* * *

During the *geographie klasse* on the train from Blanes, we passed Mataró Station and travelled along Spain's original mainland train line from 1848.

It is a half-hour journey onward from Barcelona-Sants Station to Vilanova i la Geltrú along the sea in a busy carriage with a cluster of exhausted-looking party people who, on this Saturday morning, appear as though they are dressed from last night. A woman sitting opposite wearing cowboy boots with her legs slung over her friend's lap is talking about the behaviour of a man they met last night: "I wonder: can he even remember what he said?" They laugh and hug each other as though holding on for safety on the deck of a ship in a storm; limbs akimbo, sticking out across the aisle. I'm not sure Jutta would have approved. A busker plays "Can't Help Falling in Love" on a recorder. An elderly woman turns the pages of a romantic novel. Waves break on the shore in a soapy wash and the sea beyond is brilliant aquamarine. The train from Barcelona has a relaxed, let-it-all-hang-out vibe.

We pull into a grand cream-and-yellow station with arched windows and rows of pink flowers: Vilanova i la Geltrú.

The Catalonia Railway Museum is by the tracks in a former engine shed. Forget Santiago de Compostela – this is the place of pilgrimage for train lovers in Spain; well, one of them at least, along with the Museo del Ferrocarril de Madrid.

As I have said, the odd bit of *railway stuff* never harmed anyone, and it will help keep my mind on my mission: Spain! Trains!

I enter the old shed and find myself wandering about a yard with water tanks, container wagons, weighing bridges, more container wagons, "hopper cars" (for transporting "loose bulk material"), sections of railway bridges and "track superstructures". These, I learn from an information panel, are especially important: "The railway superstructure, which has evolved over time, is available on a grading which is placed on the rails and the rest of the equipment. The tracks guide and carry great masses at variable velocities, and so they need strong fasteners." Intriguing, I'm sure you'll agree, though I do not think I understand a word of what is going on.

The best section of the Catalonia Rail Museum is beyond the "superstructure" section, where the old steam locomotives are kept. Locomotive 120-2112 MZA 168, otherwise known as Martello, dates from 1854 and is the oldest surviving loco in Spain, once with a top speed of 60 kilometres an hour (38 miles per hour). It was made in Britain especially for Spanish tracks and is painted black with a jolly red fender and a shiny brass chimney. Nearby is a delightful, perfectly polished wooden carriage from 1878 with *Ferrocarril de Valls a Villanueva y Barcelona* written on the side. According to another information panel, this company was the creation of a visionary local named Francesc Gumà i Ferran, whose family had made a fortune trading in Cuba, and the carriage itself was constructed by Harlan & Hollingsworth, a company based in Delaware in the United States. At the time this was state of the art with an "innovative, technical" bogie (undercarriage) that apparently "revolutionized passenger comfort". Next to this, leaping forward many years, is an *automotor diesel* train from 1935 that could power itself – "like a bus on iron rails" – reaching 100 kilometres an hour (63 miles per hour). Further on still, leaping backward many years, is a replica of the very first locomotive that travelled between Barcelona and Mataró in 1848 – painted green and looking sleek. This is a Patentee 1-1-1, so yet another panel says. I am not sure really what that means either, I will admit.

Just as I am thinking to myself, *Not bad at all, what a good little museum, worth the trip, I have made an effort and improved my Spanish train knowledge*, I step into another section with a great open space with perhaps twenty locomotives positioned facing outward in a circle. This is some kind of loco heaven; it's as though I have stepped into a steam-train dream. Rail enthusiasts, I can confidently say, will greatly enjoy the final part of the Catalonia Railway Museum. Engine after engine stares down, gleaming and looking ready to hurtle along the tracks. Most of the locomotives are steam powered but some are diesel, with art deco stripes and names written on the front: *Virgen de Begoña, Virgen de Covadonga, Virgen de la Bien Aparecida*. Collected like this, the cumulative effect is impressive. The Spanish word for "crazy" is of course *loco*. Here, should anyone wish to allow themselves, the rail enthusiast may quietly go *loco* over locos for a while.

Back in the reception, I ask the manager, Olga Pedra, if many very enthusiastic rail enthusiasts visit the Catalonia Rail Museum. Olga is a cool railway museum manager, dressed all in black with yellow-framed designer glasses. She immediately gets what I'm driving at.

"You mean trainspotters?" she asks rhetorically before continuing. "Yes, yes – from France and England. British people, oh yes, a lot of them. They come on their own mainly." She studies me over her yellow-framed designer glasses. "With French people it's different: French people come with families."

"Can you understand the most enthusiastic of enthusiasts?" I ask.

"I suppose so," she replies. "I do understand the British – maybe it is because the steam machine was invented there."

On the first Sunday of each month, the 1848 replica is driven round a track on the perimeter of the museum, Olga says.

Then she asks about my intended journey and replies: "Sun cream! I recommend you." She is regarding my complexion with concern. "Thirty-five to forty degrees down south! Minimum! Hat! Shorts! Sun cream!"

And with that – after checking out the gift shop with Spanish train books, Spanish train models and Spanish train-themed bottles of wine – I book into a hotel around the corner, drop off my backpack and hit the beach.

Tomorrow it is time to roll west.

CHAPTER THREE

VILANOVA I LA GELTRÚ TO HUESCA, VIA MONTSERRAT, MANRESA AND LLEIDA

NUNS, SNAILS AND RACK RAILWAYS

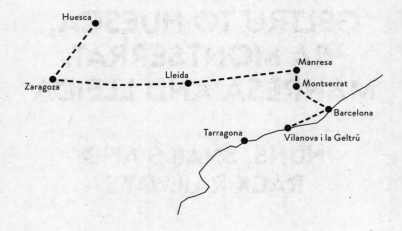

A lthough a mouthful, Vilanova i la Geltrú is a pleasant place to while away a day, so long as you watch where you dine.

After a swim beside the hot strip of grainy sand near the Habana Beach Bar, a long wander around the narrow streets lined by apricot- and salmon-coloured buildings reveals churches, a cathedral (locked) and many cafés at which men wearing yellow and white costumes have gathered. I appear to have missed a fiesta of some sort; Spanish morris dancing, perhaps. It is said that the people of Vilanova i la Geltrú *siempre tener una pierna en el aire* (always have a leg in the air), such is their proclivity to enjoy fiestas. On the evidence of my visit, this seems to be the case.

Also on display is the local passion for football. This is quite impossible to miss. While parents chatter at cafés drinking Estrella beers, children rush about just about everywhere kicking balls. In one square, Plaça de Soler, I stop to watch as a shopkeeper of a sports goods shop, appropriately, is driven mad by kids who have decided to use the entrance as a "goal". The shopkeeper flicks her fingers and waves her arms, but as soon as she is gone, they are back, with the – soft – ball thudding against the window once again. This is repeated many times until the shopkeeper simply gives up in exasperation.

The children wear purple-and-red Barcelona shirts, several with *MESSI 10* written on the back. The Argentine footballer, who some believe to be the best player ever to put boot to ball, is clearly and unsurprisingly the local hero. Let me take a moment to explain the use of "unsurprisingly" here.

Lionel Messi has, at the time of writing, scored 640 goals in 742 appearances for Fútbol Club Barcelona, where he was nurtured as a child prodigy, such was his unbelievably apparent skill. He has also, during these 742 games, created 258 "assists", set-ups for fellow players to score. So in 742 games, since starting at the age of eighteen, he is accountable one way or another for 898 goals. This is an average of 1.21 goals a game. During his time at Barcelona, the team has won La Liga, the Spanish league, ten times and the UEFA Champions League, considered the top club title in the world, four times. While playing in the Champions League, he has scored 118 goals in 146 matches so far, including eight hat-tricks (three goals in a game). This is the most ever. On one occasion in 2012, he slotted in five goals.

In La Liga, where Messi has been top scorer for seven seasons, he has scored the most goals ever: 447. This, at the time of writing, is more than a hundred goals ahead of the next-best player, Cristiano Ronaldo of Portugal – Messi's only current rival to greatness, if you put Brazil's Pelé and Argentina's Maradona to one side. He has won the Ballon d'Or, the annual award for best male player in the world as judged by football writers and coaches, a record six times, although many believe he should have been selected more often. Yes, it is true that his play for Argentina's national side has not lived up to his club performances, but Argentina has of late been going through a poor patch.

OK, so I've got that out of my system.

In short, Lionel Messi, in many ways an adopted Spaniard having lived in the country since boyhood, is some kind of miracle in footballing terms – and Spanish players themselves are not too shabby either. Since 2008, during the past eleven years, the Spanish national team has won two UEFA European Championships (best team in Europe) and one World Cup (best team in the world), while Spanish club teams have triumphed at the UEFA Champions League no fewer than seven out of ten times. This means, essentially: Spanish players are very, very good.

OK, I've got that out of my system too.

I am not bringing all of this up here simply to satisfy, or demonstrate, my own enjoyment of the game.

My point is that the Spanish are absolutely mad about football, as their great recent successes and their willingness to spend multimillions of euros on the world's greatest players such as Messi and Ronaldo shows. This passion, this thud of balls against walls and scurry-and-scuffle of feet in small towns, remote villages and big cities, is to become an accompaniment to this journey; a comforting background noise that says kids are out being kids, playing in their neighbourhood, not shut up indoors staring at screens with goggle-eyes, twitchy fingers and numbed brains.

OK, it's all totally out of my system now.

In the evening in Vilanova i la Geltrú, I eat an awful meal of seafood risotto – with hardly any seafood – served with a plate of awful olives that I did not ask for although I make the mistake of eating three and later realizing that each of these three awful olives has cost me precisely one euro a piece.

Then I go to a bar near the hotel where the barman, Ronny, who is from Bangladesh, serves a glass of rudimentary red wine, also one euro, and tells me he used to live in Windsor: "Right by the palace. I mean right by it. Next door. I was an executive chef at a pub. I seen her three times."

By "her", Ronny is referring to Queen Elizabeth II.

"Very nice. It was amazing, honestly. Three times. We have a soft corner for her here."

By "corner" Ronny means "spot" and I am unsure who "we" is.

Then Ronny goes on to say he studied in Britain to gain an MBA in business and finance. "Honestly, it was boring. Why would I want an eight-hour office job? So I change. I became a chef. I love it. Every second here is a challenge. I want to learn Spanish cooking. Sure, I have problems with the language. It is difficult to learn both: the language and cooking, but I try."

I tell him that I wish I'd eaten at his bar, not where I ended up earlier, explaining the risotto and the olives.

"You must watch for that, watch for it," he says extremely earnestly.

I tell him I will – and return to my hotel by the Catalonia Rail Museum.

"Spiritual medicine"
Vilanova i la Geltrú to Montserrat

To reach my next destination requires catching the 09:38 to Bellvitge Station in Barcelona followed by another train on the R5 Metro line that arrives in Monistrol de Montserrat Station at 11:40. From there I will take the Montserrat Rack Railway up a mountain for 5 kilometres to Santa Maria de Montserrat, a Benedictine monastery that attracts two million visitors a year, many on religious pilgrimages. I have already booked a room on the mountain at Hotel Abat Cisneros Montserrat, which is run by the monks and is right next door to their Renaissance basilica.

Obviously, the rack railway is a draw. This railway weaves up the slopes gaining an altitude of 550 metres, running every 20 minutes, taking 7 minutes each way, and is powered by a system of cogs. It was opened in 1892 by Ferrocarriles de Montaña a Grandes Pendientes (which translates as something like "Mountains and Big Slopes Railway") due to the popularity of the monastery with tourists, but closed as major repairs were required in 1957. In the 1980s interest revived in the railway and the line reopened in 2003. Also of railway interest at Montserrat are a couple of funiculars on the mountaintop, which provide access to excellent walks. I intend, for the purposes of train research, to take at least one of these funiculars.

So quite a day, train-wise, lies ahead.

At Vilanova i la Geltrú Station I enjoy a tasty chorizo baguette and a coffee (the same price as last night's olives) sitting in a leather armchair at the tangerine-coloured station café. Shortly afterward, the train arrives, retracing the journey along the coast to Barcelona. It is quiet on board – not many Spaniards seem to be on the move on Sunday morning other than a guy hauling beach blankets on a trolley. I'd seen him trying his luck near the Habana Beach Bar yesterday; it looked like a hot, hard way to scratch a living.

Again, the feeling of moving onward is calming and it is interesting to witness the line cutting through the Garraf Massif of mountains having read about the tunnels here at the Catalonia Rail Museum; construction had required a monumental feat of engineering. It is a sunny, hopeful morning and before long we pull into Bellvitge Station, where a short walk to Gornal Station is required to catch the connection to Montserrat.

There are eighteen stops on the R5 line travelling in the direction of Manresa-Baixador Station. After waiting on a platform with pea-green tiles and long strips of neon lights, the R5 arrives and makes steady progress through the suburbs into a valley and then upward with cliffs soaring above on the lead-in to Monistrol de Montserrat Station. There is a lot of oohing and aahing at the mountains as quite a few passengers on board are tourists visiting the monastery like me; this is the most popular day trip from Barcelona.

Which brings us to the rack railway. We all pile on board the narrow-gauge train and I find myself facing forward near the front with the seat opposite taken, after I sit, by a very large man wearing very tight shorts, somewhat off-puttingly.

Upward we go, crossing a milky green river and a road, and passing a mounted steam locomotive, before settling into a speed of about 25 kilometres an hour (16 miles per hour), so says a display. Rock formations shoot upward like enormous totem poles. If you stare at these rocks for long enough faces seem to emerge, as though the mountains are alive with ancient ancestors, quietly watching. This is the most beautiful ride yet, with delicate yellow shrubs, ramrod straight pines and glistening pink rocks beside the track. It is easy to understand why the monks were keen to build a monastery up here, quite apart from the discovery of the Black Virgin (*La Moreneta* in Catalan).

This virgin, also known as the Black Madonna, is the real reason the Benedictines came. The icon was unearthed in a mountain cave in AD 880 and the legend goes that the Black Virgin or Madonna, whose black features gave birth to the name, was left here by St Peter in AD 50, only to be hidden during Spain's Muslim invasion. Whether the legend is true or not, St Peter missed out by a couple of millennia or so on A Very Good Train Ride.

The wheels screech and squeal as we rise ever more steeply. Vibrations from the track cause the carriage to wobble and hum. Across the valley a mountain range rises out of the distant haze. Walkers with sticks tramp up a track below (more fool them). A train slides in the opposite direction at a section of line with double tracks while yellow and white butterflies flutter by the carriage windows. As train journeys go, this is about as heavenly as they come.

Then we enter a tunnel and pull into a station.

We have arrived at Montserrat.

After Santiago de Compostela, this is the second most visited pilgrimage site in Spain, although the crowds have yet to overwhelm the monastery today. Well-fed monks in brown tunics tied with ropes stride purposefully hither and thither, taking shortcuts up stairways and along little lanes. A small flock of visiting nuns, discussing matters as though exchanging secrets, has gathered by a cross near the station exit. Close by, a security guard rolls past on a Segway – even godly mountains require policing – and I walk up a short, paved road to my resplendent ochre-coloured hotel, next to the magnificent arched entrance to the basilica and a balustrade on a terrace facing the misty valley. All above pink-hued cliffs rise, totem-pole faces peering downward as though inspecting the day's tourist catch.

Hotel Abat Cisneros Montserrat is the perfect base for a train-orientated visit to Montserrat. Not only is it near the main station, but both the funiculars are also close by, although the one to the cave where the Black Virgin was discovered is closed for some reason I cannot fathom. So I go to the other funicular up to the hermitage of Sant Joan, waiting in a queue for a while and catching the words of a monk in conversation with one of the visiting nuns. "Some places," he says, "give you spiritual medicine…" His voice fades away.

This is true – and that is to come – but first I have another ride, a very steep one.

We are at about 1,000 metres here, but the Sant Joan funicular rises a further 248 metres, covering 503 metres at a steepest gradient of sixty-five per cent. This is the steepest funicular in the country, built in 1918.

With a beeping sound we depart in two narrow green carriages, squeezed in and watching blackberry bushes and thick forest pass by. On a flickering screen at one end images of white-water rafters and cyclists flash up, advertizing the tourist attractions of Catalonia. Looking downward, it appears that one thick cable is responsible for our remarkable rise (though I may well be wrong about this). A sound of creaking and rubbing comes from the track. The tops of the heads of passengers are almost all that can be seen in the carriage behind, phones raised filming the ascent.

Six marvellous minutes later we reach the top, where it is about a half-hour's scramble up tracks past Sant Joan's hermitage and smaller rocky paths between pines and damp caves to the mountain peak.

Boulder-like summits poke up all around, some being tackled by climbers, others with mountaineers on top resting after ascents. Plains, valleys and distant ridges spread out as far as the eye can see inland, with the haze of Barcelona to the north and a faraway glimmer of sea. Here above the hermitage of Sant Joan, beneath a solid blue sky, is a place to consider things peacefully while sitting on a quiet stone ledge. Spiritual medicine, indeed.

On the way down the path from the top, I meet one of the visiting nuns.

"Parlez-vous français?" she asks.

A little, I reply.

"Quelle direction pour Magdalena?"

I point toward Santa Magdalena Chapel, for which I'd seen a sign further up the mountain.

She had been about to go the wrong way and is grateful. *"Merci, merci,"* she says. Then she adds in English: "My name is Jen."

I give my name and she hears that I have said "John". Her eyes light up. Sant Joan in Catalan is Saint John. I correct her and she seems a little disappointed that I am not a modern-day tourist reincarnation of the saint.

Jen asks where I am from and I tell her. She says she is from Versailles.

Jen asks me what I do – Jen is an inquisitive nun. I tell her I'm a journalist.

"Oh well, I'd better watch what I say," she replies in French, before informing me in English: "My brother-in-law is a journalist."

She does not seem particularly impressed by our choices of job, although I think this may just be nun humour.

"Pray for me, Tom," she says as she clambers up the steep path, her pale grey habit disappearing into the pines.

Pleased to have met a French nun, I continue my descent, passing the funicular and taking a long winding path all the way back to the basilica.

Inside, a service is on. Hymns reverberate across packed pews above a black-and-white tiled floor embedded with crosses and quatrefoil patterns. Above the high altar the Black Virgin herself rests in a gilded alcove, gazing down upon the congregation. Brass lamps lit with candles hang below a vaulted ceiling. Murals of angels soar upward by the nave. Sculptures of biblical figures in various states of agony and ecstasy cast eerie shadows on walls.

Montserrat's famous boys' choir is singing with transcendent voices in between monks performing rituals with incense and occasionally addressing us with sermons. Bells peal. More incense is swished about and after a while the bells ring for a long time and the show is over. We all file out and I go to the hotel restaurant, where I eat an excellent chicken dish in a vaulted dining chamber served by a waiter in a smart white uniform while listening to an American grandmother and daughter discuss car hire troubles, vegetarianism, the price of wine in New York City and the granddaughter's recent boyfriends. "Most of 'em have just treated me as Miss Moneybags," the granddaughter complains.

In the bar afterward, I eavesdrop on another conversation, between a nun and two monks. The nun is drinking a large G & T; the visiting nuns of Montserrat seem pretty cool characters. The monks have just joined her, and soon large G & Ts are being delivered their way too. The nun, I gather, is to give a sermon tomorrow but is concerned about keeping her balance on the lectern. She is worried that if she looks upward she will "wobble". One of the monks, a young English monk who appears quite solid and tough, says: "Do not worry, I will be there for you." If she falls, he will catch her.

Another round of large G & Ts is ordered.

They discuss the "sense of presence" of Montserrat, before the nun raises the subject of the Virgin Mary and chastity: "What do youths think?"

The English monk replies: "Some see purity in a very medieval sense..."

But I do not catch the rest of the answer as the new G & Ts arrive and the other monk, a Spanish monk, says: "Cheers!" This is just about his only contribution to the conversation.

The nun takes over for a while. "There's something about that unity, about what Mary says about women in general..."

This continues for a while, after which the English monk says: "Yes, yes, yes."

The nun launches into another soliloquy: "Mary Magdalene, now I don't think there's a theologian who believes..."

This continues for some time too, after which the English monk says: "Yes, yes, yes."

So the pattern of conversation continues until, like students when the student union bar is closing, they all clatter their coins on the table, dug deep from habits and tunics, pay their bill and go.

The last train down the mountain for the day has long ago departed. It's just me, the monks, the nuns and the few other tourists staying at the hotel who appear to be up here on the mountain now.

Outside, moonlight bathes the faces of the totem-pole cliffs and bright stars sparkle in a deep purple sky.

Yes, staying up here is spiritual, and a little bit strange too (in a nice way).

"I am from round here... I do not do this"
Montserrat to Lleida via Manresa

Before catching the Montserrat Rack Railway down the mountain, I go to see the Black Virgin.

Yesterday the queues had been too long, but one of the benefits of staying at the Hotel Abat Cisneros Montserrat is being able to beat the crowds and walk straight in to see the ancient icon when doors open. Down a corridor on the right of the basilica I go, alone, before ascending a marble staircase flanked by paintings of saints, and enter the glittery gold and silver alcove above the high altar, where the Black Virgin resides with a figurine of a child resting on her knee. She has a long thin face bearing an inscrutable expression, holding a sphere to represent the world in her right hand, while the child on her lap has curly locks and a cheeky grin. A cleaner comes in and mops the steps around the icon while I look about. Then a family enters and each member of the family touches the sphere, which protrudes from behind a transparent partition, while whispering prayers. Although not religious, I do the same for luck when they are gone; could prove useful on the trains to come.

Next up is the gift shop. This is right by the train station and evidence that the monks of Montserrat are very canny mountain monks. Like the people of Figueres with Dalí, they know they are on to a good thing. Bottles of wine, bottles of liquor ("The alcohol is made in Barcelona but the monks make the recipes," says an assistant), jams, mustards, olive oils, pastries, sweets, cheeses, flatbreads, honey, biscuits, chocolate, sparkling wine, tea, oven gloves, kitchen aprons, magnets, caps, straw hats, "bumbags", hoodies, T-shirts bearing the slogan *Montserrat: The Best Place in the World*, pouches for glasses, bandanas, shawls, mugs, pencil cases, purses, thermometers, egg timers, leather water pouches, fans, wooden boxes, snow globes, jigsaws, walking sticks, large decorative ceramic spoons, bells, espresso cups, hotplates, smaller spoons, Christmas tree decorations, bellows for fires, crosses for walls, back scratchers cum shoe horns, religious icons, necklaces, pendants, rings, candles, plates, ashtrays, shot glasses, salt and pepper shakers, candle holders… all branded *Montserrat* with pictures of the mountains or of the Black Virgin. You've got to take your hat off to the mountain monks of Montserrat – they really know how to do tourism.

Resisting the urge to purchase a back scratcher cum shoe horn (which would stick out of the backpack too much anyway), I catch the 10:15 on the rack railway to the sun-drenched valley below.

At the hotel earlier, the receptionist had looked at me with bafflement and alarm when I had asked how to catch a train to Lleida. This historic city with a ruined old castle at its centre is in the Catalan plains, halfway on the route to Aragon, where I want to – as I have said – see the trenches George Orwell served in during the Spanish Civil War. This is as far as definite plans go for northern Spain, other than to drop by in Santiago de Compostela, as everyone seems to do that.

The receptionist's alarm had come from my idea of taking slow trains out of the mountains and across the plain to Lleida, rather than returning to Barcelona and taking fast trains to get there.

"I am not sure about this, not sure," he had said, raising his eyebrows and looking quite perturbed.

"Why?" I had asked.

"In Spain, you see, there is normally a *radial* system."

"What do you mean?"

"In Spain it is better to go to the big city," he had replied. "Go to Barcelona. Then, it is *radial*." As he said this, he had gesticulated with his hands to point outward in various directions. His point seemed to be: don't bother with the little lines, catch the fast trains that ping out of the big cities to just about anywhere you want to go.

After he said this, I showed him my *Rail Map Europe*; an onward connection from the close-by town of Manresa seemed possible.

"I am from round here," he had replied, mentioning a village further inland. "If I want to go there, I go to Barcelona. I do not do this."

So, totally ignoring the receptionist's advice, I am taking the 10:41 R4 Metro line service to Manresa.

This is a short, squeaky ride beside an olive-green river flanked by crimson-hued cliffs. Aside from the squeaks, it is a peaceful, lazy, slow journey punctuated by a couple of stops, including one at Castellbell i el Vilar Station, near an eye-catching medieval bridge that arcs high above the water. This is such a captivating spot that for a split second I consider getting off.

But the train rolls on, with the mountains of Montserrat disappearing behind and the suburbs of an industrial-looking city soon arising.

This is Manresa and the R4 pulls in at Manresa-Baixador Station, where the service terminates. A handful of passengers disembarks and I try to find the ticket office for the connection to Lleida.

There is, however, no ticket office. The station is unmanned, with just a couple of ticket machines that do not feature Lleida. I stand by the station entrance by a busy road. There must be a Renfe station somewhere near here; Manresa-Baixador seems to be just for the Metro from Barcelona.

As I do so, a short woman with a purple handbag sidles up. She asks if I am lost and I explain. She grabs my arm and says in a mixture of Spanish and English: "I go! *¡El río! ¡El río!*"

Which is how I meet Svitlana, who introduces herself as a *profesora ucraniana de psicologia* (a psychology professor from Ukraine). She is going to the *río*, which is apparently next to the station I need, and says she'll show me the way. When I thank her, she just says, "*Es nada, nada*" ("It's nothing, nothing") and leads onward.

Svitlana wears tight faded jeans, pink-and-green high heels and a tight black T-shirt. Her hair is in a blonde bob. Without the high heels she must be about five feet tall. She has quick hazel eyes and is in her fifties. She grabs my arms and pulls me onward, asking where I have come from. At a mention of Montserrat, she replies, "*Bonisimo, perficio.*" ("Very good, perfect.")

We walk along a street toward Manresa's ornate theatre as Svitlana tells me that she came to Spain twenty years ago, although she does not explain how or why. She seems more concerned about my well-being. There are many *guindon* (thieves) to watch out for, she says, grabbing my arm once again to lead me across a street.

I tell Svitlana about going to Seville. "*¡Mucha cremo!*" she says, looking at my complexion. "*¡Mucha sol! ¡Mucha cremo!*"

She grabs my arm once again, seemingly just to make sure I'm paying attention. We are walking along a narrow lane with colourful bunting above.

"*¡Muchas fiestas!*" Svitlana says, looking up. "*¡Música! ¡Violín! ¡España: muchas fiestas!*"

She pulls me onward.

We reach a square by the *río*, with what looks like a cathedral on a hill above. It is scorching now and I can see Manresa's Renfe station across the River Cardener, sitting alone below a tree-covered hill. Svitlana reminds me to drink lots of *agua*, tells me several times over to watch out for *guindon*, says *nada, nada* when I thank her, gives me her phone number and departs across the baking concrete square toward a side street, tottering slightly in her pink-and-green heels.

Very helpful, Svitlana.

In Manresa Station I buy a ticket to Lleida, discovering that the next train is at 16:43. It is just after noon now. Perhaps this is why the receptionist at the monks' hotel returns to Barcelona to move onward. However, *realmente no me importa* (I really don't care). This is what it's all about when taking slow trains: getting waylaid is just how it goes. I must embrace delays and mistakes. I must readjust. I am in Spain, not London. I am on *vacaciones*; getting away from it all. There is no hurry. As Svitlana would say, *es nada, nada*. The train will arrive at Lleida, whenever it will, though I do check the timetable. Scheduled arrival: 18:40.

Manresa's "cathedral" is in fact a church named Santa Maria de la Seu, with parts dating from the thirteenth century and additions added over the centuries.

It is, frankly, breathtaking. Stop off in an out-of-the-way place on a train in Spain – like Vilanova i la Geltrú, Manresa is not in my guidebook – and this can happen to you, I'm quickly discovering. Great places of worship the length of football pitches, with lancet windows the size of small houses, flying double buttresses, forests of stone columns, and glittering works of art from before the time of Shakespeare lurk just around the corner from your station. Some of the altarpieces here once graced chapels in Barcelona Cathedral. I am the only tourist in the vast structure and, afterward, outside, I sit by the wall overlooking the river ravine and the station simply enjoying the silence of Santa Maria de la Seu here in the depths of Catalonia, somewhere down a rattling train line through the mountains.

Then I take a short walk to visit the Cave of Saint Ignatius. In my great ignorance, I knew nothing of this before the train pulled in. Yet here it is, another religious treasure trove – the very cave, so tradition has it, in which Saint Ignatius of Loyola, founder of the Jesuit order, stopped by in March 1522 and studied in solitude for eleven months. It was here, after a pilgrimage to Montserrat, that Saint Ignatius chose to leave his military life and devote himself to spirituality, writing his classic Christian work *Spiritual Exercises* and experiencing a revelation by the River Cardener that he describes in his autobiography: "And while sitting there, the eyes of understanding began to open for him. It was not that he saw a vision, but that he understood and knew many things with such great enlightenment that all things seemed new to him."

OK, so I cannot pretend Manresa has had quite this effect on me, so far, but I do quite like it here.

Before catching my ride to Lleida, I go to the main square. Local life is in full swing at café/bars near a disused wooden newspaper kiosk, an old-fashioned pharmacy and a platform that seems to have been erected for a fiesta. Beers are being drunk on this Sunday afternoon, so I join the beer drinkers, while reading up about Manresa's shocking treatment of Jews in bygone years in streets just round the corner from Plaça Llisach.

The story of the Jews of Manresa is the story of the Jews in Spain. For centuries from around the time of Christ, Jews and Christians lived side by side on the Iberian Peninsula and the population of Spanish Jews grew to many hundreds of thousands spread across the country. Then the persecution began. In the fourteenth century anti-Semitism was on the rise – partly due to a Catholic interpretation of the New Testament that the Jews had crucified Christ – and violent attacks on Jews were common. Tensions grew and in 1391 they boiled over. Murderous anti-Semitic mobs targeted the Jewish community across Spain, leading to widespread deaths as well as conversions to Christianity for fear of loss of life. Many fled the territory and for a century afterward relations between the communities were on a knife's edge. Then, in the Alhambra Decree of 1492, Isabella I of Castile and Ferdinand II of Aragon expelled Jews from Spain altogether. While in the twelfth century Manresa had been home to a thriving community of five hundred Jewish families, mainly living in the streets near Plaça Llisach, after this there were none.

A little bit of harrowing history.

Many events, good and not so good, have happened in Manresa. One of the most important, for the region, took place in 1892. It was in Manresa during that year that the *Unió Catalanista* was signed, establishing how Catalonia could be run independently with its own language. Manresa for this reason, and because of its geographical position in the centre of the land that Angel had marked off with his pencil back in Figueres, is a key Catalonian city. The local tourist board's motto, *Cor de Catalunya* (Heart of Catalonia), written on the map I picked up at the station earlier, now makes sense. Yet, I'll say this again, it is *not even mentioned* in my (very well-known) guidebook.

Saints founding famous religious orders, devastating pogroms, declarations of independence: these are not the types of story you pick up during a wait for a train at, say, Clapham Junction, I can't help reflecting.

I order another one-euro San Miguel at Bar Restaurant Casual, served by a waitress wearing a T-shirt bearing the slogan *CHILL WITH ME*. I am already, I realize, quite happily lost in Spain.

Long may the feeling continue.

Bonisimo, perficio.

This is just how I wanted it to be.

* * *

The 16:43 pulls up and away we go. The temperature is 29°C, says a screen. The *proxima parada* (next station) is Rajadell, says an announcement. I gaze out of the window for a while, soaking up the rural scenery and enjoying simply watching the sky above. It's an interesting one with a large anvil-shaped cloud on the horizon that looks so solid it might be permanent. It is relaxing to watch this cloud as its shape subtly mutates yet holds its own.

I turn to *Homage to Catalonia*. When George Orwell clattered down this line in the opposite direction after a spell at the front near Huesca, just north of Zaragoza, it was not as quiet as on today's ride: "The train, already full of militiamen when it left Barbastro, was invaded by more and more peasants at every station on the line; peasants with bundles of vegetables, with terrified fowls which they carried head-downwards, with sacks which looped and writhed all over the floor and were discovered to be full of live rabbits – finally with a quite considerable flock of sheep which were driven into compartments and wedged into every empty space. The militiamen shouted revolutionary songs which drowned the rattle of the train and kissed their hands or waved red and black handkerchiefs to every pretty girl along the line."

A different era, but intriguing to imagine one of the twentieth century's greatest writers jolting along in the opposite direction on these very tracks, revolutionary lyrics filling the air and rabbits squirming at his feet.

There is something wrong with the door to what looks like the fuse box to this carriage. It hangs open, swaying as the train trundles along. No one else seems to notice or mind, although you can't help imagining what might happen if you flicked a switch.

We pass a huge, vulgar country house with a tower and its name written by a gate. The train begins to bounce slightly from side to side as we cut through hills. I look up Lleida, which *is* in the guidebook. Apparently, the city is best known for its fine cathedral and a ruined castle on a hill. Lleida is also famous for snail eating; locals love them (perhaps this has something to do with the proximity to France in this north-east corner of Spain).

A man lies down on a row of seats by the open fuse box and begins to snore gently as great plains spread out with pencil-grey mountains rising on the horizon. Fields of wheat are replaced by cornfields. A conductor with a purple tie checks our tickets. At Cervera Station a sign commemorates the construction of the Manresa–Lleida line, stating the dates 1860–1985. Meanwhile at Tàrrega Station, graffiti declares: *DEFENSEM LA REPÚBLICA.*

We move into a patchwork quilt of velvety green farmland with the silhouette of the bell tower of a distant town to the right. Castellnou de Seana Station is derelict, yet with a lovely old blue-white sign still gleaming. There is a toot of the horn. There are grapevines. Mollerusa Station is coloured peach-white and looks old-fashioned, like a country mansion. We traverse fields the colour of golden retrievers with only the odd stone barn and apple orchard breaking up the golden glow. A rabbit hops alongside the track seemingly oblivious to the danger presented by the train. Orderly olive groves emerge, as does a scrapyard and a burnt-out warehouse.

Shortly afterward we arrive in Lleida Pirineus Station.

I shall not dwell on Lleida, as I did not dwell here very long. I do like the place, but I do not see much of it at all. This is mainly due to deciding to buy a ticket for the 09:34 train to Huesca the following morning.

After achieving this, I go to my hotel – a tall red-brick affair, not far from the tracks, with tiny rooms, noisy neighbours and a receptionist who says: "If you want, I can give you a map" in a tone of voice that suggests a visitor might not be enthralled by Lleida. Map in hand, I stride forth into this city of 137,000 inhabitants.

I am in search of snails. The local love of eating the creatures has caught my interest. It would be good to eat some snails in Lleida. So I walk down a long road called Rambla de Ferran, close to the station, which the receptionist regarded as the place to go for entertainment in Lleida. This is a narrow pedestrianized street with a Cheapy Shop, tattoo parlours, pizza and kebab joints, swimsuit shops and the occasional smell of dope. No snail restaurants are in evidence, so I turn up a hill toward the old castle and enter a neighbourhood that feels as though I have somehow been transported to Africa.

For a few minutes I am the only white face as I walk through vibrant streets with many languages spoken as folk hang out in the early evening exchanging stories. Immigration is a big subject and one that is influencing politics on the high stage in Spain – witness the rise of the Vox party. In 1981, a total of 198,000 immigrants lived in Spain; the latest figure is about six million.

I go up the hill to the castle. Here, the jagged remains of the old fortifications are contained within the high walls, with parts dating from the ninth century. Here also the plains of western Catalonia are laid out beneath a calm pale-blue sky with a pink haze settling on a distant ridge of mountains. A slight breeze ventilates the wooden-deck terrace of Bar 1203 (this date was the year the first stone of the cathedral was laid within the fortifications). Bar 1203 is the only place to eat or drink on Lleida's hill, and it is a perfect location to dine after a long day on and about the Spanish tracks.

Snails are indeed on the menu and I order them. Each year in Lleida in May a snail-eating festival is held and, such is the city's fondness for the food, as many as 12 tonnes of snails are consumed, which makes me wonder where they come from. Are there snail farms on the plains of Catalonia?

Anyway, I eat the snails, which appear to have been grilled, while looking across western Catalonia. The snails are chewy, garlicky and rather like cockles. Swallows swoop above the battlements as I polish off two dozen of the creatures one by one, trying not to think about them sliming about too much before they reached the pot. I can highly recommend the snails of Lleida (though they may not, perhaps, be everyone's cup of tea).

Fast and slow
Lleida to Huesca, via Zaragoza

This is a surprise. To reach Zaragoza for the connection to Huesca requires putting luggage through an X-ray machine. Although only a short journey, 43 minutes, I appear to have unwittingly bought a ticket on a Spanish "fast" train that requires security. I am not, however, going to stress about this. Things like this are bound to happen and I am not going to take "slow" trains slavishly just for the sake of being "slow", although I will always try to be "slow" (if that makes sense). Spain is a large country and there is no point hanging around wasting time in stations for the hell of it. Anyway, it is not as though I intend to zoom from Barcelona to Madrid (journey time: 2 hours and 30 minutes), Madrid to València (2 hours and 18 minutes) and then València to Seville (3 hours and 58 minutes), madly pinballing about the country at 300 kilometres an hour (188 miles per hour).

There is a queue to the X-ray machine, with a sign informing us in a mix of languages: *Vigile su equipaje. Vigili el seu equipatge. BEWARE.* This is accompanied by a picture of a man sitting on a chair with *Z Z* written above his head as though he has nodded off. Meanwhile, the arm of a robber reaching for the sleeping man's luggage pokes out from behind the chair. Above the image of the thief is a red exclamation mark. If you fall asleep on a Spanish fast train, the message seems to be: *more fool you.*

At the X-ray machine, while waiting for my backpack to emerge, a woman wearing earrings that may or may not contain diamonds pushes past rudely to fetch her bag (a Gucci bag, I notice). This is even though the Gucci bag arrives after my backpack. She duly takes her place on the platform next to a guy with golf clubs and waits like the rest of us for the ride to Zaragoza. This is the thing about trains (and planes for that matter, when not private jets): there is a certain democracy regarding your arrival time. Gucci won't help you jump the queue for that.

The Zaragoza service turns up, for everyone. It's an eel-nosed beauty of a train, one of Renfe's Alta Velocidad Española (AVE) top-of-the-range fleet. The word *ave* means "bird" in Spanish, appropriately, as these things fly along. Inside is a temperature indicator (25ºC) and a speed indicator, initially reporting a sedate 35 kilometres an hour (22 miles per hour), although this moves rapidly to 48 kilometres an hour, then 88 kilometres an hour on the outskirts of Lleida.

I am given plastic headphones so I can watch a cartoon on a screen, though I do not open the pack. The seats are extremely comfortable, with a speckled lilac pattern. We move so smoothly along the tracks that it feels as though the carriage is floating... birdlike indeed. The seat comes with a large fold-down table and a convenient electricity socket.

The speed picks up as we pass thickets of bamboo followed by farmsteads and fields: 116 kilometres an hour... 121 kilometres an hour... 148 kilometres an hour... 208 kilometres an hour... eventually 299 kilometres an hour (187 miles per hour). There is a rather morbid fascination in watching precisely how un-slowly this train is travelling. Escarpments materialize. Escarpments dematerialize. Scrubland and orchards do the same. There is a smell of bacon sandwiches from an adjoining buffet carriage as we positively whistle along, devouring Spanish landscape. Although the train is going very fast indeed, there is a slight wobble that makes those walking toward the buffet carriage look as though they have had one too many drinks. After the Montserrat Rack Railway, you cannot help feeling as though you may get a nosebleed at any moment; as well as thinking: *I really hope the brakes don't fail.*

Olive trees, hayfields and rolling plains blur by. At the buffet carriage I buy a coffee from an attendant who tells me that the top speed during service is 301 kilometres an hour (188 miles per hour) "but it can do 350 kilometres an hour [219 miles per hour]". As I pay for the drink, I notice that my five-euro note has *FREEDOM FOR CATALONIA* written in ink on each side, although on one side someone has crossed out *CATALONIA* and put *TABERNIA*. This five-euro note seems to be living up to the saying *money talks* – a conversation even appears to be taking place.

I show it to the attendant. She looks nonplussed.

"But what is Tabernia?" she replies.

I return to my seat and look it up. Tabernia, it turns out, is a counter-separatist movement to those seeking Catalan independence: i.e. the people in Catalonia who do not wish to break from Spain, mainly concentrated in the region between Barcelona and Tarragona to the south. The movement is satirical, designed to mock the independence campaigners, and is supported by Vox.

When you take the train to Spain you arrive in the heart of *gran política* (big politics) that are just about impossible to ignore.

The train pulls into Zaragoza-Delicias Station at 10:15, two minutes early.

* * *

Zaragoza, however, is the capital of the region of Aragon – we are out of Catalonia now. There is enough time before the 14:35 connection to Huesca to see the sights, of which there appear to be three main ones: the Moorish palace, the cathedral and a museum celebrating the painter Francisco de Goya, who was born hereabouts.

The modern station is massive, a good 400 metres in length with a vast atrium and a budget hotel. It opened in 2003 to serve high-speed trains between Barcelona and Madrid, and is 2 miles west of the centre of town, to which the number thirty-four bus runs.

This stops conveniently right outside the Aljafería Palace, which rises in pink and cream stone with great turrets and a bridge across a dried-out moat. Inside, all is peaceful courtyards with orange trees and vines, pillars, ornate plasterwork, marble passages and Islamic geometric patterns dating from the eleventh century. A panel explains how the intricately carved designs in the latticework were based on advanced mathematics. A sweeping staircase leads to chambers with glittery gold ceilings. Marvellous palace, the Aljafería Palace.

Eating a bag of *cerezas* (cherries) bought from a nearby *frutería* (greengrocer), I stroll along the River Ebro to the Cathedral-Basilica of Our Lady of the Pillar. This faces a square the size of several football pitches with towers, cupolas and domes casting long shadows on the flagstones, and a heavy door studded with metal spikes. Inside, all is crystal chandeliers, pink-marble chapels, glorious ceiling murals, golden altars, stone cherubs, confession booths, brass railings and *SILENCIO* signs. The voice of a priest murmurs somewhere deep within. Pilgrims and tourists kiss the pillar after which the cathedral is named, where the Virgin Mary is said to have descended from heaven before St James the apostle. Out of some sort of inner tourist compulsion, I do the same. Marvellous cathedral, the Cathedral-Basilica of Our Lady of the Pillar.

Across the square on a lane is Museo Goya, housing a private collection of the renowned eighteenth- and nineteenth-century artist's works. It is not nearly as extensive in scope as the Dalí museum in Figueres and the first floor is devoted to works by others who were "references for Goya during his youth", according to a panel. Interesting enough, *but not by Goya*. Upstairs, however, portraits of noblemen with puffed-out chests, bloody battle scenes, young gentlemen with wise brown eyes, sneering soldiers and devious-looking courtiers reveal his undoubted genius for catching character and moments in time. A self-portrait depicts a man with a double chin, wispy moustache and innocent-yet-appraising eyes; not flattering at all, just somehow honest. While on another floor a series of engravings – for which Goya was, I discover, famous – show an array of gory bullfighting scenes, street brawls, stabbings, bodies taken on carts to cemeteries, raucous taverns, women balancing chairs on heads during drinking games and leering men. Real life is captured, as is a nightmarish fantasy world, in a final section of winged devils, evil-eyed cats and witches on broomsticks. What a superb insight into another era and an artist's inspiration – the work of a master who, for my money, knocks Dalí for six. Marvellous museum, Museo Goya.

Marvellous all round in Zaragoza.

Images of Moorish opulence, miracle apparitions and Goya-era debauchery swimming in my mind, I catch the 14:35 train to Huesca.

This is appropriately enough from Zaragoza-Goya Station. We are soon sliding away with a view of the cathedral to the left and then golden plains with ridges rising to the west. Storks sitting on nests balanced on old telegraph poles regard our slow progress, looking like bored policemen who would rather not be on duty and would prefer us to *move along quickly please, would you please just get a move on*. A genial middle-aged schoolteacher-ish conductor checks our tickets. The landscape becomes dry, gritty and desert-like, with plateaus dropping into ravines that must be home to a snake or two. A recorded message says in English: *"Renfe thanks you for travelling with us and we look forward to having you again. Please do not forget your luggage and personal belongings."* The announcer has a Birmingham accent and "luggage" comes across strongly as *"luug-idge"*, making me wonder how someone from the English Midlands became a translator for Renfe train announcements in the Spanish region of Aragon.

We very slowly slide to a halt. It is 15:26. We have reached Huesca.

CHAPTER FOUR

HUESCA TO BILBAO, VIA PAMPLONA AND SAN SEBASTIÁN

BULLETS, BULLRINGS AND BLOOD

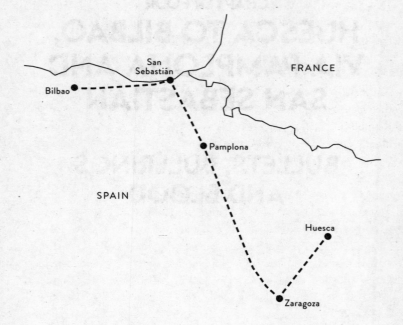

OK, so my minor obsession with George Orwell's life and works has brought me here. Over the years, one way or another, I have visited the writer's early childhood home (in Shiplake, Oxfordshire), his school (Eton College), his parents' home in Southwold in Suffolk (where he taught and began *A Clergyman's Daughter*), some of his favourite London boozers (including the Canonbury Tavern in Islington, where Orwell is said to have drafted some of *Nineteen Eighty-Four* while sitting beneath the chestnut tree in the garden) and his grave (in Sutton Courtenay, Oxfordshire). Now I'm at the end of a train line – Huesca is a terminus – in deepest Aragon in Spain to visit some of his Spanish Civil War trenches.

Never before have I made such an Orwellian effort – and I am not sure exactly where to go. Huesca was a Nationalist stronghold during the Spanish Civil War of 1936–1939 and Orwell, fighting for the Republicans, was in trenches to the east of the town, launching a forlorn, bloody and ultimately unsuccessful attack. The assault was hopelessly ineffective as Republican firepower was weak and the trenches on both sides so established, and far apart, that making breakthroughs was nigh on impossible. And it was here that Orwell almost died when he was shot through the neck one morning in May 1937. As he lay on his stretcher and was informed of the wound, his thoughts, as told in *Homage to Catalonia*, were: "I took it for granted that I was done for."

Orwell was given morphine and eventually sent to a hospital in Lleida, after which he was transported by train for further treatment in Tarragona: "They had put us into ordinary third-class carriages with wooden seats, and many of the men were badly wounded and had only got out of bed for the first time that morning. Before long, what with the heat and the jolting, half of them were in a state of collapse and several vomited on the floor."

It was a lucky escape. A centimetre's difference and the bullet might well have struck his carotid artery and he would indeed have been "done for"; no *Nineteen Eighty-Four* or *Animal Farm* among so much else.

Hoping for the best, after dropping my backpack in simple digs usually used by students, I go to Huesca's tourist office and ask how to find Orwell's trenches.

Fernando, a kind-eyed skinny man wearing a purple shirt, is sitting at a desk alone inside. The main square outside had been deserted, as had the old medieval streets near the Gothic cathedral by my accommodation. When I had tried the handle of the tourist office, I had half expected it to be locked.

Fernando looks up, a little shocked by the arrival of company, gets the gist of my request and produces a map of the area around Huesca, using a pen to mark a line near a village on the outskirts named Tierz. This is about 4 miles away and Fernando kindly calls to book a taxi.

I ask if many tourists request information about Orwell.

"We get about twenty a year," he says. The Huesca trenches are clearly not pulling them in quite like the Dalí museum or the monastery at Montserrat.

Fernando explains that many visitors interested in Orwell go to the trenches at Alcubierre, which have been well restored; these are where the writer served during his first war action, about 30 miles due south (and inconvenient by train). Of *Homage to Catalonia* Fernando says: "It is very beautiful. He says many truths. It is a very real description." For a while, Fernando seems quite passionate about Orwell, just like Josep at the botanical gardens in Blanes.

A large shiny white Mercedes pulls up outside and soon I am being driven, fast, down little lanes to Tierz, where the driver is unsure about the location of the trenches and I get out by some dusty old cottages.

No one is around and it takes a while to find a rickety wooden sign partially covered by foliage on the outskirts of the village. The sign is marked *Ruta de las Trencheras*. Following the arrow, a lane leads past two emaciated white cats and a paddock of shiny black horses, before turning into a dirt path and winding up a hill with a long ridge. Butterflies flutter as the path twists upward, getting narrower and narrower and steeper and steeper.

At the top, the track turns left and there they are, dug into the hillside with sublime views across the plain to the jagged outline of the castle on Mount Aragon: Orwell's *trencheras*. The sky is cobalt blue and the hillside is rugged and rutted, as though still marked by artillery shells, with fields of yellow crops so parched they are almost white spreading out on the horizon toward the mountains. Lizards scurry near the entrance to a narrow trench with hollows carved into the hill and crumbling stone walls facing the former front. It is now a beautiful, peaceful place.

Somewhere here, one dawn, Orwell fell after being hit by a sniper. "Everything was very blurry," he writes. "There must have been about two minutes during which I assumed that I was killed. And that too was interesting – I mean it is interesting to know what your thoughts would be at such a time. My first thought, conventionally enough, was for my wife. My second was a violent resentment at having to leave this world which, when all is said and done, suits me so well. I had time to feel this very vividly. The stupid mischance infuriated me. The meaninglessness of it! To be bumped off, not even in battle, but in this stale corner of the trenches, thanks to a moment's carelessness!"

His short time in Spain – he was forced to flee soon after his injury in June 1937 (he had arrived in December 1936) – was crucial to Orwell's world view and his future writing. His observations of the "revolutionary atmosphere" of all-togetherness disappearing in Barcelona, the Republican stronghold to which he returned after both spells on the front, with "militia uniforms and blue overalls" replaced by "smart summer suits", and his vivid description of the invidious suspicions between Republican factions, which led to imprisonments and mysteriously missing people, resonate strongly in both *Animal Farm* and *Nineteen Eighty-Four*. The changes in Barcelona were Orwell's Spanish Civil War equivalents, if you like, to "four legs good, two legs bad" mutating to "four legs good, two legs better" in *Animal Farm*, as well as Big Brother and the sense of menace in *Nineteen Eighty-Four*.

Somewhere on this deserted hill, twentieth-century literature survived a very near miss.

The last rays of the day are lighting up the rose-hued fortifications of the castle on Mount Aragon and hawks are sailing above as I walk down the hill through what was once no man's land, where Orwell was sometimes sent as a sniper himself.

Then, I return to town (quite a long, hot walk), eat a fine salmon meal at Huesca's main square and hit the sack. Tomorrow another day on the Spanish tracks lies ahead, taking me to one of the country's most famous tourist cities of all.

I also intend to do something Orwell never managed, though he promised he would if he ever returned to Spain.

"The bull got him"
Huesca to Pamplona

In a speech to motivate his troops during the Spanish Civil War, a Republican commander once said: "Tomorrow we'll have coffee in Huesca." The saying was forever after a running joke among the ranks, given the likelihood was so slim.

This was Orwell's dream – to drink coffee in Huesca. So I raise a cup to the writer at the old-fashioned Café Oscense Bar before walking down to the station via graffiti on a wall that says SOCIALISMO O BARBÀRIE (SOCIALISM OR BARBARISM) next to VEGANISMO O BARBÀRIE (VEGANISM OR BARBARISM), below both of which a wit has scrawled O BARBIE. It seems local politics are still alive and well in Huesca, as is the love of popular plastic children's toys.

The ticket assistant at Huesca Station is incredibly helpful. Her name is Isabel and she has green eyes and wears a natty green-and-purple Renfe scarf and lots of bangles. *Princesa* is tattooed on her left arm. She taps away looking for options for destinations on her computer in a station side room, interrupted from time to time by passengers needing tickets urgently for Zaragoza, before examining all the various possibilities, turning to me and pointing her hands on her head to indicate bull horns. Pamplona, she feels, should be my next destination. If I catch the 08:45 I'll arrive by 13:15, via Zaragoza. I buy a ticket.

Isabel asks me why I came to Huesca and I explain the *trencheras*. Upon hearing this, she urges me to meet the Huesca Station security guard – and leads me out into the concourse.

María-Belen has a baton attached to her belt and a gold badge on her uniform saying, *VIGILANTE DE SEGURIDAD*. She is, Isabel says, a fan of literature.

"Oh, Orwell! He put Huesca on the map," says María-Belen. "I read his book in Spanish and I like it very much." She pauses as though deep in thought. "Yes, yes, in English, I like best James Joyce. *Ulysses*: a wonderful book, very important." She pauses once again to consider her words. "I think the most important book of the twentieth century. At the beginning of the twentieth century there was a very narrow mentality in writing. He changed all that."

We stand about for a while discussing James Joyce, waiting for the 08:45. Then I board a tiny white train with purple and orange stripes, wondering if I'll ever discuss *Ulysses* with a station guard again. The odds must be pretty long, especially on a London commute (though maybe I'm being unfair: maybe James Joyce devotees are to be found lurking at ticket barriers all over the place… you just need to ask).

Anyway, off we go in a carriage with blue curtains that look as though they belong in a semi-detached house in Surbiton that has not been done up for a few decades or so. There are just two carriages and little glass doors between each – this is the homeliest train yet, slower than yesterday's one along the same line, but more comfortable. We retrace yesterday's journey – this is an example of a *radial* line from a big city – and stop at Zaragoza-Delicias Station, where I get out and wait at a café frequented by cops for the connection to Pamplona.

Out of the depths of the cavernous station, the Pamplona train emerges and my heart sinks slightly at the sight of another North Korean missile moving stealthily down the tracks to platform three. Not another fast one! (Catching slow trains in Spain seems trickier than imagined.) However, this missile has *Alvia* written on the side, not *AVE*. This comes as something of a relief – it is a *marginally slower* train than an AVE. Alvia trains in Spain run on the high-speed lines but only up to 250 kilometres an hour (156 miles per hour) and often much less.

I board. We begin to move through a long tunnel beneath Zaragoza-Delicias Station and exit into the bright sunny day with mountains to the north and a prominent ceramics factory on the outskirts of Zaragoza. Parched landscape opens out: bone-dry gorges, cacti, shrubland and the occasional village wrapped in heat haze with ramshackle abodes by the tracks, paint peeling and walls crumbling. A man sitting next to me begins watching a film on his smartphone. The conductor hands out plastic earphones. We zip along yet, according to the digital monitor, never surpass 138 kilometres an hour (86 miles per hour); dead slow for a Spanish bullet train, really. Concrete sleeper depots come and go. We pass an *alabastros* (alabaster) plant. Haughty storks on electricity pylons regard us with disdain. What peculiar creatures they are: *if only everyone would just go away!*

The scenery begins to change. Fields become steadily greener and then woodland emerges and taller and taller trees, with granite-peaked mountains looming; one in an almost perfect pyramid shape. Villages with the appearance of "cubes sprawled like a throw of dice" (a phrase used by Orwell) cling to the foothills: *dice villages*. A trackside car factory arises with hundreds of vehicles wrapped in white plastic as though mummified. These are stored on double-decker wagons on sidings. Then ugly apartment blocks on the edge of a city shoot up and you might be in a former Soviet state in Eastern Europe if it were not for the odd rail-side prickly pear and the blinding Spanish sunshine.

The train pulls into Pamplona, right on time. Many of us disembark – the train is going on to San Sebastián by the coast – and I follow a river by a busy road before cutting inland and taking a weird little (free) public lift/mini cog railway a short distance to a tiny lane with tall, narrow terraced buildings coloured green and pink. This leads to a square and another tiny lane with more tall terraces, and another, and just when I think I'm completely lost, in a very tiny lane, I find my *hostal*.

I have struck lucky in the city of the "Running of the Bulls". I appear to be in the heart of the city's *pintxos* district: the busiest tiniest little lane with the most *pintxos* bars of all, about twenty though it is tricky to count with so many people milling about drinking wine and beer and generally making merry while eating *pintxos*.

My *hostal* consists of rooms above one of the bars. I am effectively staying in a *pintxos* bar. So I dump my rucksack and start to eat *pintxos*, which are different from regular tapas in that they tend to be skewered to a piece of bread with a cocktail stick. The word *pintxos* means "spike" or "thorn" in the Basque language. Elsewhere, in most of Spain, the snacks are referred to as *pinchos* or, in Asturias, *pinchus*. Pamplona is the capital of Navarra, a medieval kingdom, just to the east of the bulk of the Basque Country with a French border to the north.

After checking in at Hostal Bearan, I stand by the bar next to two old-timers in flat caps drinking red wine and eating little sausages skewered by cocktail sticks on to pieces of bread as I proceed to consume a series of pork balls skewered by cocktail sticks on to pieces of bread, all covered in spicy sauce. In the cacophony of the bar, packed at lunchtime, voices rise and mingle in a genial din. A man bats the buttons of a fruit machine named *La Perla del Caribe Deluxe* (The Deluxe Caribbean Pearl), plastered with pictures of beaches and palm trees as though paradise awaits those who play. Three oranges flash up as winnings clatter out: a grand total of eighty cents.

More old-timers gesticulate to the barman for service. The previous old-timers leave, waving flat caps and crying *"adios"*. I polish off a selection of chicken and prawns skewered on bread, with chopped onions and a spicy sauce, accompanied by a glass of red wine, while standing in my "space" watching a sea of *pintxos* eaters shuffling by in search of skewered snacks.

Then I join the throng outside, in search of the starting point of the Running of the Bulls.

The background to this traditional festival held in a couple of weeks' time, at the beginning of July each year (7–14 July), comes from farmers leading bulls into town to be fought in bullrings. It is said to date from medieval times and has, over the years, been adapted to become an opportunity to demonstrate bravery by running ahead of the bulls. What happens is simple in theory: six bulls are released at eight in the morning and anyone who wishes may run before them. The bulls are corralled by heavy wooden fences that snake forward to the ring.

In practice, partly because so many people love to give it a try, all mayhem is let loose and people are often gored or trampled, sometimes killed. A total of sixteen bull runners have died since 1910, most recently in 2009. Each year about one million people come to witness or take part. It is very big business.

Pamplona's Running of the Bulls, which coincides with the San Fermín fiesta, is the most famous of all Spain's bull runs, partly because everyone wears white jeans, white T-shirts and red neckerchiefs during the fiesta, making proceedings especially dramatic. Television stations analyze proceedings in great depth, as though judging a gymnastic floor performance or the twists of a diver plunging from a high board. Commentators go to town, slowing down footage captured by cameras that cover every inch of the way.

The course covers 875 metres. Some of the wooden fences are already up in readiness for the fiesta. I follow these to the beginning and walk the length of the course back through twisting streets with plenty of *pintxos* bars and shops selling red-and-white clothing to the great stone circle of the bullring. On a corner here, one shop has decided to do things a little differently. In order to continue my gift shop studies of northern Spain, after Dalí and the monks, I enter to examine shelves stacked with large numbers of cans of *toro rabo* (bull's tail) and a great many unusual cakes described, perhaps a little bluntly, as *miermerienda* (shit snacks). These cakes are shaped like bull's turds, decorated with a pair of cartoon eyes and a smile. They are *smiling* bull's turds, which you can give as a present to a friend or loved one or simply eat yourself.

The twenty-something man in charge of the shop watches me as I inspect the edible turds. He wears a blue T-shirt and jeans and looks tough although he has a gentle manner. I ask him how many edible bull's turds he sells a day.

"So far today: twenty," he replies.

We get talking. There are no other customers. His name is Fermín – "like the festival" – and he is a bull runner.

"Every year since fifteen I have run," he says. "First time was with my father – we didn't tell my mother. My father said: 'Don't worry, it'll be OK.' So I did it. I didn't run a lot that year. I went to the side behind one of the barriers in less than one minute. I was so scared. It was less than one minute but it felt like an eternity. Last year, I did it three times. For me it is so much better now. I run better. Now I have grown up and my body is bigger."

Fermín pauses, and then whispers as though letting me in on a secret. "The most dangerous thing is not the bulls," he says quietly. "It is the *people*."

Then Fermín waves his elbows about madly, as though pushing his way through a jungle, imitating how bull runners behave.

"Injuries happen when you fall down or get pushed on to the walls," he says. "Last year I fell and got a scar on the back of my head. I was pushed down by someone. But there is so much adrenaline, you can't feel it. I didn't feel anything. When the bulls had gone though: then I feel it." He had to have stitches. "Actually, a lot of people say it is the same with bulls out there." He points in the direction of the bullring. "They say they can't feel it either. The adrenaline, it works for them too. I don't know about that." He frowns, looking thoughtful as though weighing up the matter.

I ask what he thinks of foreigners doing the bull run.

"Every year there are first-time *guiris*," Fermín says. *Guiris* is a slang word for *foreigner* with a pejorative edge, aimed at pale-skinned foreigners mainly. "The most dangerous thing is to look at the bulls and then run." This is apparently what a lot of *guiris* do. "You must be running already, looking backward, ready to move." Fermín shows how to do this, as though providing me with tips I may follow during the fiesta.

Has anyone ever made it all the way from the beginning all the 875 metres to the bullring ahead of the bulls?

"Nobody can do it," he replies. "Impossible! If the streets are empty, maybe, but you would have to be so physically good. It is so difficult at the start. Anyway, the streets are not empty. Impossible! Even from here just up to there." He points the 80 metres or so to the gates of the bullring. "Impossible!"

Fermín tells me about his father's attempts at the bull run. "He got injured two times: one time the horn got him here." He points to his elbow. "To here." He points to his armpit. "He was turning right and…" Fermín cuts off to imitate a bull raising horns in a vicious movement. "He go to hospital. The bull got him." His father's other goring was in a shin. "My father knows many matadors. Bull runs, bullfighting, it is in his blood. He studies the sport."

Fermín says he hopes to do the bull run this year and, as he does so, two friends arrive. It seems pretty easy to get talking to people in Pamplona.

One of Fermín's friends begins telling me, at length, that Murcia – a region in the far south of Spain – is "the best place in Spain, the best!" and that I must go there. I explain that I almost certainly will do so on trains very soon. He is delighted. Murcia is, he says, absolutely *el mejor* (the best) with *muy buen* (very good) weather and *muy amigable* (very friendly) people. We discuss Murcia in this manner for some time.

Then Fermín's friend turns to Fermín and points at him and says as though exceedingly proud of Fermín: "He is crazy… crazy!"

"Because he does the bull run?" I ask Fermín's friend.

"No! No! Not just that. Really crazy! He climbs buildings!" Fermín's friend is waving his hands about excitedly and pointing upward.

"What do you mean?" I ask.

"When he is drunk, he likes to climb buildings to get to balconies," Fermín's friend replies.

"Really?" I ask Fermín.

"Don't say that! Don't say that!" Fermín has begun to say to his friend. It turns out that Fermín is something of a local legend for this.

"Yes, it is true," he says a little sheepishly. "I do this sometimes."

With great admiration – acts of daring are, after all, what it is all about in Pamplona – Fermín's friend says: "You see! You see! Crazy!"

In Pamplona there seems to be no higher compliment: *loco* is king.

We all shake hands. I resist the urge to buy an edible bull's turd or a can of bull's tail. And I go for a walk around the big concrete and stone bullring.

There is nothing especially elegant about the ring, other than rows of neoclassical balustrades and a mosaic displaying a particularly fierce bull chasing runners dressed in white and red by the ticket office. On one side is a Hemingway Bar, a nod to Ernest Hemingway's entertaining 1926 novel, *Fiesta: The Sun Also Rises*, about a group of debauched British and American expats coming from Paris for the San Fermín festival – another big reason behind the fame of the Running of the Bulls. On the other is Club Taurino (Club Bullfighting), where matadors are said to hang out.

I enter in search of matadors and *pintxos* but find neither. The only other customers are a furtive drinker who appears to be a tout selling bullring tickets to a customer. A row of old bull branding irons is mounted above the bar. The walls, appropriately for the venue, are blood red. A calendar behind the bar shows that *junio's* (June's) bull of the month is a fearsome black-and-white beast that looks extremely pissed off by the bull-of-the-month calendar photographer.

The only food that appears to be on offer is Spanish omelette, so I order this and enjoy a fat (delicious) slice while taking in Club Taurino. Signed pictures of matadors wearing knee-high pink socks and gold-and-blue outfits line the walls. A stuffed head of a bull named *Patirrota* glares down from a corner, looking just as pissed off as *junio's* bull, as he probably was in his final moments. Money exchanges hands at the table. A pop song about *amor* plays on the stereo. Club Taurino feels as though it is at the heart of Pamplonian matters; quite relaxing in a strange way, despite the undoubted brutality, blood and controversy of bullfighting.

Back at chaotic Calle San Nicolás, I devour a series of *pintxos* with accompanying *vinos*: octopus with potato and paprika skewered to bread on a cocktail stick; black pudding skewered to bread on a cocktail stick; walnuts and cheese (served loose); a spring roll; a spinach pastry with cheese; and two spicy sausages skewered on cocktail sticks to slices of green pepper. The bald barman serving me the latter tells me these sausages "are not chorizo. Chorizo is all over Spain – these are *txistorra* sausages!" They are, he says, from the village of Arbizu. He writes the names down for me on the back of a napkin. The barman seems excessively dismissive of mere chorizo sausages and excessively pleased that I have ordered another round of *txistorra* (pronounced *chist-ora*) with another glass of *casa vino tinto* (house red wine).

However, before he pours the wine, he pauses. He has two bottles in his hands.

"Would sir prefer the *rioja*?" he asks with a snake charmer's look that suggests that the most discerning of *txistorra*-eaters obviously opt for the rioja.

I nod toward the rioja (twice the price) and the bald barman bows ever so slightly with a glint in his eye as he pours the excellent red wine.

Calle San Nicolás can be expensive for the *pintxos* tourist, but it must also be one of the very best streets for tapas in the whole of Spain.

Without climbing any buildings to see if I can reach balconies, I return to my *hostal* feeling full and, frankly, somewhere well on the way to *borracho* (drunk).

The clamour and shriek of the street is going strong as I fall into a deep slumber.

A short hop and a showdown
Pamplona to San Sebastián

So the plan for northern Spain is to take narrow-gauge trains westward all the way across the country before dropping down south to Santiago de Compostela. Renfe has a subdivision named Renfe Feve that runs narrow-gauge lines along much of the distance, with regional operators also chipping in with services.

Train gauges in Spain are not, as I mentioned earlier, a straightforward affair, and at the risk of accusations of *rail overenthusiasm* I will endeavour to explain the basics here (the best I can).

In a nutshell: the historical nervousness about a possible French invasion along the tracks meant that in the nineteenth century a gauge of 5 feet and 5 ⅝ inches, precisely, was initially preferred rather than the standard gauge of most of Western Europe of 4 feet and 8 ½ inches, precisely. This meant that those travelling to Spain by train would have to change carriages by the border. As well as using this *wider* "Iberian gauge", some local services, usually along coastlines in mountainous regions, adopted the *narrower* gauge of 3 feet and 3 ⅜ inches. Meanwhile, in an about-turn, the high-speed lines that have spread across the country since Expo '92 have reverted to standard gauge to make it possible for trains such as mine from Toulouse to Barcelona to roll all the way through and further. The fear of Gallic attack appears to have abated and the pesky days of gauge isolation are well and truly over.

There you have them: Spanish train gauges.

The 11:19 to Irun, near the French border, is another Alvia service – on *standard gauge* – which departs from Pamplona's modern station punctually, sliding through a green hilly landscape beneath leaden clouds.

The tall, curly-haired conductor asks about my journey and when I describe going west along the coast, he tells me that I should not be heading for Irun as this will mean an unnecessary detour east. Taking some time, as though in no particular rush, he patiently explains I should catch a Euskotren regional service run by Basque Railways to Bilbao from San Sebastián, where this train stops for connections.

"Cross the *río*," he says, showing on his smartphone that I need to walk from San Sebastián-Donostia Station to Amara-Donostia San Sebastián Station for the new train. "Cross the *río*! This is the narrow railway! Euskotren! Euskotren! Euskotren!"

Just before departing, he writes *1km* on the back of my current ticket and indicates that this is the distance between the two stations. Then he taps his feet together and seems to give a little salute (or perhaps this is just my imagination). What a great Spanish train conductor.

The train judders onward past timber yards before climbing into the hills. We are about to enter the Basque Country.

So here it is probably about time I explained a few of the basics about Spanish autonomous communities (the best I can, too).

There are seventeen *comunidades autónomas* covering Spain in all. I have already been to three: Catalonia, Aragon and Navarra. Across northern Spain ahead, moving west, lie Cantabria, Asturias and Galicia. Some of these autonomous communities are made up of more than one province. Aragon, for example, has three: Huesca, Zaragoza and Teruel. However, seven of the seventeen are single provinces as well as autonomous communities: Asturias, the Balearic Islands, Cantabria, La Rioja, Madrid, Murcia and Navarra.

The Basque Country is perhaps the most infamous of the *comunidades autónomas*. Comprising precisely 7,234 square kilometres with a population of more than two million, it has its own distinctive flag coloured red, white and green with crosses in more or less the same configuration as those on a Union Jack. While modern Catalonian separatism has flared relatively recently, Basque separatism has been around for many years in many formats, including a military wing named Euzkadi Ta Askatasuna (ETA), which translates as Basque Homeland and Liberty. This group, founded in 1959, was responsible for 829 deaths and many thousands of injuries and was only fully disbanded in 2018, bringing an end to the bloodshed.

There you have them: *Comunidades autónomas*, the vital organs of Spain. Strong identities, traditions and passions mark their borders.

* * *

Four Scandinavian gap-year students across the aisle begin noisily eating crisps and nachos with dips. Laurel and Hardy and Marx Brothers films begin on a screen by a temperature monitor that says 18.4ºC. There is a definite feeling of moving north, away from the sunshine here. Higher and higher up we go, in and out of tunnels, before trundling across a high metal bridge with the view annoyingly obscured by clouds and dropping into a fern-covered landscape and soon afterward entering a city.

This is San Sebastián.

I exit into a pink station decorated with stone lions. Opposite is a bridge across the *río*, the River Urumea, with pink stone masonry and old-fashioned lanterns shaped like dragons and cherubs. A close inspection of these lanterns reveals intricate carvings of tall ships next to a smart *SS* city motif. All very decorative in San Sebastián. On the opposite side a fine row of nineteenth-century buildings with palm trees growing outside lines the riverfront. Beautiful art nouveau tiles in lilac and green depict flowers on the facades. Elaborate stucco, elegant wrought-iron balconies, towers, cupolas, high arched windows, decorative columns and gates guarded by stone urns... evidence of the late nineteenth-century heyday of San Sebastián, when the seaside resort was a magnet for Spain's socialites, is all around.

But I really am not hanging around in San Sebastián.

At the Amara-Donostia San Sebastián Station, housed in a surprisingly dull concrete building, a glass boxlike information office with potted plants is to the right. Inside, an employee wearing designer glasses and a crisp blue shirt who might pass for an architect is soon filling me in on Euskotren trains to Bilbao.

"It is called the Coastline Train: two hours and ten minutes to Bilbao," he says. "It will only get you to Bilbao. You will arrive here," he says, drawing a rudimentary map of the centre of Bilbao on a piece of paper. "You need to cross this bridge and there will be a church here and a big square. From there it is a very nice train onward to Oviedo."

The Coastline Train leaves every hour. I ask the attendant whether he would recommend stopping overnight here in San Sebastián or continuing to Bilbao.

He is, initially, diplomatic in his reply. "Well, San Sebastián has a population of one hundred and seventy thousand," he begins, "while Bilbao has half a million and then there's the urban area."

A visitor should either consider a high population a reason to visit, or not – seems to be his line of thinking. It is all up to the visitor. I decide to keep moving along the coast and tell him I will buy a ticket from one of the machines in a couple of hours after going to see San Sebastián's famous beach.

"Maybe," he replies, ditching his neutrality over the competing merits of the two cities. "Maybe you may stay to live here. It is very beautiful here. That I promise."

I ask the attendant about trains in northern Spain – are they efficient with all these different narrow-gauge lines?

He shrugs. "Trains are not very useful in the north," he says. "In the south, there are fast trains. Supposedly they are making fast trains in the north. I don't think *this* will happen *fast* though."

Then he waves his hand toward the west beyond the Picos de Europa mountains, which I am due to cross after Bilbao. "The worst is in this direction," he says. Then he chuckles and wishes me a good journey.

I go to take a look at the beach.

The beach at San Sebastián is a brilliant sweep of wheat-coloured sand with a curving promenade beneath which archways with benches and another walkway are to be found (handy, I suppose, in case of rain). A huge cross dominates a wooded headland to the north and an island guards the almost perfect circle of the cove.

This is as much as I see of San Sebastián – such is the nature of a series of train rides around a big peninsula in south-western Europe – apart from the Euskotren station and its immediate environs, where a series of elderly drunks have purloined the public benches and are consuming cans of San Miguel by a bandstand. They seem rather philosophical, morose drunks; contemplative of what has led them to this state of affairs, perhaps.

Inside the station, however, all is bright and jolly. An excellent *pintxos* bar is to be found on the left with long display cabinets of delicious-looking snacks. To pass the time I count these snacks: thirty of them, a truly wonderful spread. Had it not been for yesterday's assault on the *pintxos* bars of Pamplona, I would tuck in – but as tempting as Amara-Donostia San Sebastián Station's *pintxos* bar may be, I do not feel quite ready for all of that again.

In a side room to the right of the station entrance that seems to be on the way to the toilets, the rail enthusiast at Amara-Donostia San Sebastián Station may be interested to check out a series of pictures of trains at San Sebastián, but best to ask the ticket attendant first.

In fact, this side room is the entrance to an antechamber leading to the station's offices, and if you enter and gormlessly stare at the grainy photographs for a while without permission a small man may emerge from an inner room and, even though you are doing no harm and merely ogling old trains evocative of bygone times in northern Spain, usher you out with no uncertainty before watching you with eagle eyes until you depart Amara-Donostia San Sebastián Station. My first "run-in" in Spain.

On the Coastline Train
San Sebastián to Bilbao

I board the 14:50 to Bilbao.

This is a modern, electric, narrow-gauge train – and looks quite cute. Almost all the seats are taken, but I nab one by the aisle. A screen shows a film of old locomotives, so there was no need after all to break mistakenly into the station antechamber and upset people. Teenagers goof around in the seats opposite for a while but soon give up and fall asleep like a heap of seals, backpacks all over the place. Outside, a wide olive river emerges, partially obscured by trees. We enter a tunnel of green foliage with regimented rows of vineyards, before the track opens out and glimpses of the glimmering slate-grey water of the Bay of Biscay and flashes of plunging white cliffs can be seen to the right.

The television screen switches to images of shiny, happy people riding Euskotren trains, sometimes shown in slow motion as though to emphasize the sheer timeless fabulousness of Euskotren trains. We creak past caramel-coloured stations. In places the track curves so much you can see the carriages ahead out of the window. Then we rise high above a little stream, crawling along at about the same pace as the Montserrat Rack Railway (very slow).

The teenagers depart near Euba Station. Pleasant countryside populated by cows unfurls and everything feels happily out of the way and remote, as though we have somehow rolled off the regular map of Spain for a while. Donkeys munch grass in fields adjoining tiny station platforms. Butterflies flicker above brooks. Horses swish tails in paddocks. This Euskotren – the Basque County language is known as Euskara (spoken by 750,000) – does indeed feel quite timelessly fabulous. But it can't last and as we reach the outskirts of Bilbao, wagons loaded with logs and concrete boulders rest in sidings and grim apartment blocks shoot up. Shortly afterward, we arrive at Zazpikaleak-Casco Viejo Station, where I disembark into a modern underground space decorated with striking red-and-white contemporary art.

First impressions of Bilbao on foot are: wow!

The facade of a grand theatre with art nouveau ornamental figures occupies a square by Zazpikaleak-Casco Viejo Station. The facade of another distinguished building is draped with a banner saying *I LOVE INDEPENDENTZIA* next to a large Basque flag – immediate evidence of the regional separatist movement. Across a black swirling river, a train station rises beside the water with beautiful lime, apple-green and mustard-yellow tiles and spiky grey stone embellishments. This is quite a building, shimmering like a basking reptile – a Spanish rail station version of an iguana, perhaps. If San Sebastián was showy, Bilbao is show-off.

The lizard-like station is where the train to Santander departs from in the morning. Naturally, I want to go and investigate but I hold back and trudge up a hill to find my cheap cramped room in an apartment overlooking the city's bullring. The owner, an Asian man wearing glasses, tells me breakfast is included in the ridiculously low price and shows me the kitchen.

"Yeah, sure," he says. "Help yourself. Yeah, sure: milk, soy milk, tea, coffee, whatever. Beer? Yeah, sure, you want beer, yeah, sure."

There are a couple of cans, probably left by a previous guest, in the fridge.

The owner's name is Liang and he is a very laid-back, no-nonsense character. He shows me both bathrooms, explains the various keys and – when I ask him if I am the only guest (there are four rooms and no one else is to be seen) – says: "Oh no! We are *full*. We are always *full*, yeah, sure."

Liang departs and one of the other guests enters the kitchen and begins cooking broccoli for dinner on a hob fuelled by a gas canister. This is all she eats. Maybe she has allergies. She is from the Netherlands, I discover after nosily enquiring, and is middle-aged with careful blue-grey eyes. Her name is Irma and she is staying in the little apartment by the bullring for a week. She is due to meet a pen pal in San Sebastián tomorrow, so I tell her about the Euskotren train. Irma listens but does not appear to be a train person, responding firmly: "I think I will take the bus there."

She eats her broccoli and watches me steadily with her blue-grey eyes.

I ask her what she does for a living and she says: "Information specialist, librarian. Do you know what that is?"

I sputter a bit and say something along the lines of: "Well, *information* covers quite a few areas…"

She cuts me short. "I am into health writing," she says, without elaboration – and returns to eating her broccoli.

I wish her a good evening and, still slightly at a loss as to Irma's precise work, I walk back down the hill to go and work out tomorrow's train.

Abando Indalecio Prieto Station, which dates from 1870 although it was updated in 1948, is one of Spain's finest stations. The "Abando" part of the name comes from the neighbourhood and "Indalecio Prieto" is the name of a prominent local (socialist) politician and journalist who died in 1962. Most people refer to the station simply as Bilbao-Abando Station. When I enter from the side away from the river into a busy ticket hall, I take an escalator upward and am blown away by a glorious stained-glass window beneath a high curved ceiling.

It is as though you have entered a kind of cathedral of trains. Shafts of red, green, yellow and blue light fall on the cavernous concourse where commuters stride by, so familiar with the incredible work they barely glance up. Churches, bridges, rivers and scenes from local life – including workers in steel mills, miners, and farmers in fields with bullocks and scythes – are captured in a grand sweep of intricately cut glass. The work dates from the 1948 station refurbishment and was made by the glass artist Jesús Arrechubieta out of 301 pieces of glass, 15 metres wide and 10 metres high, all based on drawings by another artist named Miguel Pastor Veiga. For a while I stand there dumbstruck, interrupting the commuter flow. Sometimes we forget how crucially important trains were in years gone by, during industrialization and the decades that followed. Here at Bilbao-Abando is evidence of a joyful *celebration* of trains, of how key they were to local life at the time that such a stupendous work of art was commissioned and installed in pride of place by the platforms.

Then I take long steps down to another section of the station close to the beautiful green and yellow facade, where the timetable for the Renfe

Feve trains to Santander is to be found. A train departs to Santander at eight in the morning or else it's a wait until the afternoon. I'll get the early one. The journey across northern Spain by slow, narrow trains is going to be slightly chaotic and by any means/times necessary, I can already tell.

Then I join an asylum seekers march.

Outside Bilbao-Abando Station, a column of marchers with banners and flags has gathered, yelling: "¡*Lobos!* Liars! ¡*Lobos!* Liars! We *do* want asylum!" *Lobos* translates as "wolves" and seems to be directed at those who are anti asylum seekers.

I fall into step with a tall twenty-something man wearing glasses named Jorge, a local, who tells me: "We have come to defend against racists here. Spain is too slow to prioritize asylum seekers. The Vox party is taking advantage of a bad situation. Racism! In some parts of Spain, like Andalusía, people have difficulties making a living. Vox has a message that people come here from overseas to take their jobs. The Vox party had very good results at the last election. Their message is racism: a move to the far right. For some people, not for all people, that message is getting stronger. People go to vote now with hate in their hearts."

With almost six million immigrants living in Spain out of a population of forty-seven million – about 12.8 per cent – demographics have become a hot topic, especially as the figure was less than one per cent at the beginning of the 1980s. Yet although numbers from Morocco have leaped, immigration from within the European Union is an even bigger consideration, with many arriving from Romania and Bulgaria… as well as, yes, the United Kingdom. It's estimated that as many as 300,000 Britons live in Spain, mostly in the far south (and many of a certain age).

But it is the image of Africans arriving by ships run by humanitarian groups carrying migrants from North Africa rescued from the sea after capsizing or falling into difficulties – not Doreen and Tony's suntrap in the Costa del Sol – that has played a big part in Vox's controversial rising popularity.

As Jorge explains this, we are marching down Avenida Don Diego López Haroko Kale Nagusia with the two hundred or so keeping up the "¡*Lobos!* Liars!" chant, while accompanied by a squadron of police and police cars. Shoppers at Zara, Lacoste and Massimo Dutti shops peer at us with some bemusement. Today is World Refugee Day – not that they know much about it. To be fair, neither did I until just now.

Jorge says that the campaigners are particularly hoping to raise awareness of the "inhumane" treatment of migrants at Ceuta, an autonomous Spanish city on the coast of North Africa surrounded by Morocco, and Melilla, a similar city within Morocco. Both were part of Spain proper until 1995 and large controversial refugee camps have grown in the cities in recent years. Both have been in the news of late. Ceuta hit headlines after six hundred migrants successfully stormed its 5-mile long security fence. Meanwhile, Melilla made international bulletins when a photograph of migrants atop its 7-mile fence went viral on social media. The refugees were pictured overlooking a well-maintained golf course within the autonomous Spanish zone as golfers calmly continued their game, seemingly oblivious to the desperate plight of those gazing down on them.

Jorge gives me a yellow badge to show solidarity with the marchers and the migrants.

He tells me that the fences at Melilla and Ceuta are incredibly dangerous. "They have," he begins, before pausing and then indicating that he is shaving his face.

"Razor wire?" I ask.

"*Sí, sí*, razor wire!" he replies, before switching tack. "One of the problems is we need to say 'no' to wars. There is business with weapons. Our companies do this business. Ships come and they collect the weapons. One came from Saudi Arabia and we protested. In the end it did not stop here. But the Spanish government just doesn't think properly about these things."

"What weapons are made in Spain?" I ask.

"Oh, I am not sure," Jorge says. "I am not sure exactly: *bombas*."

Bombs – which may eventually be used in Saudi strikes against Yemen, and some recent shipments have indeed been sent.

Jorge tells me he works in the communications department of a private dental-care clinic, although he trained originally to be a journalist at the University of the Basque Country in Bilbao. He is due to join a caravan of vehicles to Morocco to offer support to those seeking refugee status in the summer during his annual holiday. There cannot be many dental-care clinic workers in Spain, or anywhere for that matter, I can't help reflecting, who volunteer to sacrifice their time off to help desperate North African asylum seekers.

We reach Plaza Moyua, a square with a pretty garden of orange and red flowers where I find myself talking to Saioa, a twenty-five-year-old nurse, and Irune, a twenty-two-year-old social worker for asylum seekers. Saioa tells me that migrants in Bilbao come from Morocco, Cameroon, Senegal, Western Sahara and Conakry.

I ask Saioa where Conakry is, and Saioa looks at me as though I really ought to know this (perhaps I should).

"The capital of Guinea," she says.

Both she and Irune are worried about the welfare of refugees but they do not believe these concerns are shared by those running the local government. "The politicians of the Basque Country are the rich people. The high society. The *alta burguesía*."

I ask Irune what *alta burguesía* means and she tells me "upper middle class". I am learning plenty on my stopover in Bilbao.

"It is the establishment that has the power. They have a movement. This movement is to be rich and look after themselves," says Irune. "They want to prevent refugees coming: simple as that."

Santander, my next port of call, is a centre of this establishment. "Santander is very rich and very arrogant," says Irune, who raises her chin and looks down her nose at me to display arrogance. Then she says: "But I admit, I'm prejudiced. I am left wing. Most of the people here are from the left position."

Irune tells me that she would one day like the Basque Country to enjoy independence but not if the arrogant establishment that is currently in charge takes over: "Not with them. No thank you very much."

We say goodbye as cries of "*¡Lobos!* Liars!" break out again. Saioa and Irene are about to march back to Bilbao-Abando Station and want to join the front amid all the banners.

* * *

Back at the apartment I listen to the shuffle of feet in the hall, reflecting that train journeys really do take you to places and situations that you might never have discovered or experienced otherwise.

But this is just how it should be: *ir con la corriente* (go with the flow).

Tomorrow I'm taking more narrow-gauge trains via "rich and arrogant" Santander in the *comunidad autónoma* of Cantabria and onward, I hope, to Oviedo in the *comunidad autónoma* of Asturias. The longest journey yet in Spain, almost 200 miles, beyond the dramatic peaks of the Picos de Europa mountain range.

Narrow-gauge trains all the way.

CHAPTER FIVE

BILBAO TO FERROL, VIA SANTANDER AND OVIEDO

ACROSS THE TOP

Hardly anyone is around for the 08:00 to Santander on this Friday morning, not even the attendant in the ticket kiosk. A cleaner with a mop informs me that he is "somewhere" and after five minutes a man with a goatee appears from a back room and sells me a ticket to Santander. No cards are accepted and the attendant does not appear overly enamoured with my fifty-euro note. A little café up by the beautiful stained-glass window sells good coffee and is notable for being illuminated by green neon lights, a loud stereo playing hits by the rock group Queen in a loop and two female Renfe conductors in grey uniforms who are dancing to the music with pastries in one hand. The guitar squeals, Freddie Mercury's vocals soar and the conductors dance with their pastries. Dalí, you feel, would be pleased with the scene.

At one end of the platform, waiting for the Santander train, I realize that, although very close together, there are two separate stations here: one with the striking green facade by the river (where I am now), and the other up the steps to the grand concourse with the stained glass and the dancing conductors. Here I am officially in Bilbao-Concordia Station, not Bilbao-Abando Station.

Anyway, beyond the ticket barriers Bilbao-Concordia Station has fine belle époque architecture, from 1902, and long rows of lovely original wooden benches inset with blue and yellow tiles with a flower motif. Neoclassical columns lead to a tiny old steam engine loco beyond the buffers at the end of the track. Potted plants have been well maintained and a bronze bust of someone important from the early days of Spanish rail is attached to a wall by the stationmaster's office. An inscription explains this is Victor de Chávarri, founder of the Bilbao–Santander line.

A little (rather dirty) blue, yellow and white train arrives. The handful of passengers boards and we are away with a toot, heading toward a hill shrouded in thick white cloud. We move onward into the mist before shortly plunging into a tunnel.

Once out, the train rattles slowly onward and I settle into my wine-red seat with wooden armrests in the company of an elderly man across the aisle wearing a trilby. I intend to tell it how it is on this series of rides across Spain – and it is not exactly *picturesque* on the edge of Bilbao. The view shifts from endless dull apartment blocks by a river to a factory billowing steam, a *productos vulcanizades* depot, the shattered windows of an old warehouse, some cranes and a series of collapsed sheds. We pass Zorrotza Zorrotzgoiti Station (which would score rather well in Scrabble if the game had that many Zs and you were allowed to use place names). Then we begin to move quite steeply into hills, and for a while the track is surrounded by thick bamboo, ferns and brambles. We enter another tunnel and I close my eyes listening to the train, which has begun making a sound that reminds me of chickens in a coop, with an occasional additional whining noise as though straining with the incline. The man in the trilby coughs now and then. Then there is a rumbling sound and the train stops abruptly. We are still in the tunnel.

Something has gone wrong. The conductor strides past and knocks on the driver's door. A torch is visible in the driver's cab. The driver appears to turn the electricity for the train off and on in the manner of an IT guy sorting out a problem with a computer in an office; the lights in the carriage flicker off and on. This does not make any difference to our movement. In the darkness, the man in the trilby comments: *"Un problema electrico."* Then the conductor returns and informs us that two power units are required for the train, although only one is currently working.

The man in the trilby asks: *"¿Autobús?"*

The conductor replies: *"Sí, autobús."*

However, we are stuck in a tunnel, so it is difficult to work out how we will be transferred to an *autobús*. Seemingly as a joke, as there clearly is not one, a passenger further up the carriage asks whether there is a canteen. The man in the trilby chuckles. I ask whether we will get our money back. The man in the trilby chuckles. We are having a reasonably jolly time, given our current predicament.

Then the driver appears and walks all the way through the train and does something, presumably to the broken power unit at the back. He retraces his steps and the train begins to move again. The conductor makes an exasperated blowing sound as he passes us all, as though he is dealing with a rookie driver. A smell of cigarette smoke emanates from the driver's cab.

"*¿El cigarrillo?*" I ask the man with the trilby.

"*Sí, sí,*" he says.

We pass through some fields with donkeys, the train making a clickety-clack on the track and tooting from time to time. Then we stop at a station and the conductor tells us to get off. We are indeed getting an *autobús* as, apparently, there is yet another *problema*: engineering works on the track ahead.

So the passengers disembark – there are five of us – and wait in the rain, with a little shelter from the edge of a roof of a house by the tracks. All around is misty hillside. Here we wait for 20 minutes before a purple Renfe Feve bus arrives and a conductor with a Salvador Dalí moustache ushers us inside. We perform a U-turn, cross the slow-flowing River Carranza and follow a narrow twisting lane upward while listening to Michael Jackson, Amy Winehouse and Phil Collins hits on Kiss FM Santander.

The purple bus proceeds to pull into every station along the line – there are quite a few – and the conductor with the Dalí moustache, like a shepherd gathering sheep, leaps out on each occasion to check platforms for Renfe passengers. He collects five or six Renfe Feve passengers in this manner. Many three-point turns are made. Stevie Wonder and Village People hits are played. Then we arrive at another station – I have no idea where – and everyone is told to get off and join another purple bus. This one has a faster driver and we swerve onward slightly erratically.

Shortly afterward, having negotiated a series of clogged junctions and passed a port with a ferry, we come to an abrupt halt at Santander Station. It has been an awful hour on the roads of the *comunidad autónoma* of Cantabria. Going around Spain by *autobús* is not quite as wonderful as by train, that is for sure.

"We hope we arrive"
Santander to Oviedo

It is 11 a.m. Somehow or other we have arrived exactly on time. At the station I establish that the train to Oviedo, which I have set my heart on as I really do need to make a bit of progress across northern Spain, is due at 16:10 and will arrive in Oviedo at 21:10 – a very long, slow ride.

So there is time to have a look around Santander, although first I go to the station tapas bar and eat a late breakfast of a boiled egg and a ham *bocadillo* (sandwich). These I consume at a table next to another *La Perla del Caribe Deluxe* fruit machine while listening to Whitney Houston songs. It is turning into a day of pop music. Other features of the Santander Station tapas bar include a beer pump depicting a German maiden clasping large beer jugs and a barmaid who appears to be on the brink of breaking into tears, but never actually does so. Perhaps it is the effect of the Whitney Houston songs.

I venture out for some Santander sightseeing.

Santander is the largest city in Cantabria and is well-to-do partly because of its well-positioned port and partly due to being the headquarters, along with Madrid, of the renowned Banco de Santander. It is indeed rich-looking, although out on the streets I never do notice any definite arrogance, as Irune back in Bilbao had suggested. Maybe I was just lucky. From my guidebook I know there are beaches, somewhere, and that a large fire in 1941 destroyed many of the city centre buildings. The guidebook refers to the city as being *bourgeois* – and it strikes me that this is a quite old-fashioned word, redolent of bygone days. Perhaps the French word has somehow slipped across the border to wealthy Santander. People, outsiders, do seem generally to have it in for well-to-do Santander.

Near the station is an *armería* shop selling a vast array of knives. A picture of the tough-looking television adventurer Bear Grylls adorns the window, as though suggesting *knives are cool*. Beyond, a road leads to the port, where heaps of colourful cargo containers are piled and a Brittany Ferries ship is at anchor near the office of the *Estación Marítima*. French tourists, presumably passengers, are wandering about and I join them on a promenade that leads to two large futuristic shoebox-like buildings with smoked-glass windows, connected by walkways in the middle, as though the shoebox has been sliced in half.

To add to the unusualness of the structures, both buildings are mounted on stilts, so you can walk beneath them unhindered apart from one bit with a restaurant with glass panels. I stare at this apparition for a while and realize that *sliced shoebox on stilts* is not quite right. It looks more like a pair of inflated killer whales balanced on cocktail sticks. Or perhaps a pair of mounted Zeppelins. And I am guessing that if you kept on gazing at it for a while you would come up with more thoughts on what these buildings look like. And I also guess that this is the effect good modern architecture is meant to have.

This is the Centro Botín, an arts centre that opened in 2017 and is the work of the renowned Italian architect Renzo Piano, also responsible for the Centre Pompidou in Paris and the Shard in London. Bilbao, of course, has its own sparkling Guggenheim Museum by the famous Canadian-American architect Frank Gehry, opened in 1997, which I totally failed to see partly due to the march and the early train (and partly because I simply, I admit, forgot). It is said by some that Spanish cities are rather competitive when it comes to this sort of public "statement" arts centre.

Which is all jolly good if you are a train tourist who happens to be passing by within easy walking distance of the station. I enter a lift that takes you to the art gallery above and is memorable for the sound of an operatic voice singing *"sí, sí, sí"* as the lift rises. Peculiar, although I am getting increasingly used to the Spanish taste for eccentricity.

Upstairs is a futuristic white space with an art collection funded by a foundation created in 1964 by Marcelino Botín Sanz de Sautuola, a former director of Santander Bank who died in 1971. I buy a ticket from a smart woman wearing black and find myself in a room with a series of beautiful paintings. The first that catches my eye is by Isidre Nonell (1873–1911), depicting a woman reclining in a purple shawl looking thoughtful. The next is by Henri Matisse (1869–1954) of a *Spanish Woman* with tight red lips, flowing black hair with a red flower pinned within and an uncompromising gaze. Then there is a painting by Daniel Vázquez Díaz (1882–1969) of another woman in red, with a haunted, pensive expression who is taking notes with a pencil and wearing a hat. Next to this is *Portrait of My Mother* showing a woman with wide-set, glassy eyes and a crooked nose by Francisco Cossío (1894–1970). The theme of this part of the gallery, I gather, is *portraits of women*.

I mention the dates of the artists' lives here for a reason. These are sensitive, well-considered works that capture an essence of personality that is both thought-provoking and highly individual – composed during an era before "wacky" arrived (perhaps partially inspired by Dalí). After spending some time in the presence of these first-class paintings, I move on to a much more contemporary avant-garde art section at the back.

Here "wacky" takes over. First up is a video of a "desert island" with a palm tree floating along a river. Next, a pile of wooden beams, besides which rests another work: a sandbox with cork balls in the shape of ping-pongs. Yet another work comprises a wooden rack on the floor with a mirror beneath the wooden rack. Then comes a mural made up of a compilation of postcards. Then a picture of two men throwing a large "stone" to each other, except it is not really a stone and the lightweight object in question is on the floor in front of the photograph.

This work is meant, according to an explanatory panel, to represent Spain's "complicated relationship" with the years of rule by General Franco. A man regarding this photo, standing beside me, gently kicks the "stone" with his foot to test how light it is – and an attendant, who spots him, tells him to stop kicking the "stone".

The symbolic stone is followed by another photograph of several discarded ovens, a long piece of blue piping, a boiled sweet mounted on a plinth and a rope hanging from the ceiling. The oldest work from the contemporary art section seems to be from 1999; most are much more recent. To my eye, they are gimmicks, one and all. But as I said previously, I am beginning to appreciate the Spanish enjoyment of absurdity. And there is of course the argument that they have provoked a reaction and is that not what art is supposed to do?

One of the best features of Centro Botín is the view from the terrace at the top. Inland is a grand building with a huge archway through which pedestrians can walk, classical figurines and a Spanish flag the size of a tennis court fluttering on a pole above. This is the local headquarters of Banco de Santander, Spain's biggest bank, beyond which higgledy-piggledy apartments rise on a hill. Looking out to sea, a cargo ship is cruising across the wide, calm bay with a tumble of hills and a long pier tapering into the water on the far side. Down below, skateboarders are performing "tricks" and two acoustic guitarists are strumming a folksy song.

I walk around for a while, passing bronze sculptures of boys leaping into the harbour and a swanky restaurant called Real Club Marítimo, where chauffeurs are waiting in Mercedes-Benzes and BMWs outside. Evidence of Santander's richness, and perhaps its arrogant streak, I suppose. A smart couple, probably in their sixties, walks past. I can tell they are wealthy as the woman wears red high heels that are either alligator or snakeskin, while the man wears box-fresh white Nike trainers and designer jeans. Both have mirrored aviator shades and are carrying handfuls of shopping bags. A smell of expensive perfume trails behind the woman with the alligator or snakeskin high heels.

Past the headquarters of the bank are sushi bars, pricey fashion boutiques and a series of wine bars. More signs of money. Santander is indeed clearly pretty loaded.

Then on the corner of a building back near the station, an old advert for Holland America Line depicting a cruise ship with three red funnels on the high seas stops me in my tracks. Although faded and weather worn, it is simply charming. There is something about the lettering and the imagery that evokes a period when travel seemed to hold more excitement – a period when you could not simply hop on a jet and go just about anywhere for quite low fares, as you can today.

It is that feeling of slower travel that I am hoping to capture on these trains in Spain. A feeling of being one step removed from the fast lane. The advert, which has been preserved above the offices of a winery, is for trips to Cuba, Mexico, the United States and South America as well as a cargo service that covers *todos los puertos del mundo* (all the ports of the world). The destinations in Spanish have an exotic flavour: *pasajes a los Estados Unidos y America del Sur* (passage to America and South America). It is, frankly, amazing when you think of how jet planes have totally transformed our conception of travel.

But then again, not long before planes, railways did that too.

* * *

Santander Station for Renfe Feve services, as opposed to the city's main station next door, is remarkable for having a tailor's shop by platform eight.

It also has a strange system of platform numbering that appears to go: one, seven, two and eight, in that order. Where three, four, five and six have gone, I am not sure. There is a sculpture of a railway worker at one end next to a vending machine. The people of Santander seem generally to be quite arty.

The 16:10 to Oviedo departs five minutes late. It is a neat little white and yellow train with three carriages that buck up and down quite a bit and are powered by overhead electricity cables. Clouds have parted and the sky is royal blue as we move through the suburbs. We stop at many stations with plenty of *proxima parada* (next stop) announcements as we quickly roll onward through countryside beside a clear, shallow river; were there any fish, you would be able to see them. We pass a cliff with protective wires to stop boulders falling on the tracks and fields of goats and cattle. Mountains rise to the south: the start of Picos de Europa. And just when I'm slightly dozily settling into the ride, we stop at a station. Having fallen into something of a trance I do not notice that all the other passengers have disembarked and a conductor comes along and taps me on the shoulder. A diesel train has broken down ahead, he says, and we are all taking an *autobús* to Llanes (pronounced "Yannis"; the double "l" in Spanish turns into a "y"). "Yannis! Yannis!" he keeps on saying as he walks me to yet another purple *autobús* that proceeds in by-now-familiar fashion to call at every station, with the bald conductor leaping off to root out Renfe Feve passengers waiting for the 16:10 Santander train.

All of this is (I will admit) really quite upsetting; I had been looking forward to spinning through the mountains, but nothing can be done. Instead, it is hard to see the scenery from a seat by the aisle on the jolting *autobus*. Crackly, almost inaudible pop music plays through speakers. The time on the clock at the front says 1 a.m. although the time is 6.30 p.m. Everything seems a little bit wrong on this purple *autobús*. We negotiate a series of roundabouts and hurtle down small lanes, on one of which a blue and yellow sign with a symbol of a shell points the way on the Camino de Santiago pilgrimage route. Eventually we pull up at Llanes Station, where the four remaining Renfe Feve passengers on the bus (including me) get off.

Here the bald conductor ascertains that only two passengers, myself and a man wearing a purple jumper, wish to travel further down the line and tells me: "No train! Taxi! Ticket, you have ticket?" I show him my ticket. I am, he says, to travel by taxi to Infiesto Station, where I will catch a train. This will be arranged by Renfe Feve at no extra charge. The man with the purple jumper will be dropped off somewhere before Infiesto.

Our taxi soon pulls up and I tell the man with the purple jumper all about my plan to take the narrow-gauge trains of northern Spain along the coast. He seems delighted by my failed mission and begins to laugh heartily and relay the story to the taxi driver, who also has a good chuckle. I tell him about the buses on the way to Santander and he laughs even more, rigorously shaking my hand and wishing me well when he departs at a little town in the foothills of the other side of Picos de Europa. We seem somehow to have passed through the main mountains.

I move to sit in the front and the driver explains that this happens often. Problems on the track, whether with engineering work or broken trains, go on all the time and he gets good business out of Renfe Feve. After explaining this, he apologizes, makes a hands-free phone call and begins a long conversation with his wife about how it is not fair that it is always him, and not his cousins, who goes to mass with his aunt. "My position is this," he is saying. "What about those cousins? What are they doing?"

We reach Infiesto Station, where I drink a glass of *vino blanco* at a tiny railway-themed cafeteria while waiting for the forty-minute onward train to Oviedo. This duly arrives and I board the front carriage near the driver's door. The driver, who is wearing jeans and a T-shirt, pops out and I ask if the train will go all the way or if there will be more purple buses. The driver looks at me cheerfully and says: "We hope we arrive! It is always like this!"

We cross a river and descend for a long spell, travelling through fields and passing a series of Orwell-style *dice towns*. The driver has left the door of his cab into the carriage open and a soft orange sunset can be seen ahead through a grimy window. We twist and turn through pastureland with cows and sheep. A hawk soars above. An owl startled by the train flaps out from a tree. The driver blows the horn every now and then. Having passed the mountains, these plains feel like a completely different part of Spain – Catalonia and the Basque Country are way behind us; the region of Galicia in Spain's far north-west lies ahead.

At 21:10 precisely, by some small miracle that only Renfe Feve with all its purple buses and taxis could pull off, we arrive at Oviedo.

I exit into the dungeon-like depths of a modern station, where I ascertain from the *Media Distancia* board there are two choices of train tomorrow to Ferrol, a Spanish naval port at the end of the Renfe Feve line, which happens to be the birthplace of General Franco. One is at 07:30 arriving 14:44, the other at 14:30 arriving 21:44. I decide to take the earlier one and cross fingers that it makes it all the way in one go. I will not be spending much time in Oviedo, the capital of Asturias.

Way above, up several escalators, is a huge empty square surrounded by large uninspiring rectangular buildings dating, at a guess, from the 1960s onward. On the edge of this square, overlooking the station at my cheap Booking.com apartment, a landlady wearing a pink T-shirt hands me a key and tells me it is just for the internal door and that I can "come back any time, we're here twenty-four hours" but I will have to press the buzzer at the bottom of the apartment block if I want to enter. She tries to explain something else. I cannot quite understand what she is saying and she insists on taking out her smartphone and using Google Translate to write the message: *"toda la manzana es la ruta de los vinos y puedes tapear donde quieras"*, which comes up as "the whole apple is the route of the wines and you can tapas wherever you want".

Wondering what on earth she is on about, I thank her for this information, drop my backpack in a large room and keylessly – and I have to admit, a little cluelessly – hit the now dark streets of Oviedo.

Inevitably I am going to miss out on some of the sights on this slow trains tour – after all, the trains lead the way... timetables are king! That's just the way it is and, as soon as you accept this, a great weight of tourist expectation lifts. Sure, see what happens to catch your interest when you can, but do not try to cram in the whole lot. Train tourism is different from taking a weekend break with a list of "must dos" or a day trip from your hotel or villa with a specific sight in mind.

Oviedo is renowned for its medieval cathedral and pair of ninth-century churches outside town that the travel writer Jan Morris praised for their "pre-Romanesque robustness" and which my guidebook says rank among the "most remarkable" in Spain. But they are 2 miles away on a wooded slope and it is night-time and I am tired. I decide (not that I have much choice) to give the remarkable robust pre-Romanesque churches a miss. Meanwhile, the cathedral, with a chapel built by King Alfonso II in the ninth century, is closed and will not open tomorrow until ten o'clock, by which time I will be long gone on a Renfe Feve narrow-gauge train. Yes, this is a pity: somewhere in this cathedral, as Morris elegantly (as always) points out, an eleventh-century chest is to be found containing two thorns from Christ's crown, several pieces of the Cross and one of St Peter's sandals. It would be undeniably interesting to see this chest as it is not every day you come across thorns from Christ's crown on your travels. However, I have decided to move on. The train goes at 07:30. So that's that.

Outside the apartment a young woman in a miniskirt totters along the pavement looking haunted and gaunt. There are unusual goings-on near the station – seemingly tragic goings-on. The woman must be in her early twenties and appears to be a lost soul. Everything about her screams misery and desperation. She has dazed eyes and her visage has turned an unhealthy shade of yellow. A car slows as it passes and she straightens her gait. It revs onward. She totters onward, after lighting a cigarette: a living ghost by the tracks.

From the station, and its sad undercurrents, I walk down long lanes to the old town, about ten minutes by foot. This is another world: glorious squares, colonnaded walkways, elegant ochre townhouses with wrought-iron balconies, bell towers and churches. None of the shuffle and seediness of the station. The ornate facade of the cathedral is the showstopper with its high arched doorways, circular stained-glass windows, fancy honey-hued stucco and tall illuminated spire. Stars flicker in the pitch-black Asturian sky above, looking like celestial fireflies and making the cathedral look even more magical and lovely. And then, *tourism done*, I walk back to my apartment by the station, passing plenty of places to *tapas*. As the landlady suggested, it is indeed possible to *tapas* in Oviedo just about wherever you want to *tapas*. But after all the purple buses and trains, I just feel like returning, ringing the buzzer and crashing out.

But I don't do this.

Next to my apartment, singing is emanating from the doorway of what looks like yet another tapas bar. The lure of tapas in Spain, I am increasingly discovering, is strong – almost impossible to resist – especially when heavenly harmonies tempt you.

Curiosity gets the better of me, and I'm glad it does.

Inside, a group of men and women are standing by the bar in a little circle, drinks in hand while performing a chorus in which their voices seem to melt together in perfect, quite transfixing perfection. They are smartly dressed and seem to be enjoying themselves very much indeed. They are not hired by the bar, it turns out, just locals from a choral group who performed earlier at a concert hall and who like to gather afterward to drink and sing even more to wind down post show. This, I learn from the barman, is quite normal here in Oviedo and he asks whether I would like to drink *sidra* (cider). Maybe this is what "the whole apple is the route of the wines" was about. It is. The barman proceeds to put on a performance of his own: clasping a long green bottle above his head and pouring a stream of liquid in a great arc directly into the centre of a narrow glass. Not a single drop is spilled and he watches as I sip the refreshing bubbly drink, telling me that I am not in fact in a tapas bar. This is a *sidrería*, a cider bar, and Oviedo is famous for them.

Great fun, if only there was more time to drink more *sidra* and listen to more tunes in the *comunidad autónoma* of Asturias.

Into Galicia
Oviedo to Ferrol

Galicia, however, calls – as does one of the most famous places in the whole of Spain and Christendom.

Galicia is in the top-left corner of Spain tucked above Portugal. If you draw a jagged line up from the eastern edge of Portugal to the Bay of Biscay this is more or less the territory of Galicia. This *comunidad autónoma* has its own language, Galician, and a population of just under three million known as *Gallegos*, most of whom are bilingual in Galician – closely connected to Portuguese – as well as Spanish. Historical ties with Celtic peoples mean that the culture is distinct from other parts of Spain: hearty soups and stews are enjoyed, as is a great deal of seafood (there are many fishing ports on the Atlantic and the Bay of Biscay); folk music reminiscent of Irish traditional music is favoured, and some locals even play the bagpipes. The reason Galicia is not part of Portugal is to do with its connections with the ancient kingdom of Asturias, where a Christian army defeated the Moors in 722, beginning the *Reconquista*, a period of "reconquest" that lasted until the late fifteenth century. These historical loyalties outweighed claims from the south. This is the gist as I understand it... there seem to be quite a few nuanced versions.

In short, Galicia is a place apart – neither really Spanish, despite being technically so, nor of course Portuguese, despite the language similarities. It has a rugged landscape, which helped put off the Moors. It has Santiago de Compostela, the pilgrimage city to which tens of thousands walk hundreds of miles every year to visit the shrine of St James the Apostle, the saint's supposed resting place. It is a curious spot. *People play bagpipes.* This is not normal for Spain. This is not the castanets and fast-strumming guitar you tend to associate with the hot heel-thumping passions of Spanish dance. Flamenco performers down south do not usually, as I understand it, wiggle their hips to the whine, wheeze and drone of air delivered from the dried-out skins of sheep and goats.

With this image of bagpipe-playing Spaniards in mind, I buy a ticket to Ferrol from a machine at the station. Through the ticket gate and down some stairs a seemingly operative train purrs by the platform upon which a group of early-rising travellers has gathered in the gloomy depths of Oviedo Station.

A few are stragglers returning home from nights out: lads in ties and jackets and lasses in frocks and high heels. Four twenty-something men in hiking boots and backpacks are larking about attempting to shake snacks free from a vending machine. One has a fake flowerpot with fake yellow flowers attached to the top of his backpack – maybe as a good luck charm, who knows? Another is wearing a cap bearing the words *DRINK UP BITCHES*. I take them to be Santiago de Compostela pilgrims, though not perhaps the hair-shirt-wearing religious kind. Apparently, all sorts do it these days although, thinking about it, this was probably always the case if stories of overindulgence, lechery, skullduggery, blue jokes, gossip and all sorts else from Chaucer's *Canterbury Tales* are anything to go by.

A long walk in the company of friends and newly-made acquaintances, while stopping off at taverns, has, unsurprisingly, long been popular. In the Middle Ages as many as half a million pilgrims trudged this way annually in hope of respite from purgatory; some consider this period as being Spain's first taste of the mass tourism the country is so famous for today. Long before clubbing and pubbing in Magaluf, the party trail to the Santiago shrine was going strong. Interesting though that these "pilgrims" shaking the vending machine are taking the train. Maybe a little bit of walking in between a few rides is good enough to count as a "pilgrimage". I suppose so. All of this is new to me.

The train departs on time and follows a still, serene river shrouded in mist. Green undulating hills soon arise with tiny chapels the size of living rooms looking down and making me wonder if solitary monks lurk inside deep in morning prayer. Beehives are scattered by the trackside.

There are small towns with peculiar houses that look like conservatories as they have so many windows (this seems to be the local architectural fashion). A woman boards with friends at a station and joins the next-door carriage, where she begins laughing hysterically as though totally *borracha* (drunk) or else just having a simply amazing time. Perhaps she is a pilgrim. A bay emerges with a soapy wash of breaking waves. Watching this for a while induces a feeling of great contentment though I cannot quite say why. Maybe it is simply a joy to be on a slow train with a view of a sea, rolling along in no particular hurry.

The Renfe Feve carriages rattle by little half-ruined stations with peeling mustard-yellow walls. We cross a viaduct above a forest of pines and plunging granite cliffs. We disappear into a tunnel and emerge to a wide seascape of soft grey and lilac. More Santiago de Compostela pilgrims board, these ones more serious-looking with sticks, bandanas, hats, sunshades and all the right walking gear. They are extremely tanned and fit; not many ounces of fat to spare. They disembark along with the hysterically laughing "pilgrim" and her friends at a station with a blue and yellow Camino de Santiago sign. We cross another viaduct with the ghostly outline of the train mirrored in a lake below – somehow reassuring, and wonderful too.

A Spanish flag is painted alongside the word *Vox* on an electrical unit by the track; a jolting reminder of ugly politics, even in these remote parts. Otherwise all is harmony and calm as Galicia unravels beyond the carriage window beneath a low pastel grey-blue sky. The feeling of otherworldliness and escape high above the Bay of Biscay is soul-lifting and seductive. Due to economic hard times, between 1836 and 1960 it is estimated that around 500,000 *Gallegos* emigrated to Argentina. Buenos Aires is now jokingly referred to as being the biggest city in Galicia, where many *Gallegos* are said to suffer from *morriña*, a form of melancholic yearning for these parts. You can understand why on a journey down the tracks from Oviedo. This is dramatic, rugged territory on the western edge of Europe – and this is a ride to sit back and savour.

We putter slowly through a bleached-green eucalyptus forest before descending a long way in a straight line, crossing a marsh and entering a valley with plum trees and vines. Shortly afterward, we reach the edge of a city and come to a halt at Ferrol Station.

No purple buses today and – just like yesterday – the good old admittedly-sometimes-really-quite-erratic Renfe Feve is bang on time.

Posh trains and Franco
Ferrol

There is a very nice train on the adjoining platform at Ferrol Station.

It is old-fashioned-looking and painted shiny blue, gold and white with *El Transcantábrico Clásico* written on its side.

I appear to have stumbled upon one of Spain's finest trains.

El Transcantábrico Clásico travels along the lines from León, about 80 miles due south of Oviedo, in a loop along Spain's north coast via Bilbao, Santander, Oviedo, Ferrol and Santiago de Compostela. The eight-day journeys include accommodation in plush private air-conditioned compartments with gilded mirrors, oriental rugs, curtains with pelmets and double beds. All meals, which promise "a tour of the gastronomic identities of Galicia, Asturias, Cantabria and the Basque Country", with wine, are also thrown in. "Every night is a party night" in the saloon carriages, although some saloon carriages are entertainment-free for those after quiet evenings and passengers are free to explore each destination on their own as the train rests overnight at stations. Expect welcome drinks, guided excursions, tickets to attractions, a farewell gala and daily newspaper deliveries. The service is run by another subdivision of Renfe known as Renfe Viajeros (Travellers), which is also responsible for a similar service, the *Al Andalus*, operating between Granada, Ronda, Jerez and Seville in the south, as well as *El Expreso de la Robla* between León and Bilbao, although this one loops inland via small out-of-the-way towns and villages. *El Transcantábrico Clásico*, however, is the longest-running service of all, Spain's version of the *Orient Express* that began in 1983 with original Pullman carriages dating from the 1920s.

There is something captivating about the gleaming paintwork of this Spanish train jewel. Passengers have yet to arrive although luggage is being transported by porters to the sleeper carriages. Walking along and feeling as though I am somehow trespassing in this five-star world – like a hotel, the train is classed as having five stars – I peer into the *Coche Cocina*, where pineapples are resting on spotless cooking surfaces and chefs in white are consulting recipes. Further on is the *Ciudad de Gijón* dining carriage with its little wooden tables with lamps, champagne glasses for welcome drinks awaiting passengers, pale-green velvet cushions and vases with cut flowers. Another of the carriages is named *Ciudad de Ferrol*, with red velvet chairs, more empty champagne glasses and a glitzy, gold-tinted piano bar. The sleeping carriages trail a long way beyond the end of the platform and a panel says they were made in 2000… so not all carriages are Pullmans despite looking the part, a little confusingly.

Then I meet Jimmy. Jimmy is one of the staff, dressed in a smart blue uniform with gold buttons, a tie and white gloves. He is tall and tanned and with his white gloves and slickness might pass for a head croupier at a casino.

"We leave for León at five o'clock," he says, pleased that someone is interested rather than asking me to stop poking around Spain's *Orient Express*, which I had half expected. "We are here in Ferrol every other Saturday."

He has been a waiter on *El Transcantábrico Clásico* for four years and he proceeds to tell me much of what I have relayed above. "It's a job completely different to anything I have ever done before," he says. "I've never worked in hospitality. It's quite physical and face to face. I like this contact."

I ask him where the passengers come from.

"Northern Europe," he replies. "Norway, Denmark, Britain and Scotland. Then you have Brazil, Chile, Argentina, Canadians, Americans and Aussies. All over. People love trains from all over."

The way Jimmy says this, with a smile in his eyes, suggests that he is among this number.

Magicians, pianists and "cocktail shows" are laid on in the evenings and there are six waiters, two cooks, one engine driver, one technician and one tour manager. As Jimmy is about to go on, his eyes flick in the direction of the station building. The platforms are completely empty, but people are emerging from a side gate on the right.

The passengers have arrived. All is action. Jimmy and the other staff, who have been alerted, line up quickly alongside *Ciudad de Ferrol* for inspection by the five-star train travellers.

The guests – the train can take a total of fifty-four – mingle before the staff, taking pictures of the train and themselves with the train staff. A sense of euphoria seems to have overcome the group, most of whom are of a certain age, in the presence of the sparkling, polished, perfect *El Transcantábrico Clásico*. They hop about like children peering into windows and snapping photographs here, there and everywhere. The excitement is palpable and even before boarding you can tell they are already having a *muy bueno tiempo, de hecho* (very good time indeed).

And who can blame them – it does look like an excellent way to make one's way across the top of Spain.

Then I meet Nuria. Nuria is the station ticket assistant on duty at Ferrol Station, which is deserted apart from the five-star gathering by the platform and a solitary barman polishing glasses in its lime-green Cafetería La Estación (complete with grainy pictures of old locos on the walls). After explaining that I will need to catch the 08:54 tomorrow to reach Santiago de Compostela, changing at the port of A Coruña, she gets talking about trains. Nuria has been employed by Renfe for two years and is from a railway family.

"My mother worked for the railways, my aunt and my grandad," she says. "He was on the trains for a coal mine."

"Do you like working with trains?" I ask, having a strong inkling of the answer.

"Yes!" Nuria replies, like a shot. "Yes! Yes! Yes!"

There seems to be a lot of train love going on in Ferrol.

Nuria tells me all about her passion for the tracks and how she found her perfect job.

"My first work after studies was in a bank. I was in international affairs and commercial at a bank in Oviedo. But I gave it all up to come here. Each year the state has a test for those who want to work for Renfe in management. In my year five thousand people took the test and I was one of the lucky ones, one of the hundred, to get the job." Nuria is beaming as she says this. "Most of those who took the test had experience in the railways already."

This meant she had had to fight off stiff competition. "At first, they offered me a human resources job," she continues. "But I didn't like the idea of that. I didn't want to be in an office any more. I had done that for five years at the bank." Instead, she put her name down to be ticket assistant at Ferrol.

"What is it about trains that you like so much?"

"It's because all my special moments in my life have happened on trains: both romantic and sad," Nuria replies, not elaborating. "And on trains there is a feeling of always *moving*: that is what it is. That feeling of *moving on*."

When she is booking trips for customers, she says it is as though she is "travelling in my mind" as she works out how to get to places. Working for Renfe also means she uses trains more.

"It's a style of life: travelling," she says. "I feel alive when I travel by train. I have been along the tracks of Renfe Feve many many times. This line really is beautiful – it's so nice through the mountains."

Nuria recommends some cafés in Ferrol and says that the *tortilla* at my hotel is especially good. She tells me that Ferrol is famous for its "nineties architecture" and adds: "I don't mean 1990s – I mean 1890s." There are a lot of distinctive "glasshouses" in the city like the ones I saw from the train, she says. I should also visit the Roman lighthouse in A Coruña. "This I think you will like to see." She points me in the direction of the city centre and wishes me luck for the journey ahead.

What a passionate and thoughtful Spanish station ticket assistant. But as I am finding, Spanish train staff are, usually, very helpful indeed if you happen to be half lost while travelling round their country on trains.

I thank Nuria for her time.

"De nada," she says. (It's nothing.)

And with that I go out to see Ferrol, beyond its funny little station.

* * *

From 1938 to 1983 Ferrol was officially called El Ferrol del Caudillo after General Franco. *Caudillo* means "strongman" or "dictator" and such was Franco's high standing in his birthplace that it took eight years after his death for the city name to revert back to "Ferrol" and nineteen years more for a giant six-tonne statue of him on horseback to be removed from the main square, in 2002. In the period running up to the statue being dismantled, protestors against Franco had once painted the *generalissimo* pink and on another occasion placed explosives in his shoes, which had merely blown out nearby windows when detonated. At the time of its removal, a rearguard campaign by a local People's Party councillor and *franquista*, as supporters of Franco are known, calling for a referendum to vote on whether to keep the statue failed. Even in his home town, by the dawn of the twenty-first century, backing the *Caudillo* was not considered by bosses of the right-wing party to be much of a vote winner.

Memories of the Spanish Civil War, in which half a million people died (although this figure is contested with some saying more and some saying less), were painfully fresh – and the conflict that pitted friends and families against one another, Franco's Nationalists versus left-leaning Republicans, continues to be a hot topic. At the time of my train journeys many have been calling for the removal of the former dictator's body from the mausoleum in the Valley of the Fallen on the edge of Madrid, while the family of the man who established the authoritarian rule of almost four decades after grabbing power during the Civil War fiercely contests this.

What happened during the Civil War and under Franco's subsequent rule is a highly sensitive subject that Spaniards afterward mainly preferred to avoid. The *generalissimo* left Spain hugely divided to such an extent that mysteries about what actually happened continue; a hornet's nest that many considered best left untouched in the aftermath of Franco's death in 1975. And it is worth pointing out here that one of the reasons for the enduring interest and widespread reading of Orwell's *Homage to Catalonia* in Spain is that he wrote about the war as an outsider. Even though he fought for the Republicans, he was an Englishman with a pen and a sharp eye who told it how he saw it. While he hated the far-right-leaning Nationalists, he was also highly critical of the back-stabbing and infighting of the Republicans in Barcelona, which left him with "the strangest sensation of being in a nightmare". That word at least each side could agree upon – the Spanish Civil War and what followed were indeed for many a nightmare.

Mass graves are still being discovered to this day. Just before leaving on this train trip, heavy rains washed away soil at a cemetery in Madrid to expose human remains of those executed by firing squads during the period after the war. Many other such burial sites may exist. Francisco Fernandez, a leading Spanish anthropologist who has tracked the discovery of such graves, succinctly says of the matter: "Spain is a land full of secrets."

It would certainly seem that way.

This is the backdrop to a visit to Ferrol. Which I discover to be a lovely little city.

With Nuria's good directions, I find Hostal Zahara, which happens to be a lovely little *hostal* with lovely neat whitewashed rooms, smart shutters, a toilet that sounds like a tidal wave when it flushes and a fine location on a quiet corner not far from the main square.

Down lovely little lanes with lovely tall houses with lovely conservatory-style windows I head toward the square where Franco's statue once stood. These buildings with their glass-fronted balconies hang over the small streets and are known as *galería* houses, and it was these to which Nuria was referring. The style took off when workers in the naval shipyards here experimented with glass galleries to allow seamen to see further in bad weather. Such was the success, the approach was adopted in local architecture too and soon these ornate glass facades with high arched windows took over in the compact centre of the port on lanes leading away from what is still an important Spanish naval headquarters on a bluff facing the Ría de Ferrol leading to the sea.

They are wonderful. It's as though the buildings are leaning across to whisper to one another and there is a tunnel-like quality to the cobbled streets, with their little independent shops and cafés. What is endearing is that modern builders have aped the bulging "overhang" and the overall effect is as though you have entered a strange conservatory land of glasshouses with hardly any tourists about. There's a secretive, strange, beneath-the-radar atmosphere.

The square where Franco once stood is home to palm trees, kids playing football and a scattering of unusual brown pigeons with purple-tinted breasts. Sipping coffee at a café under a palm, I soak up local events (not many) at this former epicentre of so much controversy. An elderly man in threadbare clothes that must once have been elegant asks for a euro so politely that I give him two. The children boot their ball about. The pigeons coo. Dog walkers walk their dogs. Not a lot else is going on.

At a smaller square by the naval headquarters, sailors in white uniforms and peaked caps with navy-blue rims stroll along. Ferrol holds the Spanish naval distinction of never having been taken by the British during their many skirmishes with their arch foe, mainly due to regular strong coastal winds that drag blockades into dangerous waters by rocky shores. The naval influence here is strong. Franco himself came from a long line of seafarers; his father was a naval officer.

From the high walls by the square the skeleton-like cranes of the docks and three grey battleships in the harbour spread out beneath a sky the colour of lead with streaks of magnesium light breaking through. There are beds of pink and white flowers and banks of lavender in a park next to the square, where a pair of cannons rest against a wall of the HQ and a sign says: *Zona Propiedad de la Armada*.

A high society wedding is taking place at the sturdy-looking San Francisco Church, where Franco was baptized Francisco Paulino Hermenegildo Teódulo in 1892. Teenagers smoke dope on benches in the shade of cabbage palms by a fountain decorated with mermen blowing water out of conches. Graffiti on a wall near the solid-looking San Julián Cathedral declares: *UNHA LOITA ARMADA*. This translates in Galician as *AN ARMED FIGHT*, though quite what the fight is about I am not sure. Ferrol seems far too pleasantly sleepy for any armed fights any more.

I like it here; just the sort of place I hoped to hole up in on trains around Spain.

Back at Hostal Zahara I eat a tasty *tortilla* (thank you, Nuria). As I am finishing, a suntanned floppy-haired Englishman sits down at the table next to mine.

Will is from north Devon and has the look of a drifter, which I suppose I must do too by now. He asks me about my trip and replies approvingly: "Yeah, mate, yeah! You only live once."

"How have you ended up in Ferrol?" I ask. You have got to go quite out of your way to end up in Ferrol.

Will says he is here by accident, literally. He was on his way to work in a new job at a surf shop in Lagos in Portugal. "But I had a crash," he says. "Mate, I was in my van and it was a wet road with a cliff with trees down below on the right. Then this car slid round the corner ahead and the driver side of the car hit the passenger door on my side and took the wheel off. Four days ago, it happened. I bounced off the barrier by the side of the road. I would have plunged off the cliff and hit the trees if it wasn't for that barrier. That could have been pretty interesting. The funny thing is that, when it was all happening, I was so chilled. Chilled like a cucumber, mate. Then there was a sinking feeling: my house is dead."

He is referring to his camper van, his "house", which he had planned to live in when he reached Lagos. Now it is a write-off.

"The guy admitted responsibility," he says of the car driver. "He's been amazing. There was this massive language barrier, but we worked it all out."

"How?"

"On Google Translate, mate. He called and a. anged for a pick-up. We were on this random road in the middle of absolute nowhere."

Will met a British backpacker yesterday and a local man who works in the docks in quality control in a shipbuilding yard. He is having dinner with them tonight. He is aged twenty-seven and his mother has bought him a replacement camper van, which she is delivering here shortly, after catching a ferry from Portsmouth to Santander.

"She's awesome," he says.

"She sounds it," I reply.

I ask what made him want to go to work in a surfing shop in Lagos.

"Mate, I just wanted a change," he replies. "I decided a van was the answer. I took a risk – I had a little bit of money in my pocket, you see, so I bought the van. Then I arranged the job at the surf shop."

Will, who previously worked in a surf shop in Devon, is worried this might fall through due to the delay caused by the crash.

"Pizza delivery," he says all of a sudden. "Pizza. Yeah, that's another option."

This way he can work nights and surf during the day: "That's my main priority. The waves, man. Surfing."

Will finishes his drink. We shake hands – one drifter to another – and he disappears down a cobbled lane between conservatory-style buildings in search of his new-found friends.

I hope he makes it to Lagos.

I return to my neat whitewashed room.

Tomorrow I'm on a pilgrimage that has nothing to do with waves.

Otro día, otro tren... (Another day, another train...)

CHAPTER SIX

FERROL TO ZAMORA, VIA A CORUÑA, SANTIAGO DE COMPOSTELA AND PUEBLA DE SANABRIA

MEETING THE *PEREGRINOS*

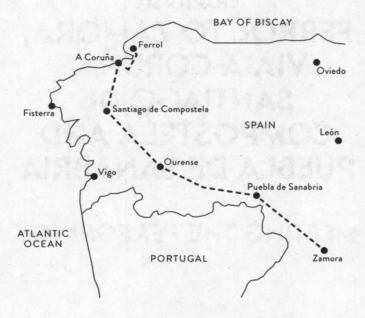

BAY OF BISCAY

Ferrol

A Coruña

Oviedo

Fisterra

Santiago de Compostela

SPAIN

León

Ourense

Vigo

Puebla de Sanabria

ATLANTIC
OCEAN

PORTUGAL

Zamora

John Betjeman statue, St Pancras
International Station

Eurostar platforms at St Pancras
International

Figueres Station

Sant Ferran Castle, Figueres

Station "above sea level" sign at Blanes Station

Locomotives, Catalonia Railway Museum in Vilanova i la Geltrú

Madrid Metro's Montserrat Station

Nun walking on mountain at Montserrat

Funicular at Montserrat

Snails for dinner at the castle in Lleida

Renfe AVE train at Lleida

Aljafería Palace, Zaragoza

Trenches in which George Orwell served in the Spanish Civil War outside Huesca

Gift shop in Pamplona

Bilbao-Concordia Station

Stained glass window at Bilbao-Abando Station

Renfe Feve narrow gauge train at Santander Station

Renfe Feve driver's cab, between Infiesto and Oviedo

Author with staff of El Transcantábrico Clásico at Ferrol Station

Renfe Avant train at Zamora Station

Roman aqueduct, Segovia

Locos at Museo del Ferrocarril de Madrid

Author on mercury mine train in Alamadén

Alcázar de San Juan Station

Ornate ceiling at Aranjuez Station

"Hanging houses" [to the left] and the Puente de San Pablo bridge at Cuenca

Street art outside Cuenca Station

Silhouette of train on viaduct on the way to Valencia

The tren turístico *in Benidorm*

Águilas train museum

Railway pier at Águilas

View from train between Almería and Granada

Torremolinos Station

Café at Bobadilla Station

Train protest in Algeciras

Calle Juan Morrison, Algeciras   *Ronda Station*

View from Alameda del Tajo, Ronda

Author on arrival in Seville

From Ferrol to A Coruña is just 30 miles. Nuria is not on duty at Ferrol Station in the morning and her replacement at first tells me I cannot pay for a ticket by card and then refuses a fifty-euro note (again, as luck would not have it, my smallest note). There is no ticket machine available. We have a stand-off over this before I am told, in a mysterious U-turn, I *can* use my card. So I do, with the ticket assistant shaking his head as though I have committed some kind of Spanish train crime, and I go to the 08:54 to A Coruña.

A pity Nuria wasn't around.

The Renfe train driver walks down the aisle before we set off, singing to himself and wearing a red-checked shirt and jeans. Drivers do not seem to be required to wear uniforms and appear ultra-relaxed round these parts. Off we go slowly along Iberian gauge tracks across an estuary and beyond a beach obscured by trees. Soft morning light flickers on the fronds of date palms and eucalyptus trees as we spin along before coming to a river with a Roman stone bridge near a pair of herons poised in reeds, their heads turned together as though whispering sweet nothings. The coastline turns rocky around here and there are grassy inlets with dark ravines disappearing into shadowy depths. We follow a river that opens into an estuary with a wide sandbank that looks like a decent place for a swim.

Further on, yellow reeds like giant feather dusters line the tracks. On a path alongside a man is walking a dog that seems absolutely terrified by the 08:54 from Ferrol. The man laughs and pats his dog for reassurance. Shortly afterward we roll past some allotments and a Renfe office with a garden with a vineyard – Renfe wine? – before pulling into A Coruña Station. The journey has taken 84 minutes, which I calculate works out at 24 miles an hour if I am doing my sums right.

Slow train in Spain indeed (and a pleasant one too).

"Somewhere nice"
A Coruña

A Coruña is famous historically on many counts. From the second century BC the port was an important outpost of the Roman Empire, which Caesar, no less, is said to have visited in 62 BC when the settlement was known as Brigantium. Toward the end of Roman rule, the Tower of Hercules, a lighthouse, was built on a headland and remains to this day; this has claims to be the oldest lighthouse in operation in the world and is the one to which Nuria was referring.

Being so far north, the port avoided the attentions of Muslim invaders. By the time of the expulsion of the Jews in 1492, a large thriving Jewish community existed, evidence of which is to be found in a lavishly illustrated Jewish Bible known as the Kennicott Bible that is now kept at the Bodleian Library in Oxford.

This is far from the only British connection. In 1554 Philip II left from here to marry Mary Tudor, daughter of Catherine of Aragon, which he did at Winchester Cathedral just two days after they met, much to the dissatisfaction of Protestants in England due to his being Roman Catholic and Mary's intention to reverse the English Reformation and reinstate Catholicism and connections with Rome. A Catholic husband for Mary was widely unpopular, leading to acts of rebellion and executions of prominent Protestants – contributing to her nickname "Bloody Mary".

Thirty years after Mary's early death from illness aged just forty-two, the Spanish Armada set sail from A Coruña in 1588 under the doomed orders of the very same Philip II to attack England, by then under the rule of Mary's sister Elizabeth I, who had reestablished the predominance of Protestantism and ordered a series of assaults led by Francis Drake in the Spanish New World. Bad relations between Spain and England continued with an English besiegement of A Coruña in 1589 in which Drake failed to capture the well-defended port and a series of skirmishes and conflicts between the two nations that rumbled into the early seventeenth century.

Fast-forward to the Peninsula War of 1808–1814 when the French under Napoleon invaded the Iberian Peninsula and A Coruña was also the scene of what the French regard as a humiliating retreat of the English troops – by now on the side of Spain against France – who fled under fire during what is known as the Battle of A Coruña, although the English prefer to describe the events of 16 January 1809 as a brilliant tactical retreat in which most soldiers survived. The British commander Lieutenant-General Sir John Moore, however, was not so lucky as he was struck by a cannonball and died from horrific injuries. He was buried by the ramparts, where there is now a mausoleum in a park.

A lot has gone on in A Coruña and much of it has been bloody.

Add to this Pablo Picasso's connection to the port, where the abstract artist lived from the age of nine to thirteen and painted his first works (his former home is open to the public), as well as the port's great fondness for the glass-facade *galería* buildings that originated in Ferrol – A Coruña is even nicknamed "glass city" – and there seems to be a great deal to investigate during a connection by train. So instead of getting the first service on to Santiago de Compostela, I buy a ticket on the 15:45 to Santiago, which will be a journey of only 40 minutes, and set off by foot down a hill from A Coruña's solid grey-stone station with a sense of anticipation and curiosity about this hotbed of Galician history.

It does not take long to reach the port along a dull dual carriageway and then past a little park with a statue of the reclining figure of John Lennon, guitar in hand, with the words *imagina que no haya nada por lo que matar o morir* (imagine nothing to kill or die for) inscribed on the plinth. Wishful thinking, perhaps, for A Coruña over the ages.

Beyond the park, the waterfront is a terrace of extremely distinctive tall *galería* facing the harbour, forming a giant wall of glass. While Ferrol's *galería* are on a series of interconnecting lanes that feel cosy and tucked away, these are grand statements of wealth and comfort with what must be magnificent sea views. Some are six storeys high and the orange and gold morning light catches the many hundreds of windowpanes, dazzling and looking at times as though the *galería* are on fire.

A promenade runs along the coast from here, past moorings with yachts and a long, solitary warship. I follow the promenade, which leads onward up a hill, eventually reaching the Tower of Hercules, about a mile away.

What a peculiar sight... and what a peculiar sound.

The tower of the lighthouse shoots up 55 metres in honey-coloured stone that does not look Roman at all; a pamphlet from the ticket office explains that the structure was re-clad during the eighteenth century. Thirty tourists at a time are permitted to climb stairs to the top but rather than wait in the queue, I wander along a path to its base, where a Galician bagpipe player is in full flow.

Maybe it is just me, but this particular Galician bagpipe player does not seem to be hitting every note. Jolly enough, but rather wobbly and with a plaintive, scratchy, discordant edge, the tune echoes across the windy yellow-gorse headland high above the Atlantic Ocean, waves crashing below. Close your eyes and you might be in the Western Isles of Scotland, except you are not: you're in Spain with *pinchos* bars and sunshine and the boyhood home of Picasso somewhere round the corner.

I pay my respects at the grave of Sir John Moore. I watch a procession of locals in colourful traditional costumes accompanied by drummers and trumpet players in Plaza da Constitución (the women wear extraordinary black headdresses that poke up like meerkats and add about a foot in height). I go for some *pinchos* at a bar where a group of British yacht owners are discussing problems with next-door neighbours. "Last time we went to sea we came back and the neighbour had redesigned the border between our properties," says a woman with a cut-glass Home Counties accent. "There was heavy machinery everywhere, obliterating things." The woman drags out the word "obliterating" for dramatic effect. "I said to my neighbour: 'What's happened to my shrubs?'" To this a companion, sipping rosé, replies as though affronted on her behalf: "You should have got David to punch him on the nose." Another of the group considers this and adds, casually, almost lazily: "Or put Coca-Cola in his car."

I leave the café, head down the hill, and board the warship in the harbour.

The warship is flying a Union Jack. A British fighting vessel is moored in the port from which the Spanish Armada set sail all those years ago – when Shakespeare was in his mid twenties. This strikes me as odd, so I go over to take a closer look.

On the edge of the dock near the warship, the HMS *St Albans*, a Royal Navy officer in a blue uniform with a tattoo of a lighthouse on his arm and a sunburned nose is sitting in a hut. In the spirit of nothing ventured nothing gained, I ask him if I can take a look at the ship from its deck and show him my passport and my National Union of Journalists card.

He says: "All right, mate, I'll try for you. Wait a moment, mate." Then he calls the ship and says into the receiver: "It's me in the caboose. Yeah, that's OK, is it?" Pause. "He seems to have legitimate ID. I'll send him through, OK?"

He clicks off. "All right, mate. Just show that ID to the guy over there: the duty officer."

So I walk along the dock to HMS *St Albans*, where a thin, straight-backed officer with pink cheeks and wearing a white uniform with shiny brass buttons is waiting at the end of the gangway. He is flanked by three men in combat fatigues with semi-automatic weapons. A sign by the gangway says: *Counterterrorism: HEIGHTENED. Threat: SUBSTANTIAL.*

Passport details are taken with eyes on my backpack. "Er, would you mind taking that off? And can we take a look inside?"

I open the backpack. Inside they can see a guidebook, Laurie Lee's *As I Walked Out One Midsummer Morning*, some crumpled clothing, a jar of vitamin pills (an attempt to stay healthy on the tracks) and the edge of my laptop; all tightly packed at the top.

"Would you like me to take everything out?"

One of the men in combat fatigues looks at the duty officer.

The duty officer nods in a way to suggest this will not be necessary.

The man with the gun says: "Satisfactory inspection given."

Then the duty officer walks me round the deck while telling me this is an anti-submarine frigate built in 2000 with a crew of two hundred.

"What are you doing in A Coruña?" I ask, mentioning that I had not expected to see a British frigate in the port from which the Spanish Armada set sail.

"We have been abroad a lot and very employed," the duty officer replies, ignoring the reference to the Armada. "We're doing maintenance support and *manpower for well-being*."

He says this phrase as though it comes out of a manual.

"A break for morale?" I ask.

"Yes."

"Rest and relaxation?"

"That, I believe, is an American term," he replies, sounding a little snooty.

We step over some neatly curled ropes heading toward the large gun attached to the bow. I ask what missions the HMS *St Albans* has been on recently.

"We are working quite closely with European allies on maritime security defending UK and NATO interests," he replies robotically before adding that he can show me around but cannot tell me anything more about the ship's activities for security reasons. Nor can he tell me his name, although he can give his rank – sub lieutenant – and says that he has been with the ship for six months.

We reach the enormous gun.

"Is it an anti-aircraft gun?" I ask, trying to get a bit of military lingo right to win him over.

He looks at me deadpan and sets me straight: "This is a medium-calibre gun for surface engagement and naval gun fire support."

"Has it ever been fired in action?"

"We use it a lot in practice," the officer says.

I ask about Gibraltar. British ships have recently intercepted an Iranian-supplied, Panama-registered tanker that was believed to be heading to the Middle East with supplies for the controversial Russian-backed Syrian regime. The sub lieutenant turns a little green and replies: "I'll not be commenting on that, I'm afraid."

A sign near the gun at the front says: *DANGER: MISSILE MAY FIRE WITHOUT WARNING*. Another by more neatly curled ropes merely warns: *DANGER*.

"We're very safety conscious here," says the duty officer.

As we return to the stern, I ask what made him join the Royal Navy and he explains that he is from a "nautical background and I always wanted to".

Then we rejoin the men with guns. I thank them all for the quick show-round and the officer, who has been glancing at his Casio digital watch, replies: "Always happy to accommodate when we can."

I walk back down the gangplank, say goodbye to the officer in the caboose hut – who tells me he likes A Coruña as it has "a few good bars and that – it was about time we went somewhere nice" – and return up the hill to the station to make the 15:45 to Santiago de Compostela.

"Wandrynge by the weye"
A Coruña to Santiago de Compostela

The train to Santiago de Compostela is white with a pointy nose at the front – not as pointy as a full-speed Spanish bullet train – and is advertized as a *Media Distancia Regionale* service. It moves away smoothly and has good air conditioning. The destination is Vigo-Guixar, according to a digital display.

We enter some tunnels, pass a few goatherds in parched fields, head up into pine-clad hills and settle into a speed of 160 kilometres an hour (100 miles per hour), although it is so smooth we might be going at half that. There is a vending machine between carriages – no buffet car – and a conductor who does not seem to mind at all that I have sat in the wrong *coche* (carriage).

Santiago de Compostela's station is busy with pilgrims with backpacks and walking sticks. The ticket hall is in a state of general mayhem and I seem to fit in pretty well as I guess I could pass for a pilgrim too. At the ticket window, I decide on the spur of the moment, while looking at my trusty *Rail Map Europe*, to take the 12:10 tomorrow to Puebla de Sanabria. I know nothing of Puebla de Sanabria, but the station seems to be in an interesting spot close to the border with Portugal and why not wing it a bit on the way down to Madrid?

When I mention Puebla de Sanabria to the Renfe ticket assistant, however, he gives me a look unmistakably suggesting: *are you sure?* Nevertheless, he prints out a ticket and takes my euros and that is that.

There is an old locomotive in a lot overgrown with plants in a corner of the Santiago de Compostela car park. Rail enthusiasts seem to have made it to this holy land; the third holiest site in Christendom after Jerusalem and Rome. A locked gate to the lot has *Asociación Compostelana de Amigos del Ferrocarril* written on a letter box attached to a post. The green and gold loco is connected to a carriage with curtains drawn. Maybe this is some sort of Spanish trainspotters' clubhouse.

It is not far up a hill to my room in student accommodation on a street with modern buildings and *pinchos* bars, and a stroll onward to little pedestrianized flagstone lanes crammed with ice-cream parlours, bars and souvenir shops selling all sorts of objects decorated with scallop shell symbols as well as restaurants offering scallops lined up on tight shelves in window displays. This symbol is used on signposts along the pilgrimage routes to Santiago de Compostela – El Camino de Santiago (The Way of St James) – and was chosen for various reasons. These are, as far as I can tell: a) because St James was a fisherman in Galilee, b) because legend has it that when St James's body was brought to Galicia by boat in the year AD 44 his body fell into the sea while being transported by horse to the shore only to emerge from the water covered in shells, and, probably most likely of all, c) because pilgrims told to make the pilgrimage as penance needed an object to show priests back home that they had actually gone to the north-east corner of Spain and not just sat in the tavern of a nearby town for a few months (although in theory that would be possible if you simply bought a scallop shell from someone and pretended you had gone).

The Spanish appear to be extremely adept at taking something that sells and shamelessly milking it for all its worth, judging by Dalí, Montserrat, Pamplona and now the scallop shells of Santiago de Compostela. And it is worth noting here that this has been going on a very long time. Scallop shell salesmen have been working the third most holy site in Christendom since the Middle Ages, aware that most pilgrims – having walked such a long way – would probably prefer not to have to make an extra effort to cover the 50 miles or so to the coast.

Myths and legends such as the one about St James's body falling in the sea seem to swirl about in Santiago. To try to summarize the whole story in one sentence is tricky, but here goes: St James, the sometimes volatile cousin of Jesus, visited Spain, where he had a vision of the Virgin Mary in Zaragoza, and then returned and was beheaded in Jerusalem by Herod Agrippa, after which his body was taken to Jaffa, where a crew-less sail-less boat transported him in seven days to Galicia, whereupon his body was buried and forgotten for 750 years before being discovered by a hermit attracted to a field lit by stars at a time when Christendom was in need of a bit of a boost due to marauding Moors, and over the years a cult of St James developed that has led to so many thousands of pilgrims visiting.

That will do.

At the end of one of the narrow lanes flanked by honey-stone buildings with souvenir shops at their bases and geranium flower boxes on upper floors – the old bit of Santiago may be chaotic with tourists but it is pretty and charming with cloisters, trickling fountains and birdsong – you come to one of the wonders of Spain. For all my cynicism about the St James connection being an historical scam, you cannot deny that Praza do Obradoiro, the main square facing the looming Gothic facade of the cathedral, is one of the finest places in this hot peninsula. This is not just down to grand architecture and the wide sweep of flagstones. It's all about the people.

If you have walked 500 miles from St-Jean-Pied-de-Port in France near the border in the Pyrenees to Santiago, the main "way", you are likely to be fairly euphoric to have reached such a beautiful place in the hills, whether you happen to be religious or not. In the middle of the square dozens of hikers are lying down on the flagstones or sitting cross-legged gazing up at the cathedral and looking thin, tanned and exhausted. Walking sticks, wooden staffs and backpacks are all over the place. There is a buzz of excitement and a sense of peace and togetherness that is hard to put your finger on… it's just there. Tourist trap, perhaps, for some. But there is another dimension, whether St James's bones are here or not. Even if you are not religious (like me) it's impossible not to feel in some way lifted by the setting.

To one side, a man on a blanket is playing Zen-like music on a stereo and holding three crystal balls in each hand, with a tray for *donaciónes*; a spiritual busker tapping into the St James story and filling one corner of the square with relaxing sounds. In another, a Galician bagpipe player is going for it with welly, the sound echoing up a lane behind the cathedral. Groups of cyclists in matching Lycra enter the square – not all pilgrims walk the route, as I noticed on the trains. A woman in a pink top with a flower in her hair passes in mid conversation with a friend and I catch: "It's the life force. I haven't been using the life force…" Her voice trails away.

In the cathedral we, the pilgrims (myself a pretender, of course), enter a passage with a *donación* machine – like a cashpoint, except *you* give money – at which a teenager has just set the amount to a thousand euros and is showing his parents. "Whaddya think?" he says. They are Americans. "Don't do that, Bradley!" replies his mother, pulling him away (he is just messing about). I wonder how many thousand-euro *donaciónes* the cathedral has had. Religion and cold hard cash never seem all that far removed in Spain.

Further in, scaffolding and sheets of plastic have turned the surprisingly cramped interior of the cathedral into a temporary building site and I queue by a row of candles in a passage with a CCTV camera. More Americans are waiting here to visit the crypt that is supposed to hold the bones of St James.

The couple behind me, from near San Francisco in California, have just walked 175 miles in nine days, starting in Porto in Portugal. This is known as the Portuguese Way; there are many different "ways" aside from the one from St-Jean-Pied-de-Port.

"What did you enjoy most about the experience?"

She, broad beaming smile and infectious enthusiasm, a secondary school teacher: "The nature! The people! Not just the other walkers. The Portuguese! So friendly!"

He, with a sideways look on things, a retired United Airlines mechanic: "I just came here to lose weight." He says this deadpan as though all the candles, incense holders, Gothic architecture and the crypt with the famous bones just happen to have turned up in front of him.

"Have you?"

"I don't know. I haven't weighed myself yet," he replies. "Carrying that backpack – boy, that was tough. Boy, did it weigh a tonne. I'm beat. Totally beat. Too tired to be spiritual. Last Sunday was a nightmare: very hot and a lot of uphill."

She: "We feel a lot healthier."

He, still deadpan: "Yeah. I'm not religious. I just did it for the walking."

She, ignoring him: "We met one guy who had walked all the way from Seville. It had taken him forty-two days. He needed a place to stay and we helped him out. It was like that on the walk: everyone helped each other out."

Both, despite their different takes on their pilgrimage, seem happy and relieved and at peace with things. Religion does not seem to matter on El Camino de Santiago.

A mother and daughter from Rijeka in Croatia, in front of us, turn to talk. Pilgrims are a sociable bunch. They too have completed the Portuguese Way.

The daughter, Marie-Anne, a biology teacher, says: "Yes, it was spiritual and friendly and nice – everything about it was positive. I could talk about life: the past, the present, the future. To anyone. After some days on the trail you build up friendships. You talk to people about these things and then they go on and you think you'll never see them again, but then you do, maybe three days later – and then you talk some more."

Her mother, Vera, a retired administrator: "We had fun."

In front of them, Tally, a real estate agent, also from California, joins in. Pilgrims really do open up. "Just being here: it's an accomplishment. An incredibly good feeling," she says. "I had never walked more than thirty kilometres in a day. Well, now I have. Oh yeah, it was tough. We had to get knee braces. There's a bit in the Picos de Europa they call the knee cruncher."

Tally and her friend Paige, unemployed from Florida, have completed the Classic Way from St-Jean-Pied-de-Port in thirty-two days.

Paige: "I was working in a wine bar – I quit to come here," she says. "I got my butt kicked pretty hard. It took a toll on the knees. Ibuprofen! Everything! Anything they sold that could relieve the pain." Then more quietly: "I think I've found a lot of clarity and self-confidence. I feel more assured. This is just the beginning."

Tally: "Yeah! We've done it!"

And with that we file through the glittery gold and silver crypt, see St James's tomb and head back out into the sunshine. They shuffle away to an office where an official certificate of some sort is given – alongside official stamps from stations along the route – to prove they are official *peregrinos* (pilgrims).

Like the retired United Airlines mechanic, I am pretty beat too. I go to a brilliant little seafood restaurant called La Cueva del Tigre Rabioso (The Rabid Tiger Cave) where I eat a plate of mussels served in an extremely spicy sauce accompanied by a large hunk of bread while listening to the analysis part of a Spanish version of the dating programme *Love Island*, playing in a corner, and a guide on a table next to mine explaining that in centuries gone by pilgrims would rest and sleep in the cathedral, which is why a very large incense dispenser was installed to help with the smell of so many sweaty unwashed bodies from the trail. "It is," he says, "the most famous smoke dispenser in the world, a liturgical tradition." Cleanliness was not always next to godliness, especially if you were a medieval pilgrim who had tramped all the way across northern Spain from the French Pyrenees.

The mussels are the best I have ever tasted: large and juicy and hot and perfect. I think the *rabioso* in the restaurant's name has something to do with this spiciness, but to be totally honest I am too tired to bother to ask, despite not having walked hundreds of miles (like most people round here). I watch a procession led by priests in burgundy robes pass by outside to the accompaniment of drummers and a brass band with a trail of *peregrinos* in their wake, some wearing simple tunics and carrying staffs. Others still have backpacks, bandanas and floppy hats from completing their pilgrimages. There is a general cacophony and the human stream down the narrow lane reminds me of football supporters squeezing toward turnstiles before a match. If you take away the upheld cameras with little digital displays filming the scene, not much can have changed since the Middle Ages when the Wife of Bath made it to Santiago as mentioned in the "General Prologue" of Chaucer's *Canterbury Tales*, which captures something of the rough and ready atmosphere of a pilgrimage here all those years ago:

> She hadde passed many a straunge strem;
> At Rome she hadde been, and at Boloigne,
> In Galice at Seint-Jame, and at Coloigne.
> She koude muchel of wandrynge by the weye.
> Gat-toothed was she, soothly for to seye.
> Upon an amblere esily she sat

> Ywympled wel, and on hir heed an hat
> As brood as is a bokeler or a targe;
> A foot mantel aboute hir hipes large,
> And on hir feet a paire of spores sharpe.
> In felawshipe wel koude she laughe and carpe.
> Of remedies of love she knew per chaunce,
> For she koude of that art the olde dance.

Which translates as something like: "She had crossed many foreign streams on the way to Rome, Boulogne, Santiago and Cologne, with a gap-toothed smile and mounted on horseback, wearing a headdress and a big hat and a large skirt with spurs on her heels. She knew how to have a (very) good time."

Ghosts of pilgrims past seem to haunt Santiago.

Then I hit the sack in my comfortable student-digs room.

I am about to head to a place I have never heard of by the Portuguese border – no famous bones, religious miracles or hordes of tourists – somewhere down the line to Madrid.

Moving south
Santiago de Compostela to Zamora, via Puebla de Sanabria

The 12:10 to Ourense is packed but silent and whips across viaducts above hills as though floating on a wind. Olive groves and pine-clad valleys scud by. Patchwork fields with green and yellow crops spread out on a plain. The soil is orange and the shadows of mountains rise on the horizon. This feels like a heavenly ride; God's people, returning pilgrims, are on a godly train flying across a gorgeous godly Galician landscape.

Perhaps the silence here is appropriate. Not long ago, tragedy struck on these tracks.

On 24 July 2013 a Renfe Alvia high-speed train derailed 3 miles outside Santiago on the Madrid–Ferrol service, resulting in the loss of seventy-nine lives and injuries to more than one hundred of the 272 passengers and crew on board. It was one of the worst rail crashes in Spanish history; the most serious for half a century.

The train was found to have been travelling at more than twice the speed allowed at a sharp curve of the track at the time of the derailment; 190 kilometres an hour (119 miles per hour) instead of 80 kilometres an hour (50 miles per hour). The driver was charged with seventy-nine counts of homicide by professional recklessness. Investigators discovered he had been talking by phone to a conductor about the route beyond Santiago to Ferrol just before the accident. "Driver error" was blamed.

Yet this is not the full story and a tape of the conversation between the driver and Renfe bosses in the immediate aftermath of the crash obtained by the Spanish newspaper *El País* is revealing. At the time, bleeding from a head wound, he is heard to say: "I had already mentioned this to the safety people, that this [curve] was dangerous, that we would get distracted one day and that would be it." He continues: "My God, I mentioned this before to the guy in safety that this is very dangerous… we are human and this can happen to us… this curve is inhuman." He goes on to say: "It's my conscience and those poor passengers."

Inquiries were launched, and safety failings were soon uncovered. A judicial report in Spain and a European Union Agency for Railways report found that an important automatic safety system known as the European Train Control System (also called the European Rail Traffic Management System) was not in place at the curve of the track where the awful derailment happened.

Since then, thankfully, safety systems have been updated across Spanish lines.

* * *

We change at Ourense, still in Galicia, and wait for the 13:08 to Madrid, which stops off at 15:08 at Puebla de Sanabria.

There is a kerfuffle of pilgrims at Ourense Station, but the Renfe Alvia service departs on time. The *Turista* carriage, in which I find myself, is comfortable with pale-green seats and is right by the buffet car. We cross a wide river and various bridges and viaducts before flying onward above rolling hills and darting into tunnels. Forests of pine trees and oaks spread out forever beneath a marble-white sky and a mist descends so the 13:08 to Madrid appears to be travelling through clouds. Empty roads wind through valleys. The landscape transforms into a wilderness of heather and low pine shrubs as though the countryside has had a barber's buzz cut. Then mysterious mountains arise almost totally obscured by rain clouds and we pass deserted farmhouses with old tin roofs and little hillside graveyards. It seems very out of the way here, near the edge of northern Portugal.

The misty scenery has a soporific effect. A monitor shows the temperature has plunged to 13°C. A downpour drenches the *Turista* carriage as we draw to a halt at Puebla de Sanabria and I disembark at a deserted station; one of only two passengers to do so.

Rain pelts down. There is no ticket hall that I can discern. There is no café. Beyond the damp grey-stone facade of the station building puddles have formed in an empty car park. There is no immediate sign of the village of Puebla de Sanabria. There is no taxi rank. There is just water. Lots of it, and a hazy landscape shrouded in cloud.

I go back to the platform and the train is still there, seemingly waiting for smokers from the train who have gathered by a shelter. So I reboard the train, return to my seat and consult the map. Zamora is the next stop, about 70 miles away. So, Zamora it will be. Puebla de Sanabria, no doubt delightful in sunshine, is just too wet and depressing.

Of course, I am now travelling without a ticket, but when the conductor comes by, I will ask to pay the extra fare.

The conductor soon appears. He is a short man with grey hair, a purple tie (clipped by a gold locomotive-shaped tie pin) and the manner of a geography teacher. When he enters the *Turista* carriage he ignores everyone else and makes a beeline for me. He seems to have noticed my movements back at the station and looks gravely concerned.

"Where do you go?" he says before I have had a chance to speak.

"Zamora," I answer, explaining that Pueblo de Sanabria did not look like the best of places to stop off on my tour of Spain by train.

"You should have told me this beforehand," he replies.

"I was waiting for you to come by," I say. "I did not know in which direction I would find you."

The conductor pauses and looks even more gravely concerned. It is possible, I realize, that I may be about to be fined for fare dodging. I show my debit card and indicate I can pay the fare to Zamora.

"No *tarjetas*!" he replies (no card payments). "Cash!"

I pull out some notes. The geography teacher conductor is visibly relieved, as am I. He sighs, takes the notes, disappears for a while, returns with a ticket and gives me a look that suggests: *I really am letting you off here and should be fining you or perhaps calling the* policía. I thank him profusely.

Yet another top-notch Spanish conductor... I'm getting very used to them.

And so the train rolls on past lakes, hayfields, olive groves, wind farms and wide ploughed fields with tomato-coloured earth. The hills are behind us and the sky has brightened. We enter a section of track surrounded by graffiti-covered walls and then an Aldi supermarket before stopping at Zamora Station, where the conductor with the purple tie watches me like a hawk as I go down the platform and some steps, just in case I attempt another U-turn.

"Morris is right"
Zamora

Arriving at a city that you had no idea you would visit an hour or so earlier is all well and good on a long train journey. Sometimes this is just how it is. Arriving at such a city in the pouring rain – the heavens have reopened – is not so great.

Zamora Station is to the north of the city centre, where I have booked a room at a *hostal*. After purchasing a cheap umbrella, I trudge down a long straight street that requires an occasional detour via a roundabout, deposit my backpack in a little room at the *hostal*, found down an alley crammed with tapas bars, and walk quite a long way onward in a heavy downpour with rivulets running all over the streets of the old quarter to the cathedral. This is due to close very soon. Given that I have already bought a ticket on the 07:05 tomorrow to reach Segovia – renowned for a marvellous Roman aqueduct that is too enticing-sounding to miss – I only have a late afternoon to explore Zamora and do not want to ignore all the lovely Romanesque architecture as I did so rudely in Oviedo. What would the great Jan Morris think of such unbecoming behaviour? It is about time I began to *try harder*.

I splash onward across Zamora – in the autonomous region of Castilla y León now – arriving dutifully at the sturdy caramel-stoned cathedral thoroughly soaked, shoes and all despite the umbrella. An expressionless, thin, nut-brown ticket-desk man tells me that the audio guides are "out of service", which is fine by me as I generally cannot stand such guides as working out the correct numbers is always a pain and the commentary tends to be delivered so drily you want to fall asleep. I ascend some stairs to look at Zamora's famous tapestries. Jan Morris has tipped me off to these, reporting that they are among the most "dazzling in Europe", featuring "a shimmer of rich colour and medievalism".

Of course, Morris is right. When has Morris ever not been? Sometimes Morris's overriding rightness just makes you wonder, in the travel writing game, whether there is any point trying to be right yourself once Morris has already righted the territory ahead.

The *tapices* (tapestries) *do* shimmer gloriously and the bloodthirsty medievalism of the battle scenes is captivating; flashing swords, grimaces, agonies, grand costumes and pageantry. What is striking is just how bloody it all is. Fierce bearded men with bejewelled helmets wring the necks of fierce bearded foes in similar garbs. Swords slice through chest-plate armour. Blood trickles from temples in the faces of stricken soldiers with eyes drifting upward as though they are about to depart this mortal coil. Arrows protrude from foreheads. Daggers flicker. Axes fly.

It is the vividness of these battle scenes that draws my attention, while the depictions of court life reveal the formality and splendour of the riches gained by all the warmongering: the glittering jewels, golden crowns, fine palaces, flower-filled gardens, abundant fields and even mounted elephants transporting princes to a parade.

For a while I completely forget that I am soaked through – and then I enter the main chamber of the Romanesque cathedral itself, where the sheer magnificence of the tall marble pillars, the rich colours of the ancient oil paintings and the high gilded dome of skylights above the altar take your breath away.

Here, beneath the dome as tower bells clang, I meet Andrés and Ana.

They have just finished placing cardboard fans on the seats of the church pews. An annual event in honour of San Pedro is about to be held in the cathedral, after the official tourist opening hours. The fans, strangely, have *Mujeres en Igualdad* (Women in Equality) written on them next to a drawing of a pair of women, and were commissioned specially as last year the cathedral had been sweltering with temperatures touching 40°C. Earlier events today, however, have been a washout and Andrés says: "We may as well put them out seeing as we've got them. I cannot understand why it is so rainy and cold today."

To check that Morris had the style of the cathedral correct, I ask Ana, the chief organizer, how she would describe the architecture.

"Romanesque," she replies quick as a shot.

Morris of course is right, almost disappointingly, once again. No point really in trying to catch her out.

Ana also tells me that the dome of the cathedral is "in the form of a chicken". By this, she explains, she means that the exterior of the dome looks like chicken feathers. I vow to take a look later.

Then Andrés and Ana surprise me.

"For three years we lived in Redhill in Surrey, near Reigate," says Ana. "We both worked for Scottish Power. I was a receptionist. Andrés was an engineer working on wind-farm designs for the Baltic Sea. Our daughter Alejandra was born at East Surrey Hospital."

At which point I am introduced to their daughter, before Ana, whose title is *presidenta* of the San Pedro festivities, rushes off to organize something.

As she departs, Andrés says: "I am just her husband", as though not to disappoint me.

Then he asks about my train travels and I explain I am due to catch the 07:05 to Segovia tomorrow and do not have much time in Zamora.

Upon hearing this, Andrés reaches in his pocket and says animatedly: "Let me show you something! You are going to laugh." Then, with a theatrical gesture, he holds up a ticket for the same train for my inspection. Andrés, who works as a hydroelectrical engineer, is going to Madrid for a business meeting to discuss work on a dam by a reservoir that I must have passed on the way into Zamora.

We discuss local trains. "Much better now," Andrés says. "Here to Madrid used to be six hours, and it takes two hours to drive. Now the train takes ninety minutes. Next year it should be one hour and five minutes, I think. They're updating all the signals."

I mention almost being fined earlier.

"We have a more relaxed attitude to fines here," Andrés says.

"What do you mean?" I ask.

"Well, so they want to give you a fine? You say: 'Here is my address. Please send the ticket to my address. No worries. I will pay when it shows up.'"

"Do you pay the fine?"

"Of course not!" says Andrés, chuckling away, before giving me a tip for a tapas bar near the *hostal* and going to take his place next to the *presidenta* for the San Pedro ceremony.

I sit in a pew to one side near a British couple from Kent, the only other tourists. They have a house in the south of Spain and are on their way down, having caught a ferry to Santander. They ask me what is about to happen and I explain what Ana told me about the service: that there is to be an hour-long ceremony with a sermon from the bishop and music. Upon hearing this, the man says quickly and a tad nervously: "We'd better go. We've got a dog in the car. It isn't fair."

The Brits depart, exit left, and a procession of figures in traditional costumes enters through the cathedral's main, high-arched doors; women in colourful velvet costumes embroidered with flowers and stars and with pink and red ribbons in their hair, while the men wear plus fours and black costumes with golden buttons. It is a veritable jamboree of colour in the pews: electric blues, lemon yellows, scarlets and deep purples. The bespectacled bishop, dressed in a tunic of white and gold, delivers his sermon in a low mumble that is hard to decipher, before sweet-toned singing and the sound of tambourines emanates from an inner chapel as children queue in the main aisle to deliver the bishop cakes wrapped in tinfoil and receive blessings.

It is a joyful hour during which I dry out partially and the rain relents.

Outside, behind the chicken dome of the cathedral, runs a grand sweep of muddy-looking Río Duero spanned by a long, arched bridge. The mottled ramparts of the city's eleventh-century *castillo* stand by a precipice on the other side of the cathedral next to a park, while rather unhappy-looking storks perch wetly on the battlements, as they do on the roofs of nearby churches next to great untidy nests of twigs and small branches.

I retrace my steps through the puddles of the narrow streets of the old quarter and eat a series of *dos que piquen* grilled pork snacks served with a *cerveza grande* at the tapas bar Andrés recommended, using his favourite order. *Dos que piquen* translates as "two that bite", which means: spicy. Again – like the mussels of Santiago – *excellent*, served on skewers and very moreish. The name of the tapas bar is *La Casa De Los Pinchitos* (The House of the Skewers).

Rubbish is scattered across the floor, old napkins and receipts, and a Spanish chat show host is rattling on noisily about convoluted romantic relationships on a screen by the door. The Spanish do like to play public televisions at an extremely high volume. This is an inescapable discovery on a tour of the country. For a while, as I eat skewered pork in spicy sauce and drink my *cerveza grande*, I wonder why and cannot come up with much of an answer. Nobody is watching the television show. It is simply on, extremely loudly so. Why does the barman not turn it down? I just don't know.

Realizing that this really does not exactly match up to the profundity of thoughts and observations of certain other renowned travel writers who have visited Spain, I decide to cut my losses and return to my *hostal* to try to work out more of a plan for the next few days. No more Puebla de Sanabrias, *por favor*, although getting lost once in a while is quite liberating (and fun). Spain by train seems to reward the lazy traveller – the more ad hoc you make it, the more you lose your way, the more the country unravels before you, revealing itself. That's the whole point of travel along the tracks in Spain. Slow down and see whatever happens to be next along the line. There is no *right* way. There is no chance you can see and understand it all. Spain is a big complicated country. Omniscience may be wonderful… but let other people worry about that. Find yourself in the gloriously Romanesque cathedral in Zamora, damp after a downpour in the midst of a celebration of San Pedro, and make the best of things. This is what it's all about for the Spanish train traveller. The joy of the unexpected; taking things in your stride.

Is this more like it? Profounder? More *beneath the skin* of the experience?

Not really, I have to admit. Not at all. Too simple: a long way to go yet.

I'm just making excuses for myself. I must strive to attain more *depth*. I must immerse myself in Spain and permit grand understandings to seep into my soul in the manner of Morris.

Let's face it: I'm going to have to work on this.

CHAPTER SEVEN

ZAMORA TO BADAJOZ, VIA SEGOVIA AND MADRID

"CAN YOU IMAGINE HOW MANY PEOPLE DIED BUILDING THAT AQUEDUCT?"

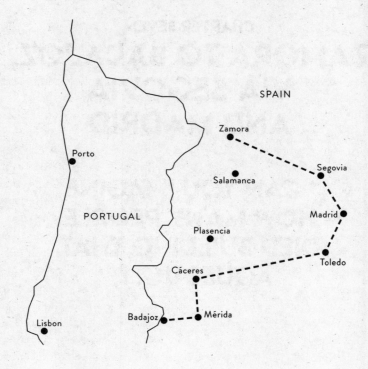

When taking a lot of trains around Spain you begin to appreciate a good station café. San Sebastián's amazingly well-stocked *pintxos* café/bar was of an especially high standard (even if I almost got chased out of the station afterward for looking at the rail paraphernalia in the side room). I rather liked Huesca's café, raised above the end of the tracks with a window for peering down on the Zaragoza trains. Good espressos there. Santander's Renfe Feve terminal café had a pleasingly down-to-earth feel and well-made *bocadillos* and good boiled eggs served to the accompaniment of Whitney Houston. Meanwhile Infiesto Station's tiny train-themed café at the end of the main platform is a must for railway enthusiasts with its cheap plonk and seats by an old beer barrel by the line.

Zamora's is another corker. It is on the right-hand side of the entrance of a honey-stoned station with a series of archways lit up by a row of eerie pistachio-green lamps. Work on Zamora Station began in 1929 and was only completed in 1958, with the Spanish Civil War having delayed matters. It is built in a Renaissance style with touches of Gothic and looks as though it belongs somewhere in Tuscany or Umbria (or maybe Gotham City). To one side is a fenced area with a preserved red-and-black steam locomotive inscribed with *RENFE 030-2214* in gold letters on the front. Poke around at Spanish trains stations and an ancient loco is invariably tucked away somewhere in a corner, often with a plaque remembering a former director of the line from the good old days.

Zamora Station's Vía Libre Café is a revelation, run by an enthusiast for 1980s pop music as well as all things train. He or she also appears to have a penchant for America's Wild West. You enter via a wide doorway with images of steam trains painted on the glass panels above. Inside, cabinets containing covers of 1980s albums take up the walls to the right: Bananarama, Pet Shop Boys, The Smiths, Donna Summer, Prince, Janet Jackson, Eddy Grant, Deacon Blue. In yet more cabinets toward the back, a collection of curling rail manuals and black-and-white pictures of steam trains that once travelled along these lines is to be found.

There are two bars, one on a raised platform to the left lit by chandeliers and lanterns in old gas lamps, with a ceiling fan and shelves of spirit bottles attached to an exposed red-brick wall. You really might be off the beaten track somewhere in Small Town USA in Arizona or Nevada. The barman at the red-brick bar on the right – complete with a model of Charlie Chaplin by yet more bottles – nods, says nothing and brings me a *café largo* (double espresso) when I eventually go over. Gloriously eccentric place.

The 07:05 is a sleek Avant bullet train with orange headlights. On board people are talking in whispers and I spot Andrés deep in thought heading for another carriage along the platform. There seem to be quite a few commuters travelling to Madrid.

We slide forward as sunlight ignites the horizon. After yesterday's downpour, a hopeful feel hangs in the air as castellated mansions, vineyards and sand-yellow wheat fields flash by. The sky is metallic blue feathered with strips of thin pearl-grey clouds that look as though they will burn away before morning is over.

This is no slow train. As I have said, the odd sprint is almost inevitable on Spain's trains these days, no matter if you prefer to take your time. The display touches 238 kilometres an hour (149 miles per hour). I am, however, feeling smug despite the speed as the journey was advertized as twenty euros at the ticket office yesterday and, somehow, my ticket cost half that price using an online promotion. It pays to keep a sharp eye on Renfe fares, which appear to have plenty of anomalies of this sort if you book at the last minute.

Swallows, crows and Laurie Lee
Segovia

Segovia has two main stations: shiny, modern, boxlike Segovia-Guiomar Station for high-speed services, on the outskirts, and the old Estación de Segovia for regional trains, closer in.

The Avant train stops at the former and I am among a handful of passengers to disembark to wait for an *autobús* to the *centro* while gazing across golden pastureland dotted with cattle. The sun beams down and the temperature is already, just after eight o'clock, heading toward 20ºC as the bus arrives. Down a hill past the town bullring of curved stone walls and rust-red doors we go, soon pulling up at a bend by the final stop. We all disembark and stare up at one of the great sights of the Iberian Peninsula.

Segovia's Roman aqueduct runs for 800 metres with no fewer than 166 arches and 120 supporting columns dating from the end of the first century. First impressions are that the town *centro* is hidden by a giant net curtain of gracefully (and carefully) placed granite blocks. I use the word "carefully" as there is not a lick of mortar holding the structure up. Yet the aqueduct has stood here for almost two thousand years, the highest point towering 30 metres above the cobblestones below. Swallows dart among the arches at the top on this sunny morning. They must be the luckiest birds right now in the whole of Spain.

On the far side, away from the road, giant shadows have created a zebra-land of light and I sit at café number two of the day in a cobbled square drinking a glass of *zumo de naranja* (orange juice) and eating a *tostadas de jamón con tomate* (ham on toast with thinly chopped tomato). Honey-coloured houses with wooden shutters and wrought-iron balconies rise near the foot of a high ridge with fortifications and a lane leading up to the heart of Segovia's old town.

As the sun warms the ancient stones, men pulling delivery trolleys rattle across the square, where a stage has been set for a fiesta that may or may not be today (who really knows when passing through in Spain?). A van brings new supplies of Mahou beer. A woman in black walks by skilfully flicking a fan. A husband and wife amble past, the husband clasping his hands behind his back and gripping a cigar in his teeth while simultaneously speaking to his wife. Quite a feat; one that must have taken years to get just right. A lottery ticket seller wearing a green jacket lurks patiently in the shadow of the aqueduct.

Above, swallows drift, dart and float like bonfire ash that will never reach the ground.

On the train from Zamora I made a four-point tourist checklist for Segovia. The first on the list is already ticked, seen straight away from the bus. But Segovia is also famous for its cathedral and its Alcázar, a castle that dates from the fourteenth century and was rebuilt in even greater medieval grandeur in the nineteenth century after a fire. So wonderfully OTT and classically "medieval" is this reincarnation that it is said to have been the inspiration for Disneyland's castle.

The final "attraction" is the site of a local miracle. And how could you knowingly pass a miracle by?

So one down, three to go.

Up the hill at the top of the ridge, Hostal Plaza is tucked to one side of Plaza Mayor, which has a bandstand at its centre and is surrounded by colonnaded walkways from which tables belonging to cafés spill out waiting for day-trip tourists from Madrid. For a few euros I have a windowless room down a dim, narrow hallway. These Spanish *hostals* come in many shapes and sizes but you absolutely cannot argue with their prices.

Out across the square, Segovia's wonderful Gothic domed cathedral arises with 167 spiky pinnacles resembling pipe cleaners and a high sturdy bell tower, 88 metres high and the tallest in Spain until 1614. It is enormous, 14,000 square metres in total (to be precise). Inside you could drive a lorry around the green marble *coro*, so wide are the passageways dividing the pews from the outer walls, along which there is access to no fewer than twenty-two chapels as well as the opportunity to regard 256 "funerary places". Columns soar above, reaching the vaulted ceiling, stained-glass windows (161 of these beautiful explosions of light) and the lofty dome, all dating from the sixteenth century onward.

The booklet you are given with your ticket is handy for statistics.

A magnificent golden organ is being repaired in the *coro*, while a hallway leads to magnificent cloisters with fragrant fir trees in the courtyard and a room to one side with more magnificent tapestries (though not as bloody as Zamora's). In a basement near the cloisters is a gallery of magnificent fifteenth- and sixteenth-century art with images of Christ and the Virgin Mary – one particularly exquisite version, known as *Virgen con Niño*, depicts Mary with ginger hair, delicate porcelain-pale skin and strange sleepy eyes, as though she has just woken up. Everything about Segovia Cathedral is quite magnificent – and obviously meant to be regarded as such. The church wanted to impress and has clearly over the centuries, to this day, achieved this very aim.

OK, two down, two to go.

The Alcázar is along a lane filling with Chinese and American day trippers, one of whom is wearing a cap mocking President Donald Trump's election slogan and declaring: *MAKE OUR WORLD GREAT AGAIN*. Nice to see. The palace, a residence of the crown of Castile from the twelfth century onward, is as fantastical as anyone could wish for, looking like something out of a fairytale dream clinging to the edge of Segovia's unusual ridgetop – all turrets and towers and battlements and flags. From this palace Queen Isabella made her way to Plaza Mayor to be crowned in 1474, while Philip II married Anna of Austria, his fourth wife here (Mary Tudor was his second), although for some years – after the royal court moved to Madrid – the building's superb vantage point was enjoyed by less regal eyes during a spell as a state prison.

You cross into this medieval Disneyland over a wooden bridge with a fearful drop below, entering chambers with shiny suits of armour, swords, crossbows and red velvet walls. "This room recreates what might have been…" I overhear on someone's audio guide. And this seems about right: everything feels *recreated* at the Alcázar, although there is nothing false about the sweeping views of the burnt-yellow hills and wheat fields between the battlements, framed by a clear blue sky.

"All the centre of Spain is on a plateau," a guide is saying to a group of Americans as we gaze out transfixed by the scenery. "Madrid is at six hundred and fifty metres. That's the highest capital in Europe. But Segovia is higher: one thousand metres here."

That's the thing about Segovia, especially with the hill at its centre. It does feel as though you have gone *up*. Zamora, like Madrid, is at 650 metres; the Avant train must have risen earlier (though somehow I did not notice).

Three down, one to go.

So to the site of the miracle – and a bit of Laurie Lee.

Santuario de la Fuencisla is a church on the northern edge of Segovia in a gorge at the foot of a sheer cliff. In medieval times criminals, troublemakers, adulterers and whoever got on the wrong side of authority were in the habit of being pushed over the edge of this "Cliff of Crows". The site is known as Peña Grajera and it was to here that Lee came during his rambunctious walking and busking adventure in Spain that began in Vigo, just south of A Coruña, in 1935, and continued as far as the Mediterranean coast between Málaga and Almería, where he was rescued by a British naval ship as the Spanish Civil War took off a year later.

By these "noisome" cliffs Lee met a priest who told him about the ancient murders and how the crows in the rockface were the "ghosts of their godless souls". The priest also related the story of María del Salto, a Jewish woman who had been wrongly accused of adultery and given the usual treatment but was saved after calling for mercy from the Virgin Mary, who answered her wishes and allowed Maria to float unharmed to the ground. She lived until 1237 and was buried in the cathedral. The church of Santuario de la Fuencisla was afterward built in María's honour and a display explains the miracle to the left of the entrance.

Lee is struck by the "harsh dry voices" of the crows on his visit, as he describes in his vivid memoir. And here they are now, flapping about still, sailing from holes in the cliff above to the trees in the park by the church and making an enormous racket: a murder of crows indeed.

While in Segovia for "not long", Lee manages to pack in a great deal, gathering juicy titbits from the priest, meeting a farmer who claims to have driven across the aqueduct on a coach and horses (Lee does not believe him), watching a film projected on to a sheet hung on a wall of the aqueduct after a supper of beans and mutton, and witnessing a "white-faced matador being carried to his car, weeping softly, attended by whispering friends" at the bullring.

His clear eye and the ebullience and poetry of his language, even during his short stay here, throw up a kind of parallel universe. It is not just the ghosts of the fallen and the crows that haunt in Segovia.

It would be bewitching to follow Lee's every move across the country. Lee had already been attacked by wild dogs while camping in the open near Vigo (he believes they may have been "Galician wolves"), suffered "pounding deliriums of thirst" on the roads near Zamora, taken a room in the house of a violent drunk in Valladolid, among much else. All of this before reaching the "half-forgotten heap of architectural splendours" of Segovia and extracting stories from farmers and priests – with the Mediterranean Sea still a long walk south.

But the trains only go where the train tracks lead.

I read Lee – enjoying his roller-coaster stories, just as I have Morris's spot-on observations – and eat tapas back at Hostal Plaza, where a bald barman with bulging eyes sings along to pop hits from the 1980s, which seem popular in these parts.

"Flashdance... what a feeling!" he croons. "Yeah, yeah, yeah!"

Pause to serve some drinks.

"The rhythm of the night... oh yeah! Oh yeah!"

Pause to serve some tapas.

"Love is in the air... oh yes! Oh yeah!"

Pause to fiddle with the till.

Resumes: "Yeah! Love is in the air!"

The barman hops outside, wiggling his hips, to check the tables.

Pause while cleaning glasses.

"Oh yeah! Oh huh huh, yeah! Red red wine…"

The barman seems to reach a point of ecstasy as he sings along to this one.

He cleans some glasses and I go outside to the square.

On the streets it is quiet – the day trippers have returned to Madrid and only overnight tourists and local families are about. The cathedral is lit up and the swallows by the aqueduct are resting above the columns by the cobblestone square where Lee watched his film. Stars flicker in the cloudless sky above the valleys beyond the Alcázar and the shadowy outline of the Cliff of Crows.

Of my pit stops so far, Segovia has been *una buena* (a good one).

"A train is on the ground, so it is better"
Segovia to Madrid

There are two options to reach Spain's capital. The first is a high-speed AVE train that takes 28 minutes from Segovia-Guiomar Station. The second is a regional service departing from Estación de Segovia that takes just under two hours but is a third of the price.

This is obviously the more appealing of the two, as enjoyable as the occasional catapult on a bullet train may be, although it involves finding Segovia's old station, which also involves convincing the number six bus driver at a bus stop just beyond a tightly packed area of houses that was once the Jewish quarter that you really do want the old station, and not the gleaming new one, which opened in 2007.

"Are you sure you want to go this way?" he asks.

"Yes," I reply. "To the station."

"Really?"

"Yes."

"I do not think you want to take this bus," he says.

"Is this the number six bus?" I ask. The woman at the tourist office on Plaza Mayor had told me this was the *autobús* to catch.

"Yes," he replies.

"Great, then this is the right bus," I reply.

"You want to catch this bus?" asks the driver.

"Yes please," I reply, a little exasperated now.

"OK, *señor*," says the bus driver, sounding extremely sceptical and with a definite underlying tone of *it's your problem,* señor, *if you get* perdido *(lost).*

And 15 minutes later the number six bus arrives at Segovia's old station, where I disembark and give the driver a little wave goodbye.

It would seem high-speed trains are so par for the course now in Spain that catching regional slow services is simply not regarded as something that *tourists do*; something I need to watch out for as going slow is so much better for seeing the scenery and I am in no particular rush.

It is worth pointing out here that the great success of bullet trains in Spain, so wonderful for getting about speedily as well as for the nation's PR in terms of international image, have come at the cost of its slower trains. In 2013 a national scheme called *El Plan de Racionalización de Servicios Muy Deficientes* (the Rationalization of Very Poor Services Plan) was put into action across the country by the Ministry of State for Public Administration's Subcommittee on Duplications to "eliminate existing dysfunctions in autonomous states".

The year 2013 was a big one for such eliminations as the economy was in the depths of a recession that lasted from 2008 to 2014, requiring a large European Union bailout, and the timetable from Estación de Segovia to Madrid, now that folk such as Andrés in Zamora were zooming in on fast trains for business meetings, took a hit. Instead of eight services a day, on some days of the week, Monday to Thursday, there would be as few as three.

Catching slow trains in Spain is not as easy as it used to be.

Estación de Segovia turns out to be in a distinguished orange-brick building with tall arched windows protected by metal grilles. It dates from 1884 and was once on a key line between León and Madrid, linking the capital with the north. Somewhere inside is a "royal room" ordered by King Alfonso XIII in 1911. Alfonso enjoyed visiting Segovia (who would not?) and wanted a bit of extra comfort during delays. These days, however, the facade looks a little run-down with weather-worn paintwork and weeds sprouting from walls. Compared to Segovia-Guiomar Station it does seem neglected.

To kill time, and eat lunch, I go to the café across the street and feast on tapas topped with super-fresh octopus and mussels washed down with *zumo de naranja* and a *café largo* for less than the cost of the ticket to Madrid. Cafés by stations in Spain really are a cut above what's on offer at, say, Crewe or Milton Keynes Central. I say this from experience, having waited around for quite a while at both.

* * *

A little red and white train pulls up and we putter down the line to the capital.

This is the 14:42, and it is soon moving through a landscape that feels quite different to anything so far on these trains round Spain.

Golden hills open out beyond the city's edge with jagged mountains rising to the east. This is heat-baked, rugged territory with prickly shrubs and dusty corrugated ravines. Frazzled grassland stretches into the distance broken only by lines of trees in folds where what little water there is must run. Pale, scratchy, defiant-looking olive trees poke out of ditches. *Aceitunas* seem to grow just about anywhere in Spain.

We – there are just two others on the slow train to Madrid – pass deserted farmhouses with ruined roofs and traverse a sun-baked field of big black cattle. The stations round here look more like country cottages. Deckchairs are propped by geranium pots on platforms. Black and white cats rest in the shade. Hardly anyone seems to be about, passengers or station staff. This is the sleepy way to Madrid.

I settle into the rattling ride, watching through the carriage window as the golden terrain turns steadily greener by degrees as we move closer to the capital. We reach Cercedilla Station, where the train stops and an announcement in English says: "End of line. Thanks for joining this service." One of the two other passengers and I get off, and a conductor points us to another train, a double-decker with tinted windows. We are switching here on to the green-coloured Line C-8 of the Madrid Metro.

The passenger who has stayed on the old train looks like a tourist, so I cross the platform and warn her of the change for Madrid.

"Oh, thank you so much," she says in an American accent and hurries across. "I'd totally zoned out."

The track between Segovia and Cercedilla is like that: extremely calming.

We wait here for five minutes. A temperature monitor shows 30ºC. Go south in Spain in the summer and mercury rises fast.

The top deck of the Madrid Metro train has low-slung lavender seats and feels far too comfortable for a commuter service; more like a retro 1970s cocktail lounge. Commuter trains in Madrid are pretty swish, it would seem – at least this one is (a cut above anything back home).

The train moves into the far reaches of the Spanish capital's urban sprawl. Houses, some with pools, line the track. We stop at Molinos Station, home to a shaded platform café with Coca-Cola umbrellas, and move on past more houses. In the back garden of one of these, right by the railway, a naked woman with – what is the permitted language these days? – *extremely ample assets* waves to the train as the Line C-8 service slides by.

Another similarly attired woman resting on a picnic blanket in the garden turns and waves goodbye as well. Muffled laughter comes from the tourist sitting behind me, who has spotted the friendly sunbathers too. Quite a send-off from Molinos Station, and again comparisons to back home spring to mind: nothing like this at Hull, Coventry or Bristol Temple Meads stations, at least not when I've been passing through.

The train begins to follow the Río Guadarrama, a tributary to the Iberian Peninsula's longest river, the Río Tagus. Water glistens at the base of a deep gorge, looking refreshing after the heat of the plateau outside Segovia.

The woman behind me turns out to be Chinese, aged twenty-three and currently living in Stockholm, where she is studying for a masters in geophysics at Uppsala University. She is from Yantai, a port city near Beijing, and is spending a fortnight's holiday in Spain, heading for Granada, having begun in Madrid. Her American accent comes from her English-language teacher back in Yantai.

"I don't like flights. I'm afraid of heights. A train is on the ground, so it is better. Stabler than buses," she says when I ask about her journey, although she did fly from Sweden.

She tells me she went up the bell tower of Segovia's cathedral yesterday. It is possible to book guided tours to do so.

"Oh yes, I climb the tower," she says, shuddering at the memory. "I thought: *OK, so I'm going to die here.*"

She really does not seem to like heights. She has beads of sweat on her nose and is petite with coal-coloured eyes that have a questioning quality. She has with her a tiny backpack, her luggage for fourteen days. She asks about what I am up to and whether I have been to China or Australia, where she has friends (I have been around both, on trains).

"Honestly, I don't know. You are like that cartoon: *The Road Runner,*" she says. She has an easy manner and a quick wit, although *The Train Runner* may be more accurate.

"Oh, Australia," she says dreamily. "I would like to go there for one year: fruit farm, whatever! My friends there, they are chasing the snow. They stay and work in hotel and the hotel gives them pass to go skiing."

In Segovia she booked a room on Airbnb. "I had a good host," she says, referring to the owner of the apartment. "Three hundred and eight yen for two nights." This is about twenty pounds a night.

"Can you imagine how many people died building that aqueduct?" she asks rhetorically. "Dreadful."

She shudders once again and pauses as we look down at the Río Guadarrama, now a long way below.

"Have you ever been to the Great Wall?" she asks.

I say I have.

"When we were growing up, we were told how many people died making that."

She returns to Segovia's Roman aqueduct. "No nails. Can you imagine building that with no nails!" she says, her arms now draped over the lilac 1970s-style cocktail lounge seat. "We have some weird structures like this too, where they make houses with no nails, just wood. The pagoda of Fogong Temple."

She asks if I have ever been to the pagoda of Fogong Temple and, when I say I have not, recommends a visit.

She pauses, then says out of the blue: "My mother said be careful and don't talk to strangers. So maybe I shouldn't be talking to you!"

Ignoring her mother's advice, she says: "Do you know couch-surfing? Local hosts let you stay for free. I always try to find *free* first."

She is an economical traveller. She is going couch-surfing in Madrid and knows how to say "hello", "goodbye" and "I am hungry" in Spanish: "My Spanish friend taught me that."

And as we pull into Madrid-Chamartín Station, at 16:35, she slips away into the crowds down an escalator soon after we all get off, and I realize I never did catch her name.

Philip II, Phillip, Deirdre and some tapas
Madrid

Given the "radial" system of Spanish railways that has evolved due to high-speed trains, it is almost impossible to avoid Madrid when travelling south from the direction of Santiago de Compostela. Not that I mind one bit. Having visited before to write about a "gin craze" that was sweeping Spain's capital for a newspaper – a tough assignment

– I have a few favourite places. I also need to do my washing and there appears to be a *lavandería automática de autoservicio* (self-service launderette) just around the corner from my apartment. And I want to see Spain's other big train museum, naturally, having not previously been. How could I possibly miss out on Madrid's Museo del Ferrocarril?

The journey by Metro from Chamartín Station to Tribunal Station costs a couple of euros. Chamartín seems a lot cleaner than London counterparts and comes complete with a tranquil fountain with water sliding down a wall near the escalators. It is ten stops to Tribunal in an uncrowded carriage in which some female passengers are using fans in the humid subterranean Madrid heat.

At Tribunal, colourful posters on the tunnel walls celebrate the centenary of the Madrid Metro. These celebratory posters seem to have taken up all the space where adverts usually go – and Spaniards in the nation's capital, judging by the huge amount of detail, appear to have a fondness for statistics.

Line 1 opened in 1919, I learn, when the population of Madrid was just 750,000. Now more than three million people live in the city and, instead of 56,000 people using the Metro each day, more than two million take to its carriages on 15 miles of tracks with thirty-three stops. The original north–south Line 1 covered just over 2 miles with eight stops, and trains had a top speed of 25 kilometres an hour (16 miles per hour). Alfonso XIII, no less, travelled on the first ride between Cuatro Caminos Station and Sol back in 1919. The king had provided a million pesetas to help finance the project, and before the inaugural journey he had his picture taken holding a top hat and cane standing by his carriage. The only problem was that he blinked during the snap. On seeing the print, however, the photographer added a pair of open eyes. This literally eye-opening fiddle is considered to be one of the earliest examples of "Photoshopping".

My apartment is not far away, past the grand pink facade of the Museo de Historia de Madrid and down a pedestrianized street with tattoo parlours, a club with blacked-out windows and *HOT* written in large red letters by the door, some street-fashion shops daubed in bright graffiti art, a series of decorations celebrating a lesbian, gay, bisexual and transgender festival and the gorgeous, tiny Virgen de la Soledad chapel with a cut-out image of the Pope staring out and gilded icons glittering inside.

Up the squeaky spiral staircase of a nondescript terrace next to a fast-food paella joint, I reach a wooden door fixed with a circular brass grille through which a pair of eyes flicker when I knock. The door is opened by a hunched elderly woman with crooked teeth and a walking stick who shows me to a small tangerine-coloured room in which towels are twisted into unusual decorative shapes on twin beds, boiled sweets placed on top. She hands me a key and, when I turn to comment that the artily placed towels are a nice touch, she is gone. I never lay eyes on my proprietress again, nor catch her name. Women seem to be in a habit of disappearing on me like this in Madrid.

Accompanied by a washing bag, I walk back past the tattoo parlour, the chapel and the HOT club to the Museo de Historia de Madrid, which, being so close to Tribunal Station, feels almost as though it is attached to the Metro – and not many Spanish Metro stations, or Metro stations anywhere for that matter, can boast *museos de historia*. Entrance is free.

Inside, a series of brilliant oil paintings transport you through the centuries: streets festooned with silks during medieval pageants; bloody battles of yore as soldiers bayonet one another during Napoleonic troubles; madcap bull runs by Madrid's main river, Río Manzanares, with bodies trampled in gutters by the waterfront; camps of pilgrims during yet more medieval pageants; and majestic kings peering down imperiously as kings in the old days tended to peer down (and a fair few still do today).

One of these is Philip II (1527–1598), who keeps seeming to crop up, I am finding, if you take a lot of trains around Spain.

After Philip's voyage from A Coruña to England and his brief marriage to Mary Tudor, Philip II was busy on many fronts. There was his failed Spanish Armada to defeat Protestantism and establish power in the north. There were the conquests and pilfering in the New World, a key source of wealth in the form of silver and gold, which helped finance what some regard as the "Golden Age" of Spain during Philip's time (Christopher Columbus had first set sail for the Americas in 1492, that key year in Spanish history, under the rule of Isabella and Ferdinand, and the dividends of exploration were paying off). There were his missions to the distant shores of Asia. Despite many setbacks, his empire spread far and wide, even reaching the Philippines, which are named after him.

Which I never knew. The Museo de Historia de Madrid is informative as well as visually captivating.

Philip II's decision to make Madrid his capital in 1561 was the moment that sealed the city's fate. Until then, Madrid had been a sleepy medieval place. Then the new king came. The old alcázar was transformed into his royal palace and Madrid became the hub of the Spanish Empire. He had chosen wisely. The city was perfect, bang in the middle of the Iberian Peninsula, with good water supplies, abundant flour mills and excellent hunting grounds. The time-consuming nomadic practice of previous royals of constantly flitting between different royal residences, such as the one in Segovia, was minimalized during the period of his rule. He was, although the Spanish Armada might suggest otherwise, regarded by many at the time as steady and sensible: a safe pair of hands. His nickname was Philip the Prudent.

There he is staring down, one hand resting on a cannonball, the other on a staff, armoured chest plates gleaming and with a frilly white collar. His eyes are wide-set and his pale-faced expression suggests: *you momentarily detain me from being quite at ease, yet I shall give you my attention. Are you almost done, artist?* He is painted sitting opposite his father Charles V, who had more than made his mark in his own right as Holy Roman Emperor and who is clearly of secondary importance, watching on proudly and lending his ambitious son an air of authority.

Philip II looks like a young gun, ready for action – which he was. As much as I am enjoying the train rides around the Iberian Peninsula, getting to know Spanish history better, I am finding, is a great pleasure – and the Museo de Historia de Madrid at Tribunal Station is a first-rate place to delve into the past.

* * *

OK, so not many trips to a self-service launderette involve such diversions but there are no rules when you are a train traveller. I collect my laundry bag from the museum's lockers and walk to the *lavandería automática*, my second such mission on this rail adventure (the other being in Pamplona). I mention this to explain the nitty-gritty of being a rail-travelling backpacker in Spain as well as how I meet an Australian brigadier and his wife. Such things can happen when you do your washing in the Spanish capital.

Deirdre and Phillip are from Sydney in Australia. We meet by the shiny steel *lavandería* washing machines and have a chat. Deirdre, "everyone calls me Dee", is a teacher/librarian at a primary school while Phillip works for a Japanese information technology company whose motto is "shaping tomorrow with you" – which is written on his card, which he gives me.

They are on a tour of Spain that will be followed by Italy and are staying at a plush nearby hotel where laundry costs "two euros for a pair of socks – they must be crazy". This is said by Phillip, who is in the middle of consulting a detailed spreadsheet with every day of his and Deirdre's journey laid out like a company's annual accounts.

"Salamanca," says Phillip. "Have you been there?"

"No," I reply.

"Salamanca. You're British. Wellington fought there. Beautiful cathedral," he says, at which point Dee mentions that Phillip is a brigadier in the Australian Army Reserve. Should anyone be planning to invade Australia, first they will need to negotiate the Australian

Army Reserve, which, judging by Phillip's arrangements for his and Dee's trip in Spain, will mean coming up against a formidable force.

Phillip has gingery hair and is in his fifties, wearing shorts, a T-shirt and hiking boots. Dee is similarly aged with gold-hoop earrings and darting eyes.

"The trains have been very comfortable," says Phillip. He and Dee have been taking trains in Spain. "Admittedly, we've been going first-class."

They have travelled to Córdoba and been to Barcelona. On their trip to Córdoba "we were given lunch and had a nice glass of wine," says Dee. "We could use the Wi-Fi and check up on Facebook."

After Spain they are flying to Verona. Their trip, although planned almost to the minute, began spontaneously after they "had a couple of drinks at a black-tie charity auction and bid for two tickets to Europe".

Córdoba is "gorgeous", as is Arcos de la Frontera in Andalucía, Ronda is "really gorgeous", while Seville is "totally totally gorgeous – I wouldn't mind living there for six months of every year," says Dee, as they begin folding their clothes, which seem to comprise mainly pairs of Calvin Klein underwear. Good to hear this about my eventual destination.

They recommend a Thai restaurant in London. They tell me that Lonely Planet is the best guidebook for Spain. "It's our Bible," says Phillip. They give me the name of a company that offers tapas tours in Madrid. Dee says that Capileira, a hilltop village in La Alpujarra region near Granada, is also "gorgeous". They finish folding their Calvin Klein underwear. They glance at their watches, consult their spreadsheet, look briefly a little concerned, and go. They must be the best organized tourists in Spain.

Feeling amateurish by comparison, I amble to Mercado de San Miguel, passing a street where the "gin bars" I once visited had been. These gin bars are gone. Madrid's "gin craze" appears to be over. However, Mercado de San Miguel is thriving, almost too much so. The market is in a wrought-iron and glass cage-like structure from

1916 that was revamped and turned into a gourmet tapas emporium in 2009. When I last came, not long after that, it was quiet and a bit of a "find". Now it has turned into a tapas zoo.

A very enjoyable tapas zoo. The market is packed. Elbows fly. Arms flail. People push by. Drinks are consumed. Tapas is consumed. Grilled octopus, marinated herrings, salt fish, smoked cod liver, pickled mussels, oysters, pies, *bocadillos*, cakes, caviar, skewered meats… all are consumed. A kind of orgy of consumption is in full swing amid a cacophony of orders and calls for *cerveza* and *vino tinto* and *vino blanco*. It reminds me of the prints of raucous scenes by Goya back in Zaragoza. And I realize I like it – a lot. Yes, this is for the tourists mainly and it is a free-for-all of the first order. But who cares? Mercado de San Miguel, just round the corner from Philip II's royal palace, is *mucha diversión* (a whole lot of fun).

Cruzcampo *cerveza* in hand, I hit the tapas and tuck into tender "codfish with honey and mustard", slices of lovely salty *jamón*, anchovies on roasted peppers with bread, pickled mussels, octopus with caviar, raw marinated salmon, and a *pollo* (chicken) pie or two for good luck. The *cerveza* flows. My euros fly. And in a heady half-hour or so I realize I have eaten a very large meal very quickly. I am stuffed and I am satisfied.

I retreat from Mercado de San Miguel. I walk to my apartment. I lie down on my tangerine bed. And I sleep for 12 hours straight.

La Marilyn, La Thatcher and southward
Madrid to Badajoz

That is (almost) that for Madrid and I do realize that by passing through that is just what I am doing.

Royal Palace: *lo siento* (sorry)! Museo del Prado, one of the finest art galleries on the planet: oops! I have shunned El Grecos and Goyas galore. I have ignored many sights of great Hispanic importance. I have mooched around and selfishly done my laundry and met Phillip and Dee from Sydney. But this is just how it is on these train rides, as I have said. You see what you see – then you move on. Impressions, whatever they may be, are what it is all about. Rail journeys around this big glorious exuberant nation in the south-west corner of Europe *rely* on them.

Impressions, snapshots… moments that may pull together into a bigger picture.

No point in pushing things and worrying too much (as I was à la Zamora). No need to dwell on internationally important art galleries, centuries-old treasures of the Iberian Peninsula or large royal residences.

Besides, there are also train matters to pursue.

In the morning I go to the Museo del Ferrocarril de Madrid, first having breakfast at a café at which a group of men from the lesbian, gay, bisexual and transgender festival – they are wearing the colours of the LGBT flag – are sitting at the next-door table. Madrid has a large LGBT scene and my apartment seems to be right in the thick of it in a *barrio* (neighbourhood) called Chueca.

"Oh, he's your *friend*, is he?" one of the men is taunting another man, speaking in English. "Just your *friend*?"

"Yes, he's my *friend*," says the man put on the spot.

"He's very hot, hot, hot for a *friend*," says the first man.

"Oh yes, I suppose you *could* say that," says the second man, coquettishly, enjoying the attention.

"We must meet your *friend*," says a third man.

"Maybe he is busy," says the second man, feigning vagueness.

"Oh, you *are* a dark horse," says the first man, sipping his cappuccino.

The group proceeds to launch into a long, detailed (unpublishable) discussion about nipples.

At another table a group of British tourists not in LGBT colours are discussing oysters.

"My old man has a little place down in Brixham," says one in a very plummy voice, talking at some length, loudly, about his father's holiday home in Devon. He could be nothing other than public school educated (in British speak: private school educated). And for a while I listen to him banging on about how the oysters in Brixham are better and cheaper than those in Madrid, which are usually transported to the landlocked city from Galicia.

"With a splash of Tabasco," he drawls, "I have to say: they're the absolute bee's knees." *Beee-zer neee-zer.*

And it occurs to me as I listen that it has been enjoyable to have travelled such a long time now in a country where class distinctions are not as immediately obvious as back home. Maybe, probably, they are to a Spaniard. Not to a train traveller rolling on by.

* * *

The Museo del Ferrocarril de Madrid is to be found in the former Madrid-Delicias Station, opened by the railway-loving King Alfonso XII and his wife María Cristina in 1880.

The *museo* is a beautiful wrought-iron and glass structure with an A-shaped roof and red-brick side buildings in which passenger waiting rooms and ticket offices were housed. It looks like one of the greenhouses at Kew Gardens, a very sturdy greenhouse with star-shaped wrought-iron adornments on the front – and a rather different collection of specimens inside.

Madrid-Delicias was the city's first grand station and it was the work of a French engineer, Émile Cachelièvre. At the grand opening of the grand station, five steaming locomotives hissed at the end of the platforms as Alfonso XII did his bit and the line from Madrid to Ciudad Real in the south and onward to Badajoz in the *comunidad autónoma* of Extremadura was given the royal thumbs up. Badajoz, very close to the Portuguese border to the south, is where I am hoping to reach by train later today.

The line from Madrid-Delicias provided a link with important coal mines and, later, a route into Lisbon in Portugal. It also offered a handy extra connection for royals from Madrid to the palace at Aranjuez to the south (although this was already possible from Madrid-Atocha Station, a mile to the north). To this day, during the spring and the autumn, a tourist day-trip train service nicknamed *Tren de la Fresa* (Strawberry Train) pulls vintage carriages between Madrid-Delicias and Aranjuez, recreating this journey of 30 miles. The farmland around Aranjuez is known for its strawberries, which are served on board.

The decline of Madrid-Delicias was gradual, mainly resulting from the rapid growth and popularity of the Madrid-Atocha Station. Over the years the usefulness of the lesser station waned and it was finally closed in the early 1970s. Fortunately, however, no wrecking balls were brought in. Instead, rail enthusiasts got hold of the site and in 1984 Madrid's collection of locomotives and railway paraphernalia was moved from another location and established at Madrid-Delicias.

So began one of the finest railway museums in the world. As you enter, a faint smell of oil and diesel carries from the platforms to the little shop and ticket booth. Just as at the Catalonia Rail Museum, no more than a handful of visitors are about and there is a strong sense of being off the usual tourist track here, well away from Prado and the palace.

"Do many people come?"

"No, not really," says the plain-speaking ticket seller, handing me my change. "Just families with kids."

Through a gate into the main station hall, you arrive at long platforms with gleaming locomotives and carriages that show how trains developed from the days of the late 1840s through the nineteenth century, when engineers in Spain initially struggled with buckling tracks caused by weather extremes. This was another of the reasons for Spain's slow train progress by comparison with other parts of Europe. Weather-damaged lines resulted in accidents, slow progress and debts among the private operators. When lines were eventually nationalized under Franco in 1941, railways were a long way behind. Journeys between Barcelona and Madrid, 375 miles, could take as long as 12 hours as late as the 1960s, which works out as 50 kilometres an hour (31 miles per hour). Very slow trains then.

The *museo* is an Aladdin's cave of Spanish rail interest. Tiny locos that look like they belong in *Thomas the Tank Engine* and rudimentary wooden carriages with fancy gold and burgundy painted decorations lead to sleeker 1930s carriages with marquetry and table lamps with pink shades. Ramps alongside windows provide vantage points to gaze upon metal-framed beds with velvet covers, bathrooms with porcelain sinks and smartly laid-out buffet cars featuring cushioned seats, crisp white tablecloths and polished cutlery.

Sleeker models from the 1950s and 1960s are suggestive of the dawn of the modern age. Curves, stripes and aluminium casing have been introduced along with rows of passenger seats similar to today, although everything seems a little wider and fancier in the silver bullet-like *Talgo II* carriage that was developed in 1950.

This used to run between Madrid and Irun, by the French border, and was pitched at business travellers and the well-to-do. Reclining seats, air conditioning, panoramic windows and an at-seat meal service all came as standard. It was state of the art and, for anyone travelling on it back then, must have made a grand statement: *we like to get about in (a lot of) style*. Farmers hunched in fields, olive pickers and grape pickers at the time must have looked up on first sight and thought: *what, in the name of St James, the bloody hell is that?*

My favourite is a diesel locomotive that ran from the mid 1950s to 1978, when it was decommissioned and brought to the Madrid collection. This was the first diesel train in Spain, initially running in Andalusía between Huelva, Seville, Cádiz and Córdoba. I like it simply because it is large and silver with a stripy green pattern on the front. Perhaps a true rail enthusiast would also be enthralled by its "class" (DL500) and the horsepower of the engine (1,600 h.p.), but for me it simply looks quite splendid. Despite having taken so many train journeys of late, I have yet to slip into the realm of *enthusiast*, although

I take my hat off to all true enthusiasts out there: it must take a lot of boning up on facts and figures.

The green loco with the stripy pattern was nicknamed *La Marilyn*, having been made in America and because of its "aerodynamic cab and the way it swayed on tick-over in a manner evocative of the famous actress," says a panel. Another nearby loco, decommissioned in 1987, is named *La Thatcher* after Prime Minister Margaret Thatcher and was powered by a Rolls-Royce engine.

There are plenty of possibly fascinating details of this sort – and much time may be spent in side rooms in the red-brick annexes, after pounding the platforms, examining old stationmaster hats, browning timetables and Morse code telegraph machines. One exhibit that stands out is the grandfather clock that was used to time Spain's very first 20-mile train journey between Barcelona and Mataró all the way back in October 1848 – an evocative link back to those heady days on the Costa Brava.

In short, the Museo del Ferrocarril de Madrid is both a mausoleum to Spanish trains as well as a celebration of progress across the decades, although the very modern era of high-speed trains (it must be said) does not get much of a look-in.

It is a relaxing spot away from the scrum of overtourism that Madrid is beginning to experience – on a minor level compared to Barcelona. The best place of all for me, though, is the buffet car of a shiny blue and gold 1930s carriage built by Compagnie Internationale des Wagons-Lit, of the sort that was once hauled by the *Orient Express*. The bar is open, tended by a man wearing a peaked cap. I buy an ice-cold Mahou *cerveza*, inspect the intricate marquetry depicting tropical birds and sit outside by a marble-topped table on the central platform, not far from where Alfonso XII must have cut the ribbon all those years ago.

I drink my *cerveza* in this holiest of holy Spanish train locations.

Then I go to catch my next train.

* * *

Madrid-Atocha Station is a beauty. Just up a hill from the *museo*, a grand span of curved glass and orange-brick arises, dwarfing little Madrid-Delicias, which never stood a chance competing against this megalithic neighbour. Madrid-Atocha was rebuilt after damage by fires in 1892, but before then, in 1851, had already seen the first trains out of Madrid to Aranjuez and beyond. The station is topped by a Spanish flag guarded by copper dragons, while above the entrance is a large clock adorned with a golden crown. Many a Spanish royal must have passed through these doors and along the tracks beyond.

Outside to the right of the facade, men are selling fake trainers, straw hats and Cristiano Ronaldo Real Madrid shirts spread on plastic at makeshift stalls. A few tourists sift through the items while the stallholders' eyes shift across the square, where several major roads converge, checking for *policía* perhaps.

To the left of the main entrance, all thoughts of moving around Spain on trains come to a halt for a while. Beyond the edge of Madrid-Atocha stands a moving cylindrical memorial to the 193 victims of the 11 March 2004 Madrid terrorist train bombings as well as a special forces officer who later died. It was the deadliest terrorist attack in Spanish history, conducted by an al-Qaeda cell. A total of ten train bombs exploded at four different sites across Madrid, three of them detonated at Madrid-Atocha Station. Each train had been travelling along lines connecting to Atocha.

It is both moving and chilling to read the messages inscribed within the high ethereal glass cylinder. May Spain – may everywhere – never see such an attack again.

Inside the station proper, I pass through a wonderful atrium of palms and tropical fronds. It is as though a little jungle has been planted in the middle of Spain's busiest station. More than 110 million passengers pass through Atocha each year, yet this is an incredibly peaceful place.

And so I catch the 16:08 to Badajoz.

Tren 194, due in at 21:26, will take me on my longest Spanish journey yet; a few minutes more than Oviedo to Ferrol. It is waiting at a side platform and on board I sit next to a polite middle-aged woman eating a banana and reading *El Señor de Ballantrae* (*The Master of Ballantrae*) by Robert Louis Stevenson. As we move off through graffitied suburbs and past many football training pitches (no wonder Real Madrid is so good, even if so many of the players come from abroad), a short, skinny, well-dressed man enters our carriage. He walks around dropping little colourful key rings with lights attached on our laps. At the far end of the carriage he speaks at some length, for at least three minutes, about how he needs money to help support his family.

What is surprising is what happens next. Instead of the reaction I would expect back home – glassy-eyed indifference or even hostile glares about having been temporarily burdened with the key rings – a dozen or so of the forty passengers take out their cash. A woman in her early twenties in the row ahead switches off her hip-hop, removes her headphones and hands across two euros. I buy mine too. So does the woman eating the banana. He smiles, bows politely and leaves our carriage. There is something about this episode that is touching. Maybe I am reading more into this than need be, but there appears to be better empathy in Spain for those who have fallen on hard times than back home. And less shame in such "begging". Just as with the elderly man who asked for a euro in Ferrol: *we are all in it together and sometimes we need a little help when things have gone wrong; who knows, one day it could happen to any of us.* Yes, maybe I am making more of a minor moment than I ought, but then again, maybe not.

A map of Spain on a screen in the corner shows our route south and west to Badajoz in a series of step-like movements beyond Toledo, Cáceres and Mérida. My neighbour pulls down the window blind almost all the way and proceeds to fall asleep with her head tilted upward in a weird position. Many bleached-yellow fields pass by, fringed by perfect rows of olives. This continues for a long time. The sky is cloudless. The train tilts. The woman next to me awakes and fixes the edge of her glasses with some sticky tape. She falls asleep once more. The woman who had been listening to hip-hop sends smartphone messages in an extraordinary blur of thumbs. I close my eyes and doze. We trundle along. I open my eyes as we pause at Mirabel Station, where a man in a straw cowboy hat runs down the platform to meet a loved one.

The landscape has turned into an African plain: rolling savannah, folds of hot dusty land. The earth is tinted orange. Rocky escarpments rise. The mountains and fertile fields of the north are long gone. This feels like frontier land, which it is; so much of Extremadura borders Portugal. We are deep in the Spanish wilds now. Tan-coloured cattle flicker in the heat haze. It is 35°C outside, says the screen, travelling at 61 kilometres an hour (38 miles per hour).

We pass a brilliant Roman aqueduct with storks on top. We stop at Mérida Station. My neighbour gets off. We reverse back past the aqueduct. We cross a lake and a marsh, the train casting long shadows in the late light. The landscape grows greener with vines and farmland. A canoodling couple in the row ahead begins to watch a steamy film on their laptop, leading actors in various states of undress. There is a hissing sound and the little arrow on the screen shows that we are very close to Portugal. We pull into Badajoz. I get off, examine the fly-splattered front of the white and purple-striped loco, nod thanks to the spindly driver and go to find my room for the night.

CHAPTER EIGHT

BADAJOZ TO ARANJUEZ, VIA MÉRIDA, ALMADÉN, CIUDAD REAL AND ALCÁZAR DE SAN JUAN

CALIENTE, CALIENTE, CALIENTE (HOT, HOT, HOT)

It is very hot in southern Spain. Svitlana, my Ukrainian psychology professor friend in Manresa, did not have that wrong.

The temperature will touch 40°C today and may reach 45°C soon. A heatwave has struck Europe. Some blame this on global warming while others say African air is passing north as a result of a storm over the Atlantic Ocean, a "Saharan Bubble" and high pressure in Central Europe. Records may be broken in France, Poland, the Czech Republic, Germany and Austria. Britain's previous highest temperature mark may be eclipsed. Whatever. It is very hot in south central Spain and the forecast is for even higher temperatures.

Heatwave or no heatwave, Badajoz is perfect for those who wish to fly beneath the radar of regular tourism in Spain. Yesterday evening I walked quite a long way from the station down a road with pink and white roses planted in the verge. There was birdsong. There was a smell of flowers. There was also a long straight footbridge above a park filled with palm trees and a wide river, the Río Guadiana. Lanterns lit the way along this bridge, the Puente de Palmas, and the sky was pale peach and hazel as night fell. White ducks quacked in the reeds and the lilies. A sign informed me that the bridge was built in honour of Philip II in the sixteenth century (but of course). I checked into Hotel San Marcos near Plaza de España, ate dinner in a narrow lane on a hill and considered my rail travel options from this baking out-of-the-way place. My idea is to somehow reach València across the middle of Spain, cut southward to Benidorm, about which I am curious, and move along the Mediterranean coast in the direction of Seville.

Today, though, I am checking out Badajoz.

In Plaza de España, I eat *tostadas* and drink three coffees over the course of an hour at a café while watching Cruzcampo and San Miguel delivery vans pass by and delivery men rolling barrels across the flagstones. A council-employed gardener waters flowerpots surrounding the low, squat Catholic cathedral. A *bombero* (fireman) sits at a table next to mine, says *hola* and begins contentedly to smoke a cigar. A sparrow hops on to my table. I give it a few crumbs of *tostada* and after a while it flutters happily away. This is the sum total of the "action" in the throbbing centre of Badajoz.

From the square it is a short walk up a hill past crimson and custard-yellow terraced houses to the battlements of the ninth-century Moorish Alcazaba fortress at the city's edge. This is free to enter. The Río Guadiana gleams way below and I walk along the ramparts by an inner park with a fountain, enjoying views across the dried yellow and patchwork green countryside to the east and Puente de Palmas to the west. Swallows flit above, reminding me of Segovia. No-one else is about and you can feel a very long way from anywhere up on the fortress at Badajoz early in the morning on a late June day.

There is a little museum here, free to enter too, with Roman sculptures depicting soldiers and maidens, ancient mosaics, prehistoric cave carvings, plus original Moorish script inscribed in marble. Meanwhile, another free museum is to be found halfway back down the hill explaining British involvement in the Peninsula War of 1808–1814, during which the *Duque de Wellington*, *militar Británico* and Napoleon, *Emperador de Francia*, squared off at Badajoz in 1811–1812. While yet another museum with no entry charge is further still down the hill, featuring works of art by Luis de Morales (1509–1586), the city's "most famous son" according to my guidebook and known as *El Divino* due to his many depictions of Christ. Some of these are here, with the most notable showing Jesus, complete with a curly ginger beard, bleeding and in the throes of agony. Another painting by a later artist imagines Morales, grey-bearded and humble, meeting a benevolent-looking Philip II. There seems to be no way of getting away from Philip II in these parts; just as there seems to be no shortage of free (rather good) museums in Badajoz, either.

So you may while away a morning in this hot, remote city near the Portuguese border.

Back at Badajoz Station, however, a further treat lies in store.

The café at Badajoz Station seems to be a local institution, popular both with passengers and locals not taking the train. Inside it is bustling with business. A fat bald man kindly warns me not to leave my notebook in my back pocket as it might be stolen. A skinny man with a full head of hair, a fellow customer, then helpfully explains that the "meat dish" being sold with *papas fritas* (chips) is *carne de cerdo* (pork). I sit outside on the café terrace waiting for the 14:30 to Mérida, a journey of just 45 minutes, while watching Badajoz Station life unfold, and enjoying the community spirit of it all. It really is a buzzing Spanish station café. A celebration of some sort seems to be going on across the way, where a group of men has gathered to drink *cerveza*. After a while, one of them stands up and begins to dance in a circle while stamping his feet as his friends clap and say *"¡Olé!"* I watch this "show", order a *cerveza* of my own from a tall, pot-bellied waiter with a hipster beard who slaps down the little glass which had been balanced on a tray with many more little glasses (before doing the same at the other tables), and buy a Cuponazo lottery ticket with a payout of between nine and fifteen million euros. I am feeling lucky. Badajoz Station café has put me in a good mood.

"For sure we are the poorest region"
Badajoz to Mérida

A *Media Distancia* train arrives and I board *coche dos*, which is air conditioned and has a humming sound. The temperature outside is 34ºC as the train rolls slowly past a herd of goats in a sandy field, followed by a row of old grain silos with storks perched on top. Olive groves emerge miraculously out of the hard, dry land. Cacti and aloe vera that I did not notice yesterday line the track. The 14:30 is retracing yesterday's route.

It does not take long to reach Mérida, passing the brilliant Roman aqueduct once again – I seem to be developing a thing for

Roman aqueducts – and I am soon talking to two of the Renfe staff at Mérida Station.

"Do you like mines?" asks ticket assistant number two after ticket assistant number one has recommended several places to visit by Renfe trains, including Badajoz, Cáceres, Zafra and Plasencia.

Ticket assistant number one is named Pedro; number two is named Juanjo. Spanish Renfe ticket assistants, I have long ago concluded, although Pedro and Juanjo help cement this point of view, are among the best in the world, if not the very best (with the odd exception).

Juanjo has a beard and jet-black hair. He writes "Almadén" on a piece of paper and hands it to me. Both he and Pedro have come around from behind the glass ticket booth to talk. There is no one else about.

"Up to a point," I reply, answering the initial question.

"There is a mine here that you must visit," Juanjo says, pressing on. "I went five years ago with my family."

"What kind of mine?" I ask.

"Iron," Juanjo says at first, before correcting himself. "Not iron! Mercury! It is a very old mine and it has a train you can go on. A very old train."

This sounds great. I say that I will visit tomorrow – I had no other destination planned – and Juanjo seems extremely pleased, informing me that it may be best to catch the 07:50 if I want enough time to go on a mercury mine tour.

We chat for a while and Juanjo says he has worked for Renfe for thirty-five years and is aged fifty-eight while Pedro has served thirty-seven years and is sixty. Pedro says he is a fan of old Fiat "Ter" trains operated by Renfe thirty years ago, one of which I was lucky enough to see at the Madrid rail museum. He also says that he used to love the *Ferrocarril Ruta de Plata* railway route (Silver Route) from Seville to Oviedo.

I say I have never heard of this.

Juanjo takes over: "It was first a Roman road. The Romans used to carry silver this way. Then it was a railway, but the government cut the line in the 1980s."

He consults my *Rail Map Europe*, which is quite battered now.

"This is a very bad map," he says. A tear in the fold has almost wiped out Mérida.

Pointing to the place on the map, Juanjo says that it was a crucial stretch of the line between Plasencia and Salamanca that was discontinued. "Now there is only a highway along here." This means that if you want to travel by train to Salamanca you need to go into Madrid.

Another example of Spain's "radial" train system at work.

"Now we are making fast trains and cutting the little routes," says Juanjo. "I don't think anyone really knows why this is. It is very sad."

The entire length of the line used to be from the south of Seville, beginning at Huelva in the Gulf of Cádiz, all the way to Oviedo in the north.

"Now there are only cargo trains to the north from here," says Juanjo. "They must go via Badajoz into Portugal and then up from there to Vigo."

They show me where to expect to see the famous windmills that feature in *Don Quixote* by Miguel de Cervantes; apparently visible from the line near Alcázar de San Juan Station. Then Juanjo and Pedro give me their emails and Juanjo says: "If you need any help, please do just write."

On this positive note, I walk up a road of terraced houses to Plaza de la Constitución, a quiet square with a couple of cafés, some palm trees and a fountain, go down a lane and find Hostal Senero.

Inside I am met by Jorge Hernández. He is in his thirties and runs the small, colourful *hostal* with his sister. They are the fourth generation of the family to do so. The *hostal* has eleven rooms and is "full every weekend – it is a very good business really".

I learn all of this rapidly – and then I learn a whole lot more.

"We have the worst trains in Spain," says Jorge, referring to the local services after asking me about my journey. "We wish they were better. One in four trains don't arrive."

"On time?" I ask.

"No," he says. "They do not arrive *at all*. There will be some sort of mistake, something broken, they have to stop for something, the air conditioning doesn't work, whatever. We are a very poor region."

Jorge seems to connect the region's poverty, well known in Spain, with the erratic running of trains.

I tell him that my train from Madrid to Badajoz was on time.

"But it took more than five hours?" he asks. He raises an eyebrow.

"Yes," I reply.

The speed between the two cities works out at about 45 miles an hour (72 kilometres an hour), not that I am concerned at such slowness.

"Once a week you hear on the news that the train from Madrid is broken," says Jorge. He sighs. "For sure we are the poorest region. We have the lowest salaries and the highest percentage of unemployment: twenty per cent in Mérida and across Extremadura."

"What about the rate among young people?" I ask.

"Oh!" he says, gesticulating upward. "Young people: forty, fifty per cent. It is incredible."

"What is the solution?"

"The solution? We really don't know. We have no industry. We have good highways and roads and we are close to Portugal…" Jorge's voice tails off.

"What about traditional industry?"

"Nothing," he says. "Yes, we have farming, but we have to buy machinery from other regions. We have no car industry. We have no industry whatsoever. We live firstly from tourism and secondly government. In Mérida, the government is situated here." The city is the capital of Extremadura. "The population here is sixty-five thousand and about six thousand work for the government."

Both Jorge and his sister have business degrees from Cáceres University. "But they are not required here." He waves his arm about the *hostal* to indicate *here*.

"Are young people in Mérida depressed about the job situation?" I ask, which I realize now is a bit of a leading question.

It is leading the wrong way.

"No," Jorge says. "They prefer to go to Madrid and Seville to work. They don't mind. There are better jobs there. Here there are no high-qualification jobs: it's a vicious circle."

The population density of Extremadura is just 27 people per kilometre against 75 in the rest of Spain (170 in Europe as a whole).

"Are people generally down about it all?" I ask, yet another leading question, I know.

Jorge looks surprised.

"It's a very, very good region to live in," he says.

"Why?"

"We are in the top happiest people in Spain," he says.

"According to who?"

"Oh, it was in a survey," he says a little airily.

"When?"

"Oh, three years ago," he says.

"Conducted by who?"

"Oh, some university made the statistics," he replies.

"Are there reasons why it is so good in Mérida?"

"The weather is better," Jorge says.

"You mean very hot?"

"Yes. Better than the rest of the regions: hotter. It only rains when it's necessary for crops. In northern Spain it's always raining. And we have more security here. I have no lock for my motorcycle. People I know from Madrid or València can't understand. Sometimes I forget and leave the key in my motorbike. Someone will come here and knock on the door and say: 'you forgot your key'. You can go for a walk in the park at three in the morning and nothing will happen. You are safe. And everything is cheaper. Salaries are lower so everything is cheaper. You want a flat? Thirty to forty thousand euros."

"For a one-bed flat?" I ask.

He looks at me as though I'm crazy and laughs. "No, for three or four bedrooms. A brand-new apartment might be sixty thousand.

Badajoz and Cáceres are more expensive – they have bigger universities."

Seeing as Jorge is so opinionated – and seeing as we are a long way from Catalonia – I ask what he thinks of Catalonian separatism.

"They think they are not with us," he replies. "They think they are better than us. The feeling there [in Catalonia] is that they give more so they should receive more. The rest of Spain thinks they should share. If we are a country, if there is a poorest part, then the wealthiest should share with the poorest."

"So you are a socialist?" I ask.

"Yes," he replies without hesitation – and looks at me steadily as though awaiting a follow-up question. We do seem to have fallen into the pattern of "interview" at the check-in desk of Hostal Senero.

His answer, however, momentarily stops me in my tracks. There are not many back home, these days, who put their hands up to *socialism*. Members of Britain's Labour Party go by various descriptions: social democrats, trade unionists and, for some, *democratic socialists*. But, usually at least, not merely *socialists*. Perhaps Jorge's answer should not be so surprising, though. The freshly elected current prime minister here is the leader of the Spanish Socialist Workers' Party, although politics is in flux and he may not be soon.

Yet for now during this train adventure, with right-wing parties waiting in the wings, *socialist workers* rule the roost.

"Why?" I ask – why is he a socialist?

"If you have more, you should share," says Jorge, as though this is a quite simple matter of logic. "I lean to the left. This is the reason I pay taxes: so the government will help those with no job or the sick."

He hands me my key. I ascend stairs to a small, neat, very-good-value room. And again, as with my reaction to the key-ring seller on the long slow train from Madrid to Badajoz, I am struck by this strong Spanish streak of benevolence, of looking after the needs of fellow citizens, that also shows its colours in the great friendliness and helpfulness of the vast majority of station staff and train conductors of the country's (mainly) well-run railways.

* * *

It really is hot in Mérida.

Yesterday I spent most of the day on a train, so I missed out on the full blistering effect of 40ºC. Today, I can report that 40ºC feels *worryingly* hot. So hot you realize you would not want to lose your way, say, on a walk in the countryside in case the temptation to curl up in a quiet-yet-baking patch of shade took over. And that might be that. It is *survival* hot. Across a big square with orange trees the heat seems to seep in waves as though, somewhere way up above, God is opening and closing an oven door and wafting the air down below.

At the far side of the square, however, is a little corner of paradise.

It is so regularly intolerably hot in these parts that a public service watery mist is provided in the main shopping street running toward the city's Roman amphitheatre. After feeling the heat, the pleasure of simply standing to one side and letting the cool water sprinkle over you is quite magnificently refreshing. I do this for a while, joining a few others doing the same. The temptation to stay here in the watery mist is strong. Yes, the amphitheatre, one of the Roman treasures of Spain, is just up a short hill. But this is a short hill without any public service watery mists that I can see.

At the end of the shopping street, where the mists stop, stands a pharmacy with a digital temperature monitor. A small group has gathered beneath and is taking pictures. The temperature reading is 46ºC. It is so hot that Spaniards consider it hot. If this monitor is to be believed, the temperature is eight degrees higher than Britain's hottest day since records began.

I go into an air-conditioned tourist office to see if there is a tourist map. There is, and Clara, one of the staff, points out the various Roman sites, which include a theatre beside the amphitheatre, a cemetery, a bridge and pair of aqueducts.

"Is this weather normal?" I ask.

"Yes, yes, very normal," she says. "It can be 39ºC, 40ºC, 42ºC in September for the first fifteen days. Now we have 41ºC." Then she says: "Normally it is 32ºC around now."

"So it is *not* normal?" I ask.

"Yes, it not normal," she concedes, switching tack somewhat confusingly. "No, no – not normal at all."

Then she says that the temperature is not really 46ºC, more like 41ºC – the pharmacy monitor is in a suntrap.

"41ºC is dangerous," she adds, confirming my own opinion. She looks beyond my shoulder as though assessing the danger level. "No, not normal at all," she says once again.

All that really need be known, I conclude, coming back to my original thoughts on the matter: *it really is hot in Mérida*.

This city was founded by the Romans in 25 BC when it was known as Augusta Emerita, a place for veteran soldiers to retire within the Roman province of Lusitania within the Roman settlement of Hispania. Along with Toledo and Zaragoza, Mérida was an important part of maintaining Roman control of central and western Spain.

A remarkable number of Roman ruins remain, all on streets without public service watery mists. I start with the amphitheatre and the theatre, both glorious structures that evoke the great sense of order and showmanship of the ancient civilization – this would have been an extremely comfortable spot to end up after the cut and thrust of various wars against the Gauls, perched pleasantly up a slope from a gentle tree-lined curve of the Río Guadiana.

Mérida must have been a happy backwater all those years ago with its huge "circus" track for chariot racing, grand arches, temples and, of course, its fresh supplies of aqueduct-supplied water.

The best maintained of these is the one by the railway tracks, providing one of the top "train views" in Spain. I inspect the amphitheatre with its information panels about how gladiators once cast 3-metre nets over opponents before attacking them with tridents and daggers. I marvel at the fine theatre, where classical music concerts are held beneath a gorgeous facade with colonnaded windows. I pay my respects at the funerary site, next to a blood-red bullring where bulls weighing 500 kilogrammes by the name of Dictadoria have been slain (heads are mounted in the passageways by the restaurant). Not far on, back toward the centre, is the Moorish citadel beside the mind-boggling bridge across the slow green river. It stretches 800 metres and both its length and its longevity seem like some kind of miracle.

My loop of Mérida takes me, via a tunnel beneath the train tracks, to the main aqueduct.

Although not quite as downright impressive as Segovia's, Mérida's has a peaceful aspect and is topped by perhaps the most singular-looking storks in Spain. Long faces stare down as though assessing your right to be anywhere near or even vaguely in the vicinity of their aqueduct: interlopers depart! Be gone!

From there, I return via the extraordinary Roman "circus", which could hold 30,000 spectators, to the centre, taking another tunnel back under the tracks into the heart of a party. A gay pride march is in full swing. Whistles screech. Drums bang. Banners with *NO HATE!* and *¡CELEBRAR!* messages are held aloft. Around a corner, another parade is on the march with religious icons balanced on shoulders, red-robed figures, the wallop of drums and trumpeters playing the Frank Sinatra tune "My Way". I duck beneath a Roman arch and drink a glass of ice-cold red wine at a bar on Plaza de la Constitución, served by a waiter wearing an Elvis T-shirt, as swallows dart in a lilac evening sky. Mérida was scorching. Mérida is marvellous. Mérida is letting its hair down. The temperature is dropping. Tomorrow, though, will be hotter still.

The mercury mine express
Mérida to Almadén

With a blast of a horn and blasting air conditioning, the 07:50 to Almadén departs, due in at 10:26. Juanjo and Pedro are not on duty as the train pulls away beneath a low orange sun illuminating little houses with horses in yards on the edge of town. We are leaving early enough that the freshness of the morning is still in the air despite the temperature already touching 20°C.

The 07:50 rattles slowly onward beyond vineyards and olive groves as a succession of images of remote rural Spain unravels. A donkey looks up at the passing train, shakes its head and hee-haws extravagantly, just for us. Pigs lollop about in muddy lots. A field of sunflowers opens up in a brilliant expanse of yellow. A deer darts from a thicket. A stork flaps upward lugubriously, seemingly disturbed by our passage. Ploughed fields of rolling orange soil spread out. Then solar panel farms emerge – modern remote rural Spain – catching the light like the sides of skyscrapers laid flat. There are hardly any settlements of which to speak. Even twenty-seven Spaniards per kilometre seems ambitious round here.

This journey is a sheer pleasure. The landscape is alive with interest as we roll along into badlands with ravines and tumbleweed. The serene mountains of the Sierra Morena arise, shards of granite towering and orange-dirt trails curling on craggy slopes. Startled sheep wobble across a field. Others rest in the shade of trees, using every inch of darkness. The result is bizarre, as though freak snowstorms have struck beneath the branches. We follow a meandering river accompanied by bushes of pink flowers in full bloom. Amid the desiccated landscape a delicious ribbon of colour snakes between escarpments. Salvador Dalí would be at home in these parts. *I am* at home. It's a long way from everything on the train from Mérida to Almadén.

If you want escapism.

Well, you'll get it here.

We roll through a cut in the hills beside a dried-out riverbed. Then we pull up at the ochre outline of Almadén Station, where a grey-and-white cat with green eyes rests on the platform, watching me and four others disembark. There are flies, a stationmaster, a bowl of milk for the cat – and not much else. Two of the passengers depart in a car. I watch them go as I work out that the station is a long way from town. As I do so, the other two passengers from the 07:50 gesture for me to join them in their battered old grey Ford Focus.

It is a ten-minute ride down a hot hill, swerving to avoid two dead cats, into Almadén as José and Clara explain they had been visiting a cousin in Mérida and tell me I must see Almadén's historic hexagonal bullring, which was built to provide housing around the edge of the ring for local miners. Cash from rent and from bullfights went toward the construction of a hospital for miners suffering from ailments caused by their work; an ingenious arrangement dreamed up in the eighteenth century.

With *buena suertes* (good lucks) they drop me by a knife and gun shop on the narrow high street of the almost deserted town where windows in houses have grilles and there is a strong sensation of being watched between the half-opened slats of shutters. I find a *hostal*, the El Cordobés Hostal, where a tiny corner room with good air conditioning is available for a reasonable price. I am officially a tourist in a remote Spanish mining settlement on the edge of the *comunidad autónoma* of Castilla-La Mancha (Extremadura has been and gone).

Almadén's mine was a world-famous mercury mine.

Following, Juanjo's advice back in Merida, I walk over to investigate. At the entrance, a dozen Spanish tourists has gathered, an extended family with local connections, and we are led forth across a hot yard while being told the basics. The extraction of cinnabar, a mineral that can be transformed into mercury in furnaces, had been going on here for two thousand years since Roman times, when the metal was referred to as quicksilver. Due to dwindling supplies, the mine closed in 2003 when an educational attraction was dreamt up in conjunction with the United Nations' World Heritage Committee.

We are given hard hats, led to a mineshaft with a cage lift and taken down 50 metres into a hill in Castilla-La Mancha.

It is dark, damp and beautifully cool after the heat in the yard above, with pullies, ropes, mule baskets, drills, shafts and tunnels.

Eusedio, a large former miner who has worked here thirty-eight years (thirteen in tourism), is accompanying the group.

"Back then we had work, we had money and we were young," he says, referring to the days before the mine's closure. "Now everyone is old. We have breathed the air of sulphur dioxide [a byproduct of mercury production]. It is a smell. It is a smell like hell. But now it is gone. The town is dying and few tourists come."

We duck beneath some beams and move along another tunnel. "It is not the oldest mine in the world," he says. "That is in Swaziland. But this was the only one in the world open for two thousand years continuously. It was the biggest mercury mine in the world, but mercury was very bad for miners. At 25°C it starts evaporating. Without good masks: dangerous. In modern times we had them. But in the old days: dangerous. It passes straight into the central nervous system. Mercury poisoning. They had to take regular blood samples and if levels were high, they would send you to the sauna to sweat it out."

We continue down long dark passages for quite some time, inspecting the occasional shaft plunging into the depths of Spain.

Then Eusedio's face brightens.

"Train!" he says, pointing ahead. "It goes four hundred metres! It is like a toy train! Train!"

We have reached the reason Juanjo recommended a stop-off in Almadén and, like Juanjo, Eusedio seems to be a Spanish rail enthusiast.

A narrow metal train with flip-up doors with grille windows awaits. We board. A bell rings and we jerk forward, rattling like crazy, cages banging, bells clanking, Spanish tourists "ohhing" and "ahhing", clattering, clanking, gathering speed and banging some more, before emerging into dazzling sunlight and coming to a screeching stop.

One of the best rides of the trip so far.

Thank you, Juanjo and Eusedio.

Ruta de Don Quixote
Almadén to Alcázar de San Juan, via Ciudad Real

Almadén is a pleasant backwater in which to idle away a day. Narrow streets with heat-cracked tarmac and shuttered houses lead to squares with cafés where, if you order *platos combinados* (combined dishes), as I do, you may be served, as I am, enough food for four people: piles of chicken, egg salads, cheeses, breads, hash browns and more. Afterward, a man with yellow teeth and his arm in a sling may offer you directions to the perfectly preserved eighteenth-century hexagonal bullring. The sound of singing may emanate from a bar near the bus station near your *hostal* on your way back from the hexagonal bullring. And in the morning guests from a wedding may be in suits and evening dresses in the breakfast room, looking haggard, making pronouncements, slapping each other on the back and drinking G & Ts as you wait for your cab to Almadén Station, which you may share with a cheerful woman bearing a tattoo that says *BE STRONG GIRL*, and your driver may be a former miner who, when you ask what it was like in a mercury mine, may tell you: "It was the same as the sea: hard. The same as the sea: exciting. As exciting as a hard sea."

And then you may catch the *Media Distancia* 10:27 to Ciudad Real after waiting for a while with the station cat and watching large ants transporting pieces of leaves across the platform.

* * *

With a screech we are off through yesterday's hills as they roll onward, as we do, before levelling out on the final stretch into Ciudad Real.

There is a chance I may have been hasty when I booked a room in Ciudad Real. The capital city of a province of the same name is just over an hour from Almadén with less than half a page of my guidebook devoted to it (admittedly Almadén has no mention whatsoever, but I had Juanjo's word and that was enough). The half page declares that Ciudad Real, a city of 75,000 Spaniards, is a gateway to "flat surrounding countryside" and further research reveals that private investors spent a billion euros on constructing an international airport that opened in 2009 only to close a mere three years later, having failed miserably to meet ambitious projected passenger numbers. Apparently, the ease of getting to Madrid's airport – by train – had made it an airport too far.

However, the city is home to the Museo de Don Quixote and Ciudad Real is at the heart of La Mancha, the landscape across which the hero of Cervantes's *Don Quixote* (full book title: *The Ingenious Gentleman Don Quixote of La Mancha*) did his chivalrous stuff attacking "monsters" (in reality, windmills) in the company of his trusty sidekick, Sancho Panza, a simple farmer who is elevated in Quixote's world to "squire". I am only a short way into the seventeenth-century novel and have already fallen for the comedy of the set-up, which shoots down the pomposity of popular tales of gallant knights from the period and involves a drily observant narrator who from the very beginning tells his readers, instantly winning them over, that he cannot be bothered to begin his story in the manner of usual tales of gallantry with sonnets and epigrams from famous poets as he is too lazy to do so and, if he were totally honest, would prefer not to write a thing about Don Quixote for fear of exposing his own lack of learning. The narrator appears on the point of dropping his whole stupid idea when a friend suggests that he merely make up his own sonnets and epigrams and take it from there. Far simpler that way.

He does so – and so begins a book that has been translated into more languages than any other apart from the Bible. It is considered one of the cornerstones of Western literature, written at a time when many others were put in place. Both Cervantes and the slightly more prolific Shakespeare died in 1616.

Then there is the tale of Cervantes's extraordinary life.

He was born to a Spanish surgeon of little means in 1547. He fought as a soldier for Spain against the Turks in Italy in 1570. On attempting to return in 1575, he was captured by pirates and made to live as a slave in Algiers. After five years and numerous escape attempts, he was ransomed and brought back to Spain. He was subsequently imprisoned twice for accounting irregularities while working as a tax collector and as a purchasing agent for the Spanish Armada. He wrote when he could, not making much money. He filed for bankruptcy. Then, in 1605 at the tender age of fifty-eight, he published the first part of his masterpiece.

Hero and author seem to have shared a swashbuckling camaraderie – and, inspired by the spirit of Quixote, I cannot pass by a museum in his name. So I hop off at Ciudad Real Station, after a journey eventful only for almost having my backpack stolen.

Thinking that I could take a decent picture of the scenery between the carriages about halfway into the ride, I had gone to look but realized immediately that the window was too grimy and had spun around to return. As I did so, a fellow passenger was leaning over to examine my backpack. Taken aback by my speedy about-face, his eyes caught mine, in that split-second acknowledging: *oops, you've caught me.* A few moments later he scurried away.

It is quite a long walk down roads baking in the ongoing Saharan Bubble heatwave to the Don Quixote museum, but I have a spring in my step as: 1) I have just avoided theft of some sort, and 2) I am looking forward to discovering more about Cervantes and Quixote.

First impressions are that Ciudad Real is not exactly a looker.

A run of dreary fast-food joints (*tres hamburguesas diez euros* – "three burgers ten euros") morphs into an equally dreary street of mobile phone and cheap fashion shops. There is a smell of drains. A man drives slowly by in a canary-yellow car playing loud music with an arm hanging out of the window while his eyes scan the neighbourhood. The fashion shops lead to a square with a statue of a soldier on a horse and benches occupied by elderly men wearing straw hats; each hat subtly different as though making minor style statements. They watch the world go by, seeming disapproving in general of the early twenty-first century whether in Ciudad Real or anywhere else for that matter. Perhaps they have a point.

I reach the *museo*, outside of which is a statue of Don Quixote and Sancho Panza. The first is on his bucking or perhaps collapsing horse, named Rocinante in the novel. Sancho Panza, meanwhile, wearily leads a donkey.

Inside, after leaving my backpack with a security guard who seems shocked by a visitor, I go down a ramp into an air-conditioned space with a series of portraits of figures from the novel. A hologram depicting Cervantes at his desk mutters some words in one corner, though I do not feel inclined to stand in front of a hologram. In a matter of minutes, I walk around this space that has been the occasion of a stop on the tracks and a diversion through the Saharan Bubble with an increasingly heavy backpack (due to an accumulation of local tourist maps of Spain).

I collect my backpack from the sympathetic guard. I cancel my booking in Ciudad Real and return to the station, where a ticket assistant, upon hearing of my journey, says: "Michael Portillo! Are you Michael Portillo?"

I explain to the ticket assistant that I am not Britain's former Secretary of State for Defence in the 1990s who has since transformed into an entertaining popular train broadcaster and writer endearingly prone to wearing mismatching colourful linen jackets and trousers and travelling the globe while clutching ancient rail guides. Whereupon the ticket assistant appears saddened and even a little depressed but sells me a ticket to a place called Alcázar de San Juan anyway.

Train two of the day departs at 14:20, arrival time 15:26.

On board the monitors are not working, but I do not need them to know it is *muy caliente* (very hot), as usual, outside. We move slowly past a lorry yard. Confirming my guidebook's analysis, extremely flat surrounding countryside soon emerges; fields with soil the colour of tomatoes spread on Spanish *tostadas*. Combine harvesters kick up trails of yellow dust before we progress into fruit orchards followed by strange ash-coloured fields, golden-velvet fields, more tomato *tostadas*-coloured fields and a section with an electricity power plant, a factory with a tall cooling tower and a winery named Rodriguez & Berger connected to perfect rows of emerald vines.

And then I see them: Don Quixote's windmills!

On the right-hand side of the train on a hill a couple of minutes outside Alcázar de San Juan, there they are. Rising on a fold of grassland, four ancient windmills stare down at the 14:20 from Ciudad Real, their sails dead still and attached to wide whitewashed bases. It was such traditional windmills that prompted Don Quixote's famous charge across the plains on Rocinante, declaring that he would put the vile monsters to a sticky end, restore natural justice and take the shares of their booty as any knight deserves after such an act of selfless bravery. Despite the protestations of Sancho Panza – "What giants? They are windmills" – he attacks one of the "giants" at top speed only to be thrown to the ground by its sails. When Sancho Panza catches up on his donkey, lifts his master to his feet – muttering, "For God's sake!" – Don Quixote is quick to put forward his theory that an enemy has magically transformed the giants into windmills and haughtily declare to his sidekick that affairs of war are "subject to continual change", upon which Sancho Panza further mutters, "God's will be done" and asks how badly he is hurt.

Pleased I no longer feel obliged to track down Alcázar de San Juan's most famous tourist sight – I had expected to go in search of these windmills but cannot see the point now – I arrive at Alcázar de San Juan Station, admire its elegant orange-brick facade decorated with yellow and blue tiles in a pretty floral pattern, and proceed down a few long empty furnace-hot streets lined by two-storey buildings with grilled windows and heavy wooden doors to Hotel Hidalgo Quijada.

This is a comfortable hotel on a side street and a good place for a siesta following a day's leaping on and off trains. It is easy to find due to its tower adorned with neoclassical columns, high arched windows, and the flags of Spain, the European Union and Castilla-La Mancha (red and white with a picture of a medieval castle). Grand enough even for Don Quixote: *hidalgo* translates as gentleman. I do like Hotel Hidalgo Quijada.

It is OK to be lazy every now and then on a long train journey around Spain. In Alcázar de San Juan, I do just this.

After a long siesta, I go for a stroll to Plaza España, where I sit at a bar, drink a *cerveza* and watch the world go by. On one side of the square is another pair of statues of Don Quixote and Sancho Panza – the Cervantes connection is flogged for all it's worth in Castilla-La Mancha, although there does not seem to be a Quixote theme park anywhere and, to be fair, it is not as though there is a booming Quixote tourist trade going on. My guidebook mentions that tourist officials in the *comunidad autónoma* have tried hard to promote a *Ruta de Don Quixote* but to little avail. Hardly anyone is about. Just locals stopping to chat to one another.

It is noticeable not only that Spaniards like noise generally but also that they like to talk quite animatedly at most times of day. And fresh from my siesta I have a theory. While most northern Europeans are wearily checking their watches or perhaps, as in Britain, enjoying a cup of tea at four o'clock and hoping this will suffice to provide an afternoon lift, the Spanish seem always to have just woken up from a nap and to be full of beans because they are well rested. Shops close from two o'clock until five o'clock in the afternoon. That is a reasonable length of time for a good snooze. Restaurants are closed from about four o'clock until eight o'clock or even nine o'clock. Plenty of time to catch some Zs. And I am sure others have different siesta patterns. The result is that days meander somewhat but go in little energetic bursts, meaning encounters have greater gusto than usually mustered in northern climes. This I offer as an *insight into Spanish culture* after *cerveza* number two from my vantage point at a table at a bar on Plaza España in Alcázar de San Juan. Admittedly, I do not feel as though I am breaking any particularly new ground here à la Morris, but one ought to, I suppose, at least give it a try.

Church bells ring in a jaunty tune across the rooftops of Alcázar de San Juan. Down small lanes, tapas bars and the odd smart restaurant are to be found. Neither wanting tapas nor an expensive meal, I arrive at a kebab restaurant near Hotel Hidalgo Quijada. Inside I order *bocadillo de jamón y tomate* – decent – as well as a crunchy potato-like side dish that I bite into and crunch for a short while before realizing I am eating part of a mussel shell and should not be doing this. When I stop eating the shell, this side dish is fine too. Spain is playing Germany at football in the under-twenty-one European league and regulars are glued to the game. Spain is winning and everyone seems happy.

I go back to the hotel and order a glass of *vino tinto* at the reception bar, where pictures of the hallowed windmills and bullfighting posters decorate the mustard-yellow walls.

The *vino tinto* tastes off.

I ask if there is another *vino tinto* available.

"But it is *rioja*," says the barmaid, stressing the wine region as though to suggest: *the very best, the absolute undisputed very best*.

"Perhaps," I reply. "But it doesn't taste right."

The barmaid looks utterly confused by the possibility.

Another *insight into Spanish culture* I have been noticing is the almost unfailing faith in wine from the Rioja region. I may have touched on this in Pamplona.

"Oh," she says. "I do not drink red wine. I will get you another."

So conclude my experiences of Alcázar de San Juan, apart from sleeping, checking out and walking back to the station.

Down by the Río Tagus
Alcázar de San Juan to Aranjuez

The journey to Aranjuez is less than an hour. At the station, portraits of commuters gaze down from the window of a long train carriage in a colourful mural on a wall facing the main platform. Some wear cocktail dresses and pearl necklaces. Others are in business suits. A few indulgently drink glasses of wine. Yet more are gossiping, while one couple is locked in a romantic embrace *sin ropa* (without clothing) and a character wearing a beret and glasses at the very end of the carriage, who may or may not be the artist, peers expressionlessly across Alcázar de San Juan Station as if considering who he will include in his next work.

Great stuff.

I catch the 10:55 to Aranjuez, which pulls up a few minutes late, unusually for Spanish trains in my experiences so far.

Sure, George Orwell had his troubles with punctuality, but everything has seemed timely up to now if you ignore the idiosyncrasies of Renfe Feve, which I actually quite enjoyed, looking back on it.

We fly along the flat fertile La Mancha plains at 159 kilometres an hour (99 miles per hour).

Aranjuez has been a royal estate since the time of Philip II in 1560 – the ever-busy king wanted a hideaway south of his new capital and liked the look of the meadows by a peaceful bend of the Río Tagus. The countryside hereabouts is renowned for its good hunting as well as its abundance: asparagus, tomatoes, potatoes, strawberries, beetroots, sunflowers, artichokes and jalapeño peppers all flourish. This is a *gorgeous* corner of Spain, as Deirdre and Phillip back in Madrid might have put it.

The name Aranjuez is believed to have come from the Basque word for hawthorn: *arantza*. Many important events have taken place at its palace, including the signing of a document to cede parts of northern Africa to Morocco in 1781, while in 1801 Spain gave back Louisiana to France in a document agreed there. As I learned at the Madrid rail museum, Spain's second railway line, from Atocha Station, began in 1851 – which gives an idea of its place in the pecking order of Spain. Aranjuez is now a World Heritage Site and a big tourist attraction.

And it is home to a rather fancy station.

Inside it is hard not to stare upward and admire the majestic ceiling of wood carvings painted in Moorish geometric shapes set within rectangular spaces that look like a series of carpets that you might find in a mosque (except they are on the ceiling). Despite the expulsion of the Arabs so many centuries ago, the artistic influence of the Moors clearly lives on here, as it does in so many of the restored fortresses across Spain, with some of the finest to come in the south. Walls are clad in yellow and blue tiles with a floral pattern and a mysterious *AZM* motif. Outside, high arches are framed by neoclassical columns and the roof is adorned by rows of unusual bobble-shaped stonework with a grand clock perched way above the entrance as though for the benefit of passing birds. The Moorish style is continued on the facade with further tiles and geometric patterns. There is almost an art deco look to the whole building which is hard to pin down architecturally: a kind of modernization of an old Arab palace for railway purposes. I am not surprised to learn it was built in the 1920s and the *AZM* turns out to relate to an old train company that once operated on this line: *Compañía de los Ferrocarriles de Madrid a Zaragoza y Alicante.*

There is a name for the style that mixes Moorish and Western European architecture: *arte Mudéjar.* Aranjuez Station seems to be a very good example.

In the ticket hall I enquire about the *Tren de la Fresa* (Strawberry Train) between here and Madrid. It is definitely not running at this time of year. I buy a ticket on the 07:02 regional service to Cuenca for tomorrow, from where I intend to move on to València the following day.

Very soon I will be back by the Spanish seaside – the last time I saw waves was on the deck of the British frigate back in A Coruña, which feels like quite a long time ago now.

What a joy it is to potter about in Spain on trains – you end up in all sorts of unexpected spots.

CHAPTER NINE
ARANJUEZ TO ALCOY, VIA CUENCA AND VALÈNCIA

SIN RUMBO (AIMLESSLY) WITH PLEASURE

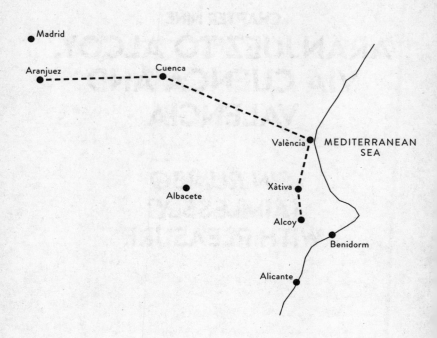

Aranjuez is a sleepy sort of royal Spanish town. It is a mile from the station to the centre and, keeping up my rule not to take a cab in Spain unless it is provided free by Renfe Feve or the one from Almadén to the station, I walk this distance in the heatwave, crossing a housing estate and weaving through side streets to Hostal Castilla.

My room here faces a peaceful yard with geranium pots and has a window with a grille and apricot-coloured walls. The *hostal* is next to a *mercería* (haberdashery) and across the road from a *vulcanizadora* (tyre repair shop). Plane trees line Carrera de Andalucia, which leads straight to a grand square, presumably for royal parades, with a fountain in the middle and Aranjuez's official tourist information office on one side.

"Monday is the unlucky day for tourists" are the opening words of the tourist information officer. The royal palace is closed. "But you may enter the gardens for free and take photographs of the gardens. Get your camera ready for action!"

He points at various faded blown-up pictures of gardens on the tourist office walls. "They are open until nine thirty tonight. This is the Garden of the Island." He points at a map and draws a big sloppy circle round the garden. "It has many mythological fountains." He points at another garden on the map and draws another sloppy circle. "And this here is the largest fenced garden in Europe."

"Bigger than Kew Gardens?" I ask.

"Fence! Fence!" he says, defending Jardín del Príncipe's "largest fenced garden" status – suggesting, it seems, that Kew does not qualify.

"But isn't Kew fenced off?" I ask.

"It depends how you define 'fence'!" he replies, as though daring me to do just that. His name is José-Manuel and he is a middle-aged bundle of energy with an unconventional tell-it-as-it-is tourist-information-office style. He wears high-top Converse trainers, rolled-up jean shorts and a T-shirt. His hair is cropped and he has a big elastic grin that exposes long rows of bright white teeth.

I say that I suppose Kew has walls as well as fences. "There, there, you see!" he replies. "Fences! Fences! You can look it up on the internet!"

There are parts of Jardín del Príncipe that are not open to the public. "Here!" He points on a map to one section. "This is not visitable."

The royal palace is free to visit on Wednesdays and Thursdays at certain times, he tells me, "for people from the European Union and Latin America". He pauses. "Just show your passport – you will be OK until Brexit."

He grins a big elastic grin and hops to another counter to tell new tourists about the unlucky day.

* * *

It does not feel that way to me. Yes, I would have liked to see inside the Palacio Real, but the palace is closed and that is that and, anyway, there are plenty of palaces in Spain and I can see this one from its garden for free.

The sun is fierce but the royals of old knew what they were doing and there are plenty of shaded walkways leading round the giant square into the royal gardens. Here are many more fountains, various sculptures of partially dressed classical figures, stone urns, a channel of diverted water from the Río Tagus (with a strange feature that looks like a weir at one end) and a multitude of shaded paths leading between trees with plants irrigated by small streams. A breeze crosses the island, created by the diverted water channel, and it is refreshing and cool at the back of the palace. The old royals knew what was required for a Spanish summer.

The palace itself – this one built in the eighteenth century with the idea being to establish a Spanish version of Versailles – is a large solid orange-brick building that looks a bit weather-worn and must have hundreds of rooms. It does not live up to Versailles, but there is something splendid about its location by the river and it is easy to understand its regal appeal. Isabella II, who ruled in the nineteenth century until being deposed and exiled in 1868, is believed to have enjoyed the palace in particular; often, it is said, in the company of men who were not the Duke of Cádiz, her king consort.

Maze-like box hedges zigzag just about everywhere and the smell of lavender fills the air. Fountains trickle beside magnolia trees and cicadas rattle away. It soon becomes evident, from inspecting the classical figures more closely, that the old Spanish royals had a good sense of humour and a taste for the absurd. One sculpture is of a semi-clothed man peering upward as though in raptures of haughty ecstasy with an eagle resting by his feet. Another depicts a maiden with a hand clasped to her bosom while her right foot stamps on the head of a large, vicious-looking fish whose tail curls round her legs leading to her private parts. Nearby, a naked man is shown pulling open the jaws of a lion. Yet another maiden, with a serene and casual expression, is in the middle of tussling with a goat. Cobras strangle antelopes. Three-headed dogs howl. Crocodiles smile. Toads grimace. Herculean figures wrestle one another, fountain water spouting from their gaping mouths.

Compared to the grandiose fountains and figures of Versailles, Aranjuez's garden embellishments have a definite comical edge. It is as though the Spanish royals are taking the mickey out of the pomposity of their northern neighbours – having a bit of fun at the expense of the French aristocracy, who often appear to have got up their noses if historical stories of meddling Gallic nobles are anything to go by.

On one occasion in 1714, Elisabetta Farnese, the new Italian-born queen of Spain by marriage to Philip V, famously threw out French advisers who had been exerting great influence on Philip's rule, thus gaining her widespread popularity. It was around this period that Philip V had the palace remodelled, and Elisabetta – considered by many to have been the power behind the throne to such an extent that she in turn was soon quite unpopular – enjoyed coming here very much. It was at Aranjuez that she died in 1766, aged seventy-three, having effectively ruled Spain for large spells during the eighteenth century.

Philip V, the first member of the House of Bourbon to rule Spain and a grandson of France's Louis XIV, had been a weak king prone to bouts of depression and rising from his royal rooms each day at two o'clock in the afternoon, by which time Elisabetta would have seen to most of the state affairs of the day one way or another from her queen's chamber. Unusually for a king, Philip V shared this chamber; most had separate rooms from their queen. The irony of all of this is that the French advisers who Elisabetta ejected as her first act as queen – arresting them and having them escorted to the border – had selected her as they had been informed, quite wrongly, that she was as weak and malleable as Philip V. This would have suited their shadowy influence. Fresh from various parties along the way from Italy to Spain, including a bash with the Prince of Monaco, Elisabetta was, however, not exactly a shy and retiring type.

Events of the past seem to hang in the air down by the Río Tagus.

The biggest fenced garden in Europe (perimeter: 7 kilometres) is indeed large, with few people about down by the waterfront, just the odd noisy goose. I walk around for a while, enjoying a stroll after so many hours spent on the trains of central Spain.

Yet the most marvellous thing about Jardín del Príncipe is, for me, just outside the main gate not far from a statue of Alfonso XII, one of Isabella II's progeny; possibly or possibly not anything to do with the Duke of Cádiz.

El Rana Verde (The Green Frog) is a superb restaurant with fine dining and a casual menu too. Here, you may eat a hot pork sandwich with jalapeno sauce, a speciality recommended by the waitress, at a table beneath a watery mist spray, rest your feet and feel quite at one with the world as you let an hour drift lazily by.

Excellent food. Excellent service. Excellent watery mist spray; you soon learn to love watery mist sprays in the hot plains of Spain.

I return to Hostal Castilla for a siesta.

I fall fast asleep for quite a long time.

I seem to be slipping into Spanish ways – and I like it.

Turísta de arte abstracto
Aranjuez to Cuenca

Hostal Castilla is a quirky one. A collection of painted tin soldiers in a glass cabinet and a collection of rocks laid out on a tray are to be found in the hallway by the reception. This space is also home to an old sewing machine, a stone lion painted gold and a grainy black-and-white photograph of a steam locomotive pulling bulky wooden carriages across a bridge on the Río Tagus (should any rail enthusiasts be considering stopping by). There is barely room to move between geranium pots in the courtyard, which has a community feel as apartments above the rooms of the *hostal* are occupied by locals. In the evening, after tapas at a bar in Plaza de la Constitución, I am greeted by three elderly women who say *"hola"* in unison as I pass below, returning to my room.

A good pit stop for Aranjuez.

Yes, I may have sung the praises of Spanish *hostals* before, but they really are quite perfect for this type of trip: down-to-earth, reasonably priced and friendly. Hostal Castilla is another *eleccion perfecta* (perfect choice) and in the morning my trio of balcony friends waves cheerily with *buenas dias's* and *adios's* as I move on to the station.

The café at Aranjuez Station is a quirky one, too: chaotic and popular with commuters, serving good black coffee in a tiled side room with beams and a rubber tree plant. Sipping *café largo* number two, I set my thoughts to the journey ahead. The regional service departing at 07:02 is scheduled to arrive at Cuenca at 09:16 and I have picked this route toward València, Spain's third city, deliberately for its slowness. It is possible to reach Cuenca from Madrid on an AVE high-speed service in 54 minutes or from Madrid all the way to València in 1 hour and 40 minutes. This regional ride is genuinely *lento* (slow).

The 07:02 pulls up.

A stationmaster in a red peaked cap blows a whistle and flaps a red flag. The train putters and hums away, with a blood-orange sun rising beyond a line of firs on a spur of land on the outskirts of Aranjuez. The feeling of renewal – another train in Spain – is strong. This is all part of the pleasure of catching a lot of rides on the Iberian Peninsula. Stop… look about… move on.

A kindly conductor with her hair in a bob pulls down a blind on the opposite side of the almost empty carriage as she notices the sun is in my eyes.

"Better?" she asks before checking my ticket.

There are not a great number of excitements on the train to Cuenca.

At Santa Cruz de la Zarza Station a man with a plastic bag disembarks while a man with a wheelie bag embarks. We are in deep countryside surrounded by vines. A rabbit hops along by the track. Two women board at Tarancón Station and begin to gossip. A group of four young men joins at Huete Station and one of them begins to play Arabic music quite loudly on his smartphone, whistling annoyingly to the tune. This goes on for some time before a deer skips across a wheat field and the guys in the gang turn to look, the whistler pausing in his whistle and pointing at the deer. The leader of the gang, who wears shades and a baseball cap pulled low and has a gravelly voice and a fierce face, breaks into a wide smile – and the gang peer out, enjoying the sight of the deer gambolling away.

Arid hills with deep walnut-like contours mark the approach to Cuenca, where a nondescript station awaits, as does a walk along nondescript streets into town, following a man with dreadlocks so long they reach the back of his knees. This man is a giant, well over six feet tall. His dreadlocks alone must be about the length of the height of an average Spanish man (five feet eight inches) or average Spanish woman (five feet three inches). Extraordinary.

At Hostal La Ribera del Júcar beside the quiet, green Río Júcar, Fernando, the receptionist, hands me an air-conditioning control, a television control, a room key and a map. He is in his twenties and has cropped black hair and a black T-shirt, looking more like a singer from an indie band than a typical *hostal* receptionist. People so far in

Cuenca – or maybe this is just misleading first impressions – seem to have an alternative streak.

"Here," he says loudly, pointing on the map. "The abstract art museum. Beautiful! The best in Spain!"

He pauses and reflects on this.

"Actually," he says more quietly, "the second best, after the one in Madrid."

He points to Plaza Mayor. "Very beautiful!"

He points to Puente de San Pablo. "Very beautiful also!"

The same is said of the cathedral, a convent, some "hanging houses" on the edge of a cliff and a church on a hill. The very beautiful bits of Cuenca are up in the old town, not on the walk from the station to the *hostal*.

Then Fernando says that, although he enjoys the *tranquilo* (calm) of Cuenca, "my personality is more suited to northern Europe. It is much too hot for me here."

He looks at the map again and recommends walking to the top of the hill in the old town: "Very beautiful!"

And, as he is about to make further tourist-sight suggestions, a British couple with a Staffordshire bull terrier enters the reception.

Paul and Gill are from close to Manchester and caught the ferry from Portsmouth to Le Havre in France, from where they drove to Spain after breaking the journey with an overnight stay near Bordeaux. He is an aerospace engineer and she is a retired social worker.

Like Fernando, they have been suffering from the heat. "It said 48ºC at the pharmacy in Burgos," says Gill, trumping my pharmacy 46ºC. "It was 38ºC in the shade."

It is almost impossible for fellow northern Europeans visiting Spain in the summer not to talk about temperatures.

They have had a sweaty night. "When we arrived yesterday there was an electric storm and it shorted the air conditioning," says Gill.

Paul cuts in: "We have two things to tell you." These are, firstly, that they are visiting his sister who works at La Manga sports club in the south of Spain. He explains her duties at the club for a while.

"The second thing?" I ask.

"Oh yes," Paul says. "Close to Saint-Émilion on the drive down we visited some catacombs and it was lovely down there: 13°C."

Their dog is named Flynn after Errol Flynn. They wear sandals and sensible clothing in shades of blue and grey. They drive a Mercedes-Benz and are booking hotels and *hostals* "on the hoof using the internet", just like me. To pass the time in the car, Gill is reading out loud the Treaty of Versailles. They have an interest in history.

I ask them what they like most about their journey.

"Well, you see, you've got me there," says Paul. "You've got me."

"Why?" I ask.

"Well, you see, I'm not a man of words." He pauses. "Words." Further pause as he tries to nail the right ones. "The spirit of adventure?" I suggest tentatively. "Yes!" he booms. "Yes! There you have it. Yes! This time we haven't even booked a return ticket! I've left the lads running the business." Making parts for planes. "Yes, that's right, no ticket back. We're saying to everyone: it's an adventure!"

Paul is on a roll. "As an engineer I've enjoyed seeing all these Spanish cities," he says. "The buildings, the structures: I look at them as an engineer and think: *How did they do that five hundred years ago? It's incredible.*"

They give me their email before departing for the next leg of their drive south – and I relate this encounter as it seems as though driving round Spain can be liberating too, even if going by train is obviously far superior and generally better all round.

* * *

Fernando's many recommendations make an excellent guide to Cuenca.

From the *hostal* it takes 15 minutes to walk along the green river, cross a footbridge and ascend a steep lane to the old town. Cuenca (population: 56,000) is built on a hill with gorges dropping below as two rivers converge and the scenery is, I can confirm, *muy hermoso* (very beautiful). Rose-hued granite cliffs plunge into tight valleys. Pines cling to slender, scar-like ridges. Birds soar in the lavender-blue sky.

The *muy hermoso* old town is squeezed on to the hilltop and ancient buildings are painted in a kaleidoscope of yellows, pinks, greens and purplish reds. From the far side of Puente de San Pablo, a red metal-framed bridge that spans one of the gorges, you get the best view of the cliffs beneath the cathedral and of the *casas colgadas* ("hanging houses"), fifteenth-century wooden houses with cantilevered balconies dangling over the cliff edge.

Inside the houses, Spain's second finest abstract art collection (I am not sure which one exactly Fernando regards as better in Madrid) turns out to be a series of minimalist whitewashed rooms containing minimalist mainly black-and-white works of art mainly from the fifties and sixties. There is a clinical coolness to them, and absence of colour, that may not be to all tastes. But that is to miss the point, I realize after a while, as the subtleties of the works take time to emerge and the whole point is to stare for a while and allow the shapes to bring to mind landscapes, figures, planets, rivers and seas. Anyway, this is what I assume on the basis that so many are named "ravine" or "countryside" or "little pilgrims" or whatever – and look *nothing like these things* until you give it a good go.

The paintings here, many completed locally, taking advantage of the remote setting and clear skies during its mid-twentieth-century artist-colony heyday, follow on from the groundbreaking works of Pablo Picasso (1881–1973) and Joan Miró (1893–1983). Salvador Dalí of Figueres (1904–1989) seems to have been creating a tradition of his own that perhaps passed by the abstract artists of Cuenca.

Museo de Arte Abstracto Español opened in 1966. One of the best things about the collection, gathered by the artist Fernando Zóbel (1924–1984) and later overseen by a wealthy financier, is the setting. The cliffs and the sky are framed in the windows of the six-hundred-year-old cantilevered balconies, providing nature's glorious sun-baked contrast to the mainly monochrome art. The scenery complements the art. And there is another factor. Standing right by the windows, knowing you are way up above the gorge, your feet held above this gorge by a six-hundred-year-old wooden structure, takes a leap of faith. While you are wondering what on earth the art is about and marvelling at the views, you are also secretly considering standards of workmanship of several hundred years ago in central Spain. At least you are if you are me.

As Paul back at the *hostal* so rightly commented: *how did they do it?*

This question is even more relevant at the cathedral, a medieval masterpiece with its towering columns, vaulted ceilings, enormous stained-glass windows and cloisters. All teetering on the edge of a cliff as it has done for a very long time. Cuenca Cathedral, just like so many other cathedrals in Spain, was built where there was once a mosque. Classical music plays from discreet speakers and at the back in a hidden-away chamber are intricate carvings from an ancient facade that was torn down to be replaced by another facade in the eighteenth century. Stone figures play flutes or sit crossed-legged looking thoughtful or scratch their heads as if at a loss or possessively clutch bags of coins – fragments of a medieval world that seem forgotten in this tucked-away back room.

This is my favourite art in Cuenca. I do afterward go to the Fundación Antonio Pérez, yet another major modern art gallery, although this one, in a former Carmelite monastery by another precipice, is more chaotic than the Museo de Arte Abstracto Español.

Think crumpled oil cans, traffic signs with "STOP" wittily turned into "POTS", washing pegs fashioned in the shape of wastepaper baskets, shelves of blue bottles, plastic cocktail stirrers twisted into erotic forms, tables of randomly scattered objects, sets of photographs of rusting tractors in fields and stark video displays with discordant music. Dalí would feel more at home here.

At the top of the hill the views are as *muy hermoso* (very beautiful) as Fernando promised. Skinny cats prowl by tourist bistros while below a Spanish Grand Canyon spreads out and you realize you are very glad you stopped off on the line on the way to València. A guitar twangs across a ravine and somewhere way down below the thin green snakes of Ríos Júcar and Huécar meet to form a bigger green snake.

Having had my fill of art and views, it is a pleasant walk back down to Barrio de San Anton near the *hostal*. Here a man is practising the jazz trumpet in a cycle repair shop; a Spanish Miles Davis lurking amid spare chains and tyres. His music drifts into the lane towards an almost empty bar with a quiz show playing loudly in a corner. I order a glass of eighty-cent wine accompanied by free anchovies and olives

This is a friendly family-owned bar and the middle-aged daughter of the owner asks me about my trip. Then, after another eighty-cent wine is poured, she opens up. All is not so well with her right now. "With the crisis we have gone from bad to worse," she says, referring to the Spanish recession from 2008 to 2014. "The economy of the country is down, and people cannot find work. There is nothing. The banks do not give credit. People have to march to protest. The students who finish studies have to go to other countries to work as there is nothing here. Two of my nieces have gone to other countries as there is no work. I have a mortgage to pay and bank troubles. The bank has taken my home and has enriched itself."

She says all of this in a matter-of-fact manner, as though this is simply *the way it is* for her and others. The crisis, it would appear, is far from over for everyone – not just in Extramadura, as Jorge back in Mérida had said.

Beautiful station, beautiful city
Cuenca to València

The ticket office and main hall at Cuenca Station are closed in the morning, shutters down; I have arrived early for the 09:18 to València and the stationmaster has not turned up yet. Across the street, I now notice, is a fine work of *abstracto* street art representing a Renfe train haunted by alien-like ghosts with purple tidal waves of paint pouring down from one side and a mysterious hand rising from out of nowhere clasping a ticket marked *sin rumbo* (aimlessly).

So much so normal for Cuenca.

The Ulises station café, to one side, is open and I drink my morning coffee at a table on the main platform, noticing something unusual. Cuenca Station is popular with dog walkers. A woman strolls by in the company of a Dalmatian. Another leads a white fluffy poodle. A man steps across the tracks with his pit bull terrier; there are no trains and he must know the timetable. No one is around to stop him, anyway. A floor-mopper from the café smokes a cigarette while listening to pop music on her phone and watching the dog walkers. The stationmaster arrives. The shutters are raised. I buy a ticket.

Not long afterward, the train for Spain's third largest city arrives.

If yesterday's train was *lento*, this one is *muy lento*, taking four hours to cover 102 miles. It rattles off five minutes late. The conductor is the same one from yesterday, Señorita Hernandez, who says: "Hello again." She inspects my ticket. "You going to València now, eh? *Muchas gracias.*" As before, she fixes the blind to keep out the low morning light. I am beginning to recognize and get to know Spanish train conductors.

So begins what has to be one of my favourite rides in Spain.

Outside town we are soon sliding past a sea of golden-yellow crops with forest-clad hills rising on the horizon. Ravines with orange-tinted soil open up as we slip across a viaduct with the shadowy outline of the train crossing the arches in the field below. Soon jagged orange rock formations fill the windows, before disappearing and more golden-yellow crops flooding the landscape as far as the eye can see, these ones being worked by combine harvesters. Then the train rises again, moving slowly along viaducts above gorges and valleys of fir trees. One elevated section of track along which the train tilts sharply has a *20 kilometres an hour* (13 miles a hour) speed sign. It is so *lento* now you could just about outrun this train.

I have the carriage to myself as vineyards, fruit orchards, ramshackle farmhouses and little stations with red roses in plant pots come and go. Yet more rocky landscape leads onward, and pink ribbons of flowers follow hidden riverbeds, just as they did between Mérida and Almadén.

The scenery is so enticing it almost puts you in a trance. As one o'clock approaches, I snap out of it as skyscrapers rise to the right and we traverse a wide dried-out river. Families seem to be living in old cargo containers next to a scrapyard close to a dual carriageway on the run-in to València-Sant Isidre Station, where the train stops and reverses direction. We move along a tunnel of graffiti with apartments almost hanging over the tracks and arrive at Estació del Nord in the centre of València.

What a ride... and what a station.

The train from Cuenca has pulled up at a platform outside an enormous wrought-iron shed with a skylight with green glass that sends delicious shards of emerald light across the platforms as the few passengers of the 09:18 shuffle toward the station entrance where, inside the station hall, I stop in my tracks. Perhaps I am developing a thing about the train stations of Spain, but this really is a good one. To the left is a row of original wooden ticket booths fitted out with high smoked-glass windows and fluted wooden panels inset with tiles decorated with red and orange flowers. Way up above a ceramic mosaic of leaves and flowers fills the gaps between exposed wooden beams held up by columns with yet more mosaics of oranges on branches surrounded by lamps shaped like tenpin bowling balls. The walls to the shed are decked out in pink ceramic mosaics with more orange fruit decorations, while the far wall by the station front comes complete with stained-glass windows and great mosaic panels bearing the message *good journey* in several languages in gold tiled lettering, including Chinese, Italian and Spanish, naturally: *buen viaje*.

A beautiful wooden clock is positioned in pride of place at the far end with a clock face embedded with wooden numbers and a panel of yet more oranges, while beyond this is an amazing antechamber that appears once to have been a waiting room, perhaps for first-class passengers. Here, the mosaic artists have gone to town installing murals depicting country houses surrounded by palm trees, maidens picking flowers, church bell towers, gardens alive with blossom, cascading waterfalls, and glistening lakes with sailing vessels and ducks. All of this in an explosion of colour that combines to create a visual feast that has quite a few train travellers, like me, staring upward and all around in wonder.

Outside, the station facade is just as extravagant – a flamboyant custard-cream-coloured palace of towers and turrets with stucco in the shape of oranges and flowers, tiled panels of maidens and water nymphs, and a statue of an eagle proudly spreading its wings at the very top above the Spanish and European Union flags.

Despite its name, the station is just to the south of the *centro* – the old Compañía de los Caminos de Hierro del Norte de España railway line used to arrive here – and dates from 1917. Estació del Nord is considered a fine example of Valèncian art nouveau architecture that some prefer to call *modernista*. It is, quite simply, superb.

It takes a good half an hour to drag myself away, down past the Plaza de Toros and along Avenida del Puerto to a hotel that turns out to be close to the beach, stopping halfway at a no-nonsense, good-value bistro for a bowl of delicious peppery *gazpacho* tomato and garlic soup served with *tortilla*, broad beans and black-eyed peas (after the fiery mussels in Santiago, my best meal so far in Spain). I seem to be having excellent luck today all round: dreamy train rides, fancy stations, fantastic lunches at neighbourhood hang-outs. Not a tourist, other than me, in sight.

I could go on here to describe how the room at my hotel is the most comfortable of all the many rooms I have stayed at in Spain, with a charming little balcony with a table and chairs right at the top. I could continue by recounting my lovely stroll to the port with the hum of cargo ships and ferries across the water and little bars serving chilled wine to the sound of ambient dance tracks spun by

DJs wearing mirrored shades. I could supply purple prose aplenty about the long sweep of soft sand beach in the late afternoon heat and the beautiful people and the laid-back vibe by the marina with the yachting crews and scuba divers returning from days out on the water. I could relate how marvellously relaxing it is simply to rest on a wall by the long row of palms on the promenade by Playa el Cabanyal and listen to the congo beat and the trumpets and the trombones of a Latino-reggae street busking band as the sky turns pink and then lilac as the last of the sunset fades and the sound of water laps gently on the shore. I could describe how the heat of the day thereafter gently softened and bathers splashed at jetties with cordoned-off swimming zones by snazzy cultural centres with crowds of smart young Valèncians happily gossiping as singers performed soulful Spanish songs accompanied by toe-tapping guitarists. I could finish off with a little mention of how pleasant it is afterward, back on Avenida del Puerto, to stop at cosy one-euro *tapas* places amid the chatter of locals before returning to your private balcony and gazing up at the stars and thinking back to the day's journey across long, high viaducts above the dramatic ravines and honey-coloured plains of south-eastern Spain while feeling quite at peace with the world.

But I would not want to make anyone jealous. Let's just put it this way: València, without even bothering with its *centro*, is a fantastic place to find yourself after crossing the hot dusty tracks all the way from the border with Portugal.

Oh, what a perfect day and what a great place to reach the *Mar Mediterráneo* on the slow train from Cuenca.

* * *

It is impossible really to do justice to València when just passing through. The city of 2.5 million may get overlooked by most "city break" tourists to Spain, who tend to be drawn to Barcelona and Madrid, yet this is a Spanish metropolis to savour in more than a couple of days. A week would be about right, allowing yourself to slip into its easy rhythm of life, of which I only just have a taste.

A quick rundown – and some voices – will have to suffice.

Spain's third city has had two big, physical upheavals in its quite recent past. The first was the dismantling of the fine city walls in 1871 to make way for a ring road; the remnants of these walls can be seen at two grand stone gates, one of which is just to the north of the old town on the edge of the lively Barrio del Carmen (aka Tapas Central) and was where Republicans kept treasures moved from Madrid's Prado museum safe during bombardment in the Spanish Civil War. València was the last Republican city to fall.

The second was a decision in the late 1950s to divert the Río Túria after a devastating flood in 1957 during which more than eighty people died and some neighbourhoods were under 5 metres of water. The result of this necessary shifting of the river has been to create one of the finest urban parks in Europe – or perhaps anywhere. Instead of allowing developers to move in willy-nilly with residential blocks or offices, city officials declared the former riverbed to be mainly parkland, with the odd tennis court, five-a-side football pitch or mini Ferris wheel permitted in the very centre and an extraordinary futuristic Ciutat de les Arts y Ciències (City of Arts and Sciences) complex built on the far southern edge, a sort of theme park of the future with concert halls, cinemas, science museums and a vast aquarium.

Paths for walking, jogging and cycling were laid all the way along the old riverbed, and now València is one of the best cities in Europe, or perhaps anywhere, for cyclists. I have never seen so many bike-rental shops.

Add to this a past rich with Romans, Visigoths, Moors and the story of a *real* knight whose exploits caught the popular imagination of the Spanish; from whom Don Quixote, you could say, owes his lineage. El Cid was a maverick twelfth-century knight, a brilliant soldier-for-hire who terrified large parts of Spain before taking València from the Moors for himself in 1094. Such were his powers of command that he became a respected (and greatly feared) ruler among Christians and Arabs alike. It is said that when he died, many were petrified to watch as his body was taken by horse for burial in Burgos.

Add to this medieval churches, an old Gothic silk exchange, first-rate *modernista* architecture, a ceramics museum (which helps explain the OTT train station hall), tapas culture in abundance, some of the best nightlife in Spain, brilliant food markets, outdoorsy living, beaches, warm weather and a lack of the overtourism of the country's two principal cities, and València has *a lot* going for it. You pick up on this straight away, even on a layover by train after travelling in an enormous zigzag around the country.

Now to the voices.

After the cacophony and excellent freshly squeezed pineapple juices and first-rate *jamón bocadillos* of the wrought-iron-framed Mercado Central near the mighty cathedral – and after climbing to the top of the bell tower and seeing the glistening golden chalice (Holy Grail) said to have been used by Christ at the Last Supper – I settle with a glass of tiger nut milk at a café outside.

Here I meet a succession of Valèncians full of praise for Spain's overlooked city.

Man with slicked-back hair and thick dark eyebrows: "This is the right city: not so big that you get stressed and not so small you get bored. I like the dimensions. A lot of variety. For me this is the quality... the quality of life. If you have normal work, it is OK. You enjoy the food. You do not have to be rich to have a good life and be happy. If you are looking for green, you have green. It is nature. It is natural. The seaside! Oh, the seaside!"

Woman with curly hair and green eyes cuts in: "Yes, go to the beach for the nice fresh air. If you want good paella, you go to the beach too. Good restaurants there. I love the city centre of València: everything is very near, you can walk, you can cycle. It is like a big town, not a city. I hate Barcelona and Madrid. They are big cities: Barcelona and Madrid. I want to go home from work: fifteen minutes, not one hour. People in Barcelona and Madrid have to take Metro: fifty minutes, one hour."

Tall man, eavesdropping on us: "No rain here in València! No rain!" I query this.

"OK, some rain," he concedes. "But in thirty minutes you don't notice that it has rained."

He is from Argentina and emigrated to València after a holiday here.

"I was just passing by in 2007," he says. "After the third day I knew this was my spot. In my opinion it has the perfect balance: the sights of the city, the Metro, the airport. A large city but not a crazy city. You can bike-ride everywhere. I'm a bike rider. All along the city you can go. Just look at the river: in thirty minutes you can get everywhere. The main avenue has a bike lane. I called my mum and asked her to empty my apartment – my rental apartment in Buenos Aires. I said: 'Mum, I'm not coming back.' She was really not very happy."

Woman wearing shades, who emigrated here from Italy, drinking a *café largo*: "Yes, not too big and not too small. The Túria gardens are a very good idea. Clean, and you can move easily by bike, bus and Metro. Good for children. Lots of play parks. This city. I really love this city. Good weather all year round."

I know, I know, this is just an impromptu straw poll... but they do all seem to like València a lot.

I do too.

I meet one more "voice", a busker on the shiny marble Plaza de la Virgen, beside the cathedral.

He has a thick ginger beard and wears a floppy sun hat and sandals. A crowd had gathered round earlier but when I pass, he is packing up his guitar and possessions. From his pale complexion, I take him to be from abroad, and having read all about Laurie Lee busking in *As I Walked Out One Midsummer Morning* I am excited to meet a modern-day version. At least, I am at first.

"Laurie Lee?" I ask as an introduction, expecting the name will break the ice.

He looks at me blankly.

"Laurie Lee," I repeat, in case he has misheard me.

Blank face.

"Who?"

I explain and he asks me to write down the name in his journal. I do so alongside various scrawlings from other people he has met on his travels. He looks at Lee's name and the title of the book and says nothing.

"How long are you in Spain?" I ask, after he tells me he is from Germany.

"That's a very odd question," he replies stiffly. "If I want to stay longer I will. Two days, a week."

He glares at me.

"Ah, OK," I reply.

"It is just like that," he says.

Another glare.

"Philip" does not sound very German – he sounds British and I suspect he may be having me on, just for the hell of it. Anyway, he is behaving oddly. I ask where he is from in Germany.

"You know, from the south," he says, extremely vaguely, before adding: "Bavaria."

I do not believe him – not that it matters much.

"What do you like most about València?" I ask.

"It is really nice," he replies, perhaps straining his brain for this description or perhaps not: he does not appear to want to give much away.

He is succeeding.

"Where are you going next in Spain?"

"I thought I might stay at one place for a long time. A farm. Organic stuff. You know. If I want to go to a farm, I will," he says, as though I am an inspector who has come to deny him access to organic farms.

"Are you camping?"

"Yes," he says, before asking me what I am doing in Spain and making his only definite-sounding reply: "I don't want to star in a book."

He tells me his age – twenty-nine – when I enquire if he is on a gap year after university.

He glares at me once more.

I offer him a euro for his tip basket.

His right hand shoots out and his fingers open slowly as my euro drops in. They close quickly and his hand slides smoothly into a pocket. "Philip" says nothing, smiles faintly and we part.

On this peculiar note I head for Estació del Nord.

The Petroleum Revolution
València to Alcoy

The ride to Alcoy is just under two hours from València's beautiful *modernista* station. It is a faster line than the one from Cuenca, passing close to an IKEA warehouse on the edge of the city before entering a flat plain of fruit trees. Beyond are many miles of vineyards. We stop at Xàtiva Station, where the battlements of a castle peer down from a hilltop. Afterward, towering cliffs rise as the landscape becomes wilder with bamboo thickets by the tracks. We curl round bends above ravines. Ridges and peaks emerge through the heat haze. The train slows and begins to squeak and strain. Another castle looms high on a clifftop, and soon afterward we stop at a tiny terminus: Alcoy Station.

Alcoy is a totally random pick.

On the rail map of Spain, the town sticks out at the end of a line leading in the direction of Alicante, tucked away in the mountains. Trains used to run onward from here to the big city, where I intend to go tomorrow after retracing my steps to Xàtiva and taking a connection. The old lines round here, which proved uncommercial and erratically run, were abandoned in the late 1960s under Franco. I say "erratically" as there were never any toilets on board and a system operated by which passengers who needed to "go" simply made this clear to the conductor and the driver before using a station toilet while the train waited, often causing delays. There are also stories of stationmasters, postmen and engine drivers playing card games at stations holding up trains to finish important hands, as well as of reversals up the line to retrieve forgotten packed lunches belonging to drivers; in one instance travelling backward more than 10 miles. Passengers back then, it seems, would reach their destinations... eventually. Now the old lines have been turned into popular trails for cyclists and walkers, with no current plans to resume services.

I am simply curious about Alcoy, sometimes spelled Alcoi, with its population of around 60,000 and its isolation up in the southern Alicante Mountains at 600 metres.

This altitude, I am soon to learn, has had many interesting consequences over the years.

One was that Alcoy became a key Spanish industrial hub in the nineteenth century. The steep landscape means the Río Serpis flows rapidly downward toward the plains, which back then provided energy for major metal works and mills producing paper, textiles and flour.

The result was great wealth – and, as I am soon to discover, a fair bit of strife too.

A piece of modern graffiti by an anarchy sign on a wall in an empty lot opposite the station hints at the troubles of the past – *CONTRA EL CAPITALISMO Y EL PATRIARCA (AGAINST CAPITALISM AND THE PATRIARCH)* – on the walk down to a bridge high above the gorge to the main square, where I am soon engrossed in the bloody story of the Petroleum Revolution of July 1873.

For five days that summer Alcoy was at the centre of Spanish events after workers protesting at poor working and living conditions during a general strike were fired upon under the orders of the mayor, who was besieged in the town hall before being dragged out and killed. Independence was declared under a workers' state that lasted just five days before government troops arrived from Alicante, quashing the uprising and issuing death sentences for its leaders.

Such was the high profile of the Petrol Revolution, so named as its leaders held aloft torches soaked with fuel, that it drew the attention of Friedrich Engels, co-author of the *Communist Manifesto* with Karl Marx. Engels was highly critical of the revolutionaries' organization. He believed that too little thought had gone into what exactly would happen next once "victory" was achieved. What was the point of taking the town and then waiting for the soldiers to come? Similar tensions were being felt across Spain at the time, and Alcoy's example was a setback to any wider revolution in the country. Yet lessons learned in southern Spain may well have influenced others further afield.

There is nothing I can find about the Petroleum Revolution on the tourist information street signs or in leaflets from the tourist office. But in the town hall on the main square, where the mayor was beaten and killed in 1873, two vivid paintings hanging by the grand staircase leading from the central hall to the first floor capture the dramatic uprising.

One shows workers holding batons and standing in a road blocked by a chaotic tumbledown barricade of broken carts, tables and chairs. Petrol cans rest by their feet and each revolutionary clutches a baton, spade or rifle while peering out beneath cloth caps as though resigned to the likelihood of their fates. The other painting is more disturbing, depicting a howling mob watching as a pair of bare-chested men haul a rope attached to the trouser-less legs of the mayor, whose torso is out of the picture. He is about to be dragged across the cobbles.

On the first floor outside some administrative offices – I am not really sure I should be poking my nose so far into Alcoy's town hall, but no one seems to want to stop me – is a simple memorial to the mayor, Agustín Albors, bearing the words: *Víctima de los luctuosos sucesos* (Victim of the mournful events).

At a bookshop on the edge of the town hall square, one of the staff, José Luis Santonia, explains Alcoy's reticence about the Petroleum Revolution.

"These years are very difficult to talk about: the conflict between the bosses and the workers," José says. "To this day no one is sure where the first shot came from, the town hall or the people. We're not proud about it."

He pauses to search for the right words.

"Let's just say: sanity did not reign at that time."

There *is* a tiny display about *El Petróleo*, as the uprising is referred to locally, in Alcoy's little history museum, down in the gorge. So, to be fair, events have not been entirely swept under the carpet.

* * *

It is unusual being in this out-of-the-way Spanish Manchester in the hills.

Plaza de Dins behind the town hall is almost empty, as is a neighbourhood of streets lined with magnificent examples of *modernista* buildings. These were constructed on the proceeds of Alcoy's manufacturing heyday and the tourist office has an excellent map showing exactly which industrialists lived in splendour at exactly which address. To accompany this map, another "industrial route map" pinpoints the old red-brick factories, some still with towering chimneys, where the workers toiled to pay for all the fancy architecture.

Alcoy, it turns out, despite its almost complete lack of tourists on my visit, is remarkably tourist-friendly.

As well as the history museum, which explains how nomadic tribes gathered in the hills here sixty thousand years ago, a separate archaeology museum is crammed with flints, arrowheads, skeletons and coins, much of which were unearthed in ancient caves in the surrounding hills. I "do" both museums. I "do" both maps. And, just as I am thinking *that's it, tourist stuff well and truly "done"*, I discover that beneath the main square by the town hall a cathedral-like space has been somehow dug out, creating the effect as you descend the steps of having entered the whitewashed innards of an enormous whale. This is truly extraordinary, completely unexpected and hard to get your head round. Inside, an exhibition of multicoloured *abstracto* art is on display, and a leaflet explains that the hall was completed as a community venue in 1995 by the renowned Valèncian architect Santiago Calatrava.

All I can say is: *bravo, Santiago!*

Alcoy is full of surprises (if not tourists).

Mulling over this, I post a large quantity of Spanish city, town and village maps home at the post office. I eat a fine fish dinner at my *hostal*. I drink a Mahou *cerveza* in Plaza de Dins, which comes alive with locals at eight o'clock. I drink a local coffee liqueur named *Alcoyanos* back at the *hostal* bar, listening to *policía* who seem extremely bored by the evening's lack of crime.

Then I look properly at tomorrow's train timetable.

Then I realize I have messed up.

CHAPTER TEN

ALCOY TO GRANADA, VIA ALICANTE, BENIDORM, ÁGUILAS AND ALMERÍA

"AT NIGHT YOU NEED TO BE CAREFUL"

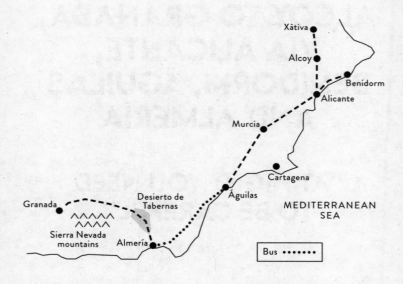

Xàtiva

Alcoy

Benidorm

Alicante

Murcia

Cartagena

Águilas

Granada

Desierto de
Tabernas

MEDITERRANEAN
SEA

Sierra Nevada
mountains

Almería

Bus ·······

It is not a disastrous mistake, however. If I catch the 08:50 from Alcoy, I will arrive in Xàtiva at 10:04 from where I need to catch an onwards connection to Alicante departing at 15:29, scheduled to arrive at 16:28. So there will be a 5 hours and 25 minutes' wait in Xàtiva.

I mention all these details as this is, after all, a story of train travel. Timetables, as much as anything else dictate the "plot" (so much as one exists).

Spending a few hours in Xàtiva will not be the end of the world. Apparently, people take day trips from València to see its castle. I will treat my impromptu stop as an unscheduled *day trip* to visit the castle, which is described according to various sources as "worth the ascent" and "stunning". The old town meanwhile is "pleasant". Many "scenic" and "tranquil" treats lie in store.

What could be better than that? Pleasant, scenic tranquillity with stunning vistas... some people will go a long way and dish out plenty of euros for that.

Alcoy Station has a shelter for refugees attached on one side. It is an official *Cruz Roja* (Red Cross) *albergue de transeúntes* (shelter for transients). I go to ask about their work and someone on reception politely asks me to leave after telling me that five African refugees are currently staying at the hostel and then deciding all of a sudden that this is the full amount of information he wishes to impart about the *albergue*. He cannot tell me anything further, he says.

I go to the platform, where I ask the station guards if I can buy a ticket in advance from Xàtiva to Alicante. This, I am informed, cannot be done at Alcoy. It must be done at Xàtiva. A complicated ticket reason lies behind this that I do not understand.

A red Renfe train arrives.

This follows the tracks of yesterday through a fine pink morning mist back to Xàtiva Station, whereupon I ask a ticket assistant with a beard whether I can buy a ticket for Alicante. He tells me "no" and that I must return to València if I want to go to Alicante. I point out that I would like to travel on the 15:29 to Alicante and that I know it is scheduled – and that the station guard at Alcoy said this would be fine. The man with the beard regards me silently for a few seconds and says this ticket will cost what seems like a very high price. It is so much more than I had expected that I say I need to think about it.

Sitting in the waiting lounge, I go online to Renfe's website and discover I can buy the very same ticket for about a third of the bearded man's price.

So I buy it and I am very tempted to go and show my new friend that I now have the ticket for a third of his fare.

But I don't.

I go to see the stunning, pleasant, tranquil castle on the hill.

* * *

It is a long way up to the top, following a hot, steep, poorly signed path that eventually turns into an easy-to-follow road. The views, I can report, are indeed momentarily inducing of an inability to move due to their sheer indescribably wonderful loveliness and fantastically nerve-relaxing qualities. I.e. stunning

You also get a fine bird's-eye view of the little town of Xàtiva with its terracotta roofs spread out below like a pond of pink beside the railway.

For as long as people have wanted to fight each other, this castle has been an important spot. This much I gather from the tourist signs. The Romans had a base up here, it is said. Well, they would have been fools not to. With high walls and good supplies of ammunition, nobody would have too much of a chance against you up here. I breathe in the aromatic herbs and enjoy the sound of the cicadas, before heading down for lunch and the train to Alicante.

This departs bang on time.

It's soon rattling along at 95 kilometres an hour (59 miles per hour), rising above a parched valley. The carriage has smart blue leather seats and a few *americanos* on board.

"We're looking for a place to live," says one sitting across the aisle.

"Where?" I ask.

"Near Alicante," she replies.

"Why there?" I ask.

"Too much of an earthquake risk back home," she says.

"Where is that?" I ask.

"California," she says.

Her friend leans over. We are crossing farmland planted with cornfields and olive groves.

"I like it here because I don't like to stay in one place for too long," she says. "I like to move."

It transpires they are only looking for a temporary place to live near Alicante. They have all their possessions in a few large bags. It seems they are on the run – from what I do not know. There is, as I am soon to find, an escapist quality to life on the Costa Blanca.

We enter a tunnel that leads to Alicante, where we arrive at a shiny modern station that I do not like much at all after València's *modernista* palace.

From the station to my bargain-basement room in an apartment run by a Romanian woman next to a takeaway pizza joint run by a Uruguayan takes half an hour's walk between concrete blocks.

Here, my late siesta turns into a long night's sleep.

At the risk of laying myself wide open to accusations of resorting to dreadful clichés that show how narrow-minded and ill equipped to have opinions I am – but who cares? – I seem to be turning even more Spanish by the day.

"Look at it, good God!"
Alicante to Benidorm

And so to Benidorm.

The words "lobster red" and "lager louts" and "high-rise hell" may spring to mind when considering this huge popular beach resort that was once a simple fishing port on a headland with two long fine-sand beaches on each side: Playa de Levante and Playa de Poniente. I will admit it: they do with me. The resort has long been popular as a place to enjoy sun, sand and seafood for Spaniards. Small hotels have existed on this highly attractive piece of coast since the 1920s. But then something happened. Put simply, mass tourism happened, on the back of jet planes in the late 1950s. Boeing 707s, bought in great numbers by the glamorous airline Pan Am, started to shrink the planet. In 1958, when this plane that was going to change travel forever went into service, Frank Sinatra captured the zeitgeist with his album *Come Fly with Me*. The sense of escapism offered by the new jet age was tangible. "Lovely days" were to be had "weather-wise" on journeys gliding through "rarified" air, transporting you to "exotic booze" down in Peru and Acapulco Bay. Flying was exciting. Boeing 707s, the precursor of the larger Boeing 747 (the Jumbo), which began in 1970, changed forever our conception of travel. "Trolley dollies" became a term. The world got smaller (and was soon to become very small indeed when budget airlines emerged in the 1990s). Yes, back in the late 1950s tourism to hot places already existed, but this was different.

In his travel book about life during three summers at a fishing village in the Costa Brava after the Second World War, Norman Lewis describes the shock of loud, well-moneyed, scantily clad outsiders arriving in sports cars and throwing their pesetas about. *Voices of the Old Sea*, published many years later in the mid 1980s, is my favourite travel book about Spain (although Laurie Lee's is a very close second). Lewis's story of the change from one way of life based around fishing traditions to a completely different life devoted to pleasing wealthy outsiders is poignant and elegiac. At first the locals in his fictionalized village, Farol, are taken aback by all the loose indulgent behaviour of outsiders, deemed "basically irrational, when not actually mad". But this quickly softens when it dawns just how much cash can be had from the addition of breeze-block extensions with a bed or two; as Jordi said of his own family back at Hostal Regina back in Blanes.

What happened in the Costa Brava was to balloon in Benidorm thanks to Boeing and its great rival Douglas. Lewis's "invasive barbarities", as he described holidaymakers' behaviour, became very invasive and very barbaric, very quickly. A concrete jungle by the beach rose that has become a kind of template across the Mediterranean – and the world – for how *not* to do tourism. Its hotels were not merely skyscrapers – they were the country's tallest buildings. For four years until 2006, Gran Hotel Bali was the tallest structure in Spain at 210 metres. There are plenty of others not far behind this concrete peak.

Planes have a lot to answer for (even when you do not consider all those fumes). Trains, I think we can all agree, are so much nicer.

* * *

On the street outside my extremely cheap apartment not far from El Mercado Central in Alicante a party is going on at seven thirty in the morning. People are dancing in trance-like circles with their arms in the air to music emanating from someone's mobile phone. A dissolute man in white trousers with designer rips staggers by smoking a cigarette. I make my way down to the port, where a few gin palace boats are moored and a great crowd of people who do not appear to have slept has gathered to eat fries and McMuffins outside a McDonald's. A big hotel, the Meliá Alicante, lies at one end of the port and I walk toward it along a promenade where a man with a dog is setting up a stall selling DVDs and books. I stop to look and as I do so am conscious of a loud barking sound of what appears to be another dog greeting the stall owner's hound. The noise is not coming from a four-legged creature, however. A topless woman with one arm draped around a companion and a cigarette in her other hand is "barking" at the stall owner's dog. She stumbles onward laughing and barking and wearing virtually nothing.

In Norman Lewis's Farol, local bylaws had stated – before the tourists arrived – that gentlemen could only wear shorts if they tied handkerchiefs over their knees, while two-piece bathing suits for women were banned (one young offender around the time of his stay was sent to a correctional institute for wearing one). These outdated rules were abandoned within a year of the first tourists arriving; one of the few plus sides of the influx of outsiders.

Things seem to have moved on quite a bit in Alicante since then.

The semi-naked barking woman heads off down a side street and I find the Puerta del Mar "Station", little more than an empty platform with a timetable at the end of the promenade by the hotel. Shortly afterward an orange and grey electric train arrives, and I board to find three conductors having a chat near the ticket machine. They explain that I need to change at Sangueta Station for Benidorm, which I do a few minutes later, waiting on my own at a platform with a view of Alicante's ancient hilltop, Castillo de Santa Bárbara, before catching another ride in an empty carriage between cliffs and beaches along the palm-tree-lined coast.

Not many people seem to want to go to Benidorm by train today.

The metallic-grey sea glimmers to the right as we rise on a slope and then cut inland across craggy landscape with the odd apartment block. A sign by my seat warns that being aggressive toward or intimidating the train staff could result in four years in prison. I am joined across the way by a woman with dyed red hair, a blue butterfly tattoo, long fake nails and a lot of rings. She appears to be an expat; about seven per cent of Benidorm's population is British and I get the feeling she is one of them, but she has headphones on so I do not ask.

A total of around 71,000 people now live in Benidorm, which had a population of 3,000 in 1930. By 1950 this had risen to 25,000, and Benidorm had a princely total of four hotels in 1959. Then the Boeing 707s came and the rest is a high-rise history of both tourists and expats from northern Europe, Britain in particular and the Dutch and Germans too.

The TRAM Metropolità d'Alacant service hums along. A temperature monitor shows 31ºC. We stop at quite a few stations and enter a tunnel or two before a high camel-hump-shaped mountain rises to the north, as do quite a few skyscrapers, ahead to the south-east. One of them from a distance looks like a giant cactus, another like an enormous finger with a broken nail. We stop at a station specifically for the Terra Mítica theme park, where a few disembark, before passing outlet warehouses and cranes on building sites of what could pass as Eastern European housing estates from the mid twentieth century.

We arrive at Benidorm Station, from where it is 20 minutes down a hill to my seafront hotel close to the old town on the headland.

In the spirit of frankness, which the Costa Blanca seems to draw out of you and I cannot quite say why – perhaps it is the breezy no-nonsense approach to *turistico* pleasures – my experiences of Benidorm can be summarized thus: a pint of Stella Artois at the Coach and Horses; a wander into the old town to inspect the *I ♥ BENIDORM* T-shirt shops and pick up the local English papers (more of which later); another pint of Stella Artois at the Coach and Horses and a chat with the barman and David, an expat; a steak and kidney pie with a pint of Amstel at the Four Kings pub and a chat with Carole and Kevin, more expats; a ride on the *tren turistico* to see the sights; attendance of a drag artists' comedy night; and a final pint at Pub Rumbo and a chat with the barman and Terry, a regular Benidorm-going tourist from Hull.

So you can see, I am quite busy.

And yes, it is a concrete monstrosity on the scale of which all other concrete monstrosities of the Mediterranean must bow and say: *you truly are more monstrous than us.*

It is not particularly *Spanish*, but then again is not tourism now so embedded in Spain that *what counts as Spanish* in many parts of its sunniest coastlines and islands is exactly what I have before me today: Benidorm. Tourism, after all, makes up fifteen per cent of the country's economy – although estimates vary quite a lot – with international visitor numbers second only to France. One in every seven euros earned in Spain comes from holidaymakers such as myself and my fellow Benidorm-goers. The culture of much of tourist Spain is the culture of Benidorm, though perhaps not distilled in such virulent form as round here.

With these thoughts in mind, I go to catch the *tren turistico*.

The *tren turistico* is quite fun. It leaves from outside the Four Kings pub. It is coloured blue and takes an hour and this is what we see: the Bulldog pub, complete with artificial grass terrace; the Pizza4U restaurant; Bowling Benidorm tenpin bowling; the Playland Slot Machines centre; a man revving his motorbike very loudly; a traffic jam; the big mountain that I saw from the train, though from this angle a highly unusual gap at the top is revealed, looking like a missing tooth; the Tartan Bar, which has cacti in its garden; a shop selling "XXXXL large sizes"; Silver City Sports Bar, all lit up in neon; the Jungle bar, where people who should really know better at their age are dancing a little too enthusiastically for this time in the evening; an establishment with a picture of the *Only Fools and Horses* comedy sitcom stars offering I am not sure what as I only catch a glimpse; the Lazy Cow British Bar; a "Pizza-Kebab-Curry" restaurant (smart move to cover so many popular foods); and, of course, a whole load of skyscrapers.

A jazzy oboist begins playing on the stereo as a recorded commentary tells us we are about to receive "interesting information" about the skyscrapers. I keenly await this intelligence as a red train from another *tren turistico* operator passes in the opposite direction. Both trains toot at each other, whether out of friendliness or rivalry I do not know. There seem to be many *tren turisticos* on the prowl in Benidorm, like taxis in New York City. "Although originally dedicated to fish," the recorded commentary suddenly kicks off, "holidaymakers discovered Benidorm in the twentieth century." This much I know to be true. We pass a restaurant with a terrace where elderly couples are ballroom dancing. Which is touching.

We learn that Benidorm "takes care of its beaches all year round" and that there are 4 miles of beaches. The jazzy oboist lounge music gets cheesier than ever at this point. "Benidorm is also about gastronomy, we can assure you... excellent fish!"

Good to hear! We go up a steep hill while being told that Benidorm is an avant-garde city that has always "looked to the sea". At the top of an escarpment we pause to regard the grand sweep of concrete apartments and hotels as a man in the row behind says: "Look at it, good God!" And I am with him in his assessment, though from here, I have to admit, if you squint your eyes a bit: Benidorm is quite beautiful. A mist rises off the placid water and the skyscrapers and the sweep of sand are enveloped in an apricot-coloured evening sky. The strange mountain rises in delicious shades of grey and waves lap on a distant little island shaped like a shark's fin.

The commentator mentions Barbary pirates of the fifteenth, sixteenth and seventeenth centuries, before the lounge music kicks in and the *tren* snakes onward between a forest of skyscrapers whose heights are mentioned and I realize that, when you look at them close up, each is architecturally interesting with a subtlety of shapes and patterns. I am sure architects visiting Benidorm would take some pleasure in assessing the imagination that has gone into making each one *a little bit different*. "Seventy buildings have more than twenty-five floors," says the commentator and, for some reason I do not quite understand, the commentator continues, this makes Benidorm an example of sustainability.

There is more lounge music as we return to the Four Kings pub along a street with a Factory Price shop, a casino, a tattooist and a henna parlour. We are told that Benidorm attracts more than eleven million overnight stays each year. "This is an amount that very few places can display," says the commentator.

And we all get off – and I walk back to my hotel, pausing to listen to a drag queen comedy act in the old town. "I'm what's known in the business as a cock in a frock," says a Liverpudlian man in a blue sequin dress, a blond wig and high heels, who begins to heckle his audience. "We're in the old town of Benidorm here. The posh part. Not like that bit down there where you are from." He points in the direction of the Four Kings. "Don't talk during the performance," he says. "It's like going to a brothel and having a wank." Then, satisfied that the audience will be well behaved, he says: "OK, shake your tits and smash the place up for Shakira!" And the man in the blue sequin dress with a blond wig departs and a man in a red sequin dress with a blond wig takes the stage and begins singing: "*We are the world...*"

* * *

Some voices from my pub crawl.

Barman, the Coach and Horses. "Over there," he says, pointing to the part of town where I take the tourist train. "That's the English zone or the *guiri* zone. That's what they call foreigners: *guiris.*" The root of this word, which I first heard about from Fermín back in Pamplona, is uncertain although it may be connected to the Basque word *guiristino*, applied to outsiders during wars in the nineteenth century. "Yeah, that's what they call us. You don't want to go there," he says, pointing again. "That's the young side. Generally, they want to get paralytic, all the time. At night you need to be careful. Literally, there are girl muggings. Prostitutes will group up on you and put hands in your pockets."

David, a retired supermarket employee from Nottingham. "Brexit," he says. "We shouldn't be leaving Europe. I can't believe it, but hundreds and hundreds of expats here voted for it. Like turkeys voting for Christmas."

Kevin, retired publican from Wakefield, and Carol, retired pharmacy technician from Liverpool. "The only thing that lets Benidorm down is the Brits," says Carole. Kevin: "They're trying to make it more respectable." By "they" he is referring to the local authorities. Carole: "They get drunk and they sleep on the floor." By "they" she is referring to young Brits, not the authorities. In the morning they find people sleeping it off at the foot of their apartment block. "Daily we see this," says Carole.

Barman at Pub Rumbo. "My old man used to run this place," he says. "He passed away five years ago. Back in the 1980s we used to get Liverpool players coming here. He knew some of them."

Terry, construction company owner from Hull, drinking at Bar Rumbo. "Fifty times I've been to Thailand, but no matter what, we always come back here. Our youngest son is now twenty-three. We first brought him here when he was four. We class this as our second home. Must have been to twenty or thirty different hotels. Where we are staying now there was nothing when we first came in the early 1990s. Just a wasteland, where we are now."

Kevin is especially chatty. He was brought up in South Africa for part of his childhood and has connections there. "My uncle was shot in the head and robbed," he tells me unexpectedly. "They caught the man responsible and put him on death row. They were the last hangings in South Africa. I couldn't watch, but my wife did." He waves over at his wife, who waves back.

And then I return to my hotel.

A strange place, Benidorm.

I sit on my balcony and watch the lights flicker along the coastline for a while before getting an early night (by local standards).

I have a train or two to catch in the morning.

Clickety-clack south
Benidorm to Águilas

Águilas is 140 miles to the south-west. To get there I must return to Alicante and catch the 12:05, due in at 15:42 via a connection in the city of Murcia, capital of a *comunidad autónoma* of the same name. Águilas is another tourist resort relying heavily on overseas visitors, but nowhere near on the scale of Benidorm. Having gone along the northern coast of Spain by train, I want to try to do the same in the south, and Águilas seems a sensible target.

The sky has a bruised colour today and the sea melds into the horizon in a blur of grey. I make the change at Alicante from the tram service on to a Renfe train at Alicante's dull main station, where the ticket machines are not working, and I wait for quite a while in a ticket office with a number system. Of all the places I have visited so far, I am probably least keen on Alicante; something about it gets me down though I know I am probably being unfair basing my opinion on a morning's debauchery and the dreary station.

My graffiti-splattered train departs in rain from platform fourteen, and I read in my guidebook that Murcia is particularly fertile and considered the "orchard of Europe". As if to confirm this, we pass through long lemon, orange, apple and fig groves, branches bending with the weight of the fruit. Lemons have fallen from the trees and the effect in places is like spilled yellow paint. A Ryanair plane soars above, presumably heading to or from Alicante Airport. Fruit pickers wearing pink overalls bend over a low green crop. Then barren, bald hills appear, although the line is along rich flat farmland. We arrive at Murcia Station, where major works are going on to accommodate future high-speed trains and I quickly buy a *bocadillo* before catching the connection south and soon moving through more lemon orchards, making me think of just how many "ice and a slice" G & Ts these parts supply. Answer: must be quite a lot.

Orange trees… peach trees… fig trees… abundance! We go so slowly at times we might almost be overtaken by a farmer's tractor. Then after Pulpí Station, the landscape turns dustier and dustier as we pass through more barren sun-drenched tumbleweed hills. The rain has gone, and the heat is back on. There is a fine view of the sea ahead. The track makes a *clickety-clack* sound and an island emerges in the distance. This is named La Isla del Fraile (Monk's Island), where an eccentric Scottish merchant (and possible spy) once lived. Many British lived in Águilas in the nineteenth century, a large proportion involved in mining.

Cacti with beautiful scarlet flowers grow out of the rocky landscape as we curve downward to the town. On this stretch huge greenhouses are to be found; vast fields of plastic tended by farmers wearing sombreros. A circular fortification on a rocky headland marks what appears to be the centre of town and we are soon pulling up at a dusty empty station with ochre walls. It has been a great ride.

* * *

Águilas makes an excellent pit stop – at first.

Hotel El Paso is on the other side of the railway tracks from the port. I have a room with a door on to an atrium with potted plants and a view of a dirty wall in a side street. I look at the receipt the receptionist has given me and find it is in the name of Thomas James McNally and for another date. Then I look at a brochure placed on the desk for a *ruta del ferrocarril* (railway route) in Águilas. There is, although I totally failed to notice, a railway museum connected to the station, while not far from there a section of historic mining railway and a preserved steam locomotive made in Glasgow in 1889 are to be found.

Really, it is quite extraordinary quite how much train love there is out there in Spain, if you scratch the surface a bit.

The train museum, my third in Spain, turns out to be in a vault in the basement of the station tended by three elderly men wearing straw hats, who sit outside gossiping when there are no museum goers, which would appear to be most of the time. Inside one of the men switches on a model railway and a little train goes round. Other excitements include old station clocks, uniforms, machine parts, lanterns, an old safe and a gallery of black-and-white pictures of former railway employees. It is cluttered and charming and worth seeing just for the early photographs of Águilas before tourist development took off in the 1960s, when a fence and a thin line of sand near a fishermen's yard seemed to be all there was at Playa de las Delicias, one of the main beaches.

The elderly man attempts to sell me a bottle of red wine with an Águilas train museum label, which I am tempted to buy but do not want to carry around town while following the *ruta del ferrocarril.* When I leave, he turns off the model train and returns to his friends.

Stop number two on the *ruta* is along Playa de las Delicias and up an embankment, where a mining train once ran into a tunnel and out on to a high pier from which minerals and esparto grasses would be transported on to cargo ships.

This is more interesting than it sounds and the pier itself, known as Embarcadero del Hornillo (Hornillo Pier), is excellent, pointing out toward La Isla del Fraile and looking as though it is built for trains to ride along and plunge madly into the sea below. Inside the tunnel, panels explain how various honourable Yorkshiremen and Lancastrians were involved in the construction of the pier, which was opened by the Great Southern of Spain Railway in 1903 (and closed in 1970).

To complete the *ruta*, I admire the old Scottish locomotive, which was in use from 1890 to 1967 and had a top speed, should anyone be burning to know, of 85 kilometres an hour (53 miles per hour). This is close to the port, where I visit the castle, with its old cannons and views of a much more developed, Benidorm-like section of Águilas along Playa de Poniente as well as the weird plastic fields of greenhouses that begin on the edge of town. I don't much like these fields.

And then, while eating dinner beneath a palm tree in Plaza de España, I realize something.

I really have messed up this time.

There is no train line onward to the city of Almería, where I had planned to go next, about 80 miles to the south-west. It looks as though a bus ride from here makes sense unless I return to Murcia for a long, complicated journey round.

On Hope Street, by the sea
Águilas to Almería

So yes, I take the *autobús*.

It gives me no pleasure to have broken the chain of attachment to Spanish train tracks, however there is no point in churlishly spending hours on complicated rail journeys just to stick to an unwritten "principle", and anyway, I had to take the buses and the taxi when Renfe Feve let me down up north.

Almería is wonderful, partly because it is so very cut off.

The bus drops its passengers at Almería Station, a squat modern grey-stone building with two shifty characters on a corner who shamelessly regard the bumbling new arrival (me) as if assessing exactly how best to liberate my possessions, in particular my wallet. I had been joined on the bus by a similar "character", who had chosen to sit across the aisle in the almost empty vehicle and furtively monitor my movements before having a long loud telephone conversation about meeting a contact. The bus ride, run by a company called BAM, although perfectly timely, had been generally quite awful after all the lovely train rides, lurching between roundabouts and chilling its passengers with air conditioning in the manner of supermarket products on shelves. The windows were far more heavily tinted than those on trains as we traversed salt plains and fields of white plastic greenhouses that made it look as though the entire landscape had been turned into a giant refugee camp. There was something sinister about these greenhouses as seen through the tinted windows that I could not quite put a finger on.

Although Almería Station is unremarkable, it sits next to a distinguished original station that is in the middle of being restored. This one dates from 1895 when a line from here to Guadix was opened, principally to transport iron ore from the interior to Almería's port; this line was extended to Linares in 1899, connecting the port with the rest of Spain. I like its brickwork: orange, burgundy and painted green in a mesmerizing Moorish pattern framed by neoclassical stucco and high arched windows. What a marvellous *arte Mudéjar* mix! A pink balustrade runs along the roof and in the centre is a pavilion of glass and wrought iron that reminds me a little of Mercado de San Miguel back in Madrid. Spain went through a phase of "iron architecture" around the turn of the twentieth century.

The contrast between the two stations is stark. The modern one devoid of almost any architectural merit and mistakable for a supermarket warehouse. The 1895 station so alive with interest and colour. Station-making people knew how to do things with a bit more style back then.

I have a few objectives in Almería. The first is to visit the cathedral. The second is to see the Alcazaba Moorish fortress on the hill. The third is to get my washing done. And finally, I would like to track down a couple of parts of the city mentioned in a brilliant memoir of life in Spain written by Gerald Brenan, a well-connected Englishman who lived in the mountainous Alpujarra region of Andalusía for spells between 1920 and 1934 (one of the guests to visit his home in the remote village of Yegen was none other than Virginia Woolf). Brenan captures the aromatic isolation and splendour of the landscape and draws crisp pen portraits of the villagers, delighting in the intrigue and gossip of local life. The book was published in 1957. In one chapter I have just read, he visits Almería, the Big Smoke in these parts, and it would be interesting "book tourism" – which is, I suppose, what also drew me to Huesca – to go and see if the port remains as he described. He had a peculiar time when he came calling at various brothels near the Alcazaba; on an entirely anthropological basis to gather stories, as he is at pains to point out. Almería seemed to have a seedy risqué edge back then. Perhaps nothing much has changed, although I very much doubt it, but then again you never know. Either way, it will give me something to do after the main sights.

* * *

Pensión Americano is, appropriately, on Avenida de la Estación, close to its junction with Avenida Federico García Lorca, the main artery in Almería leading down to the port and another old disused railway pier by a harbour where cruise ships dock. I am guessing that the name of the *pensión* has something to do with Almería's connection with the many cheesy spaghetti westerns that were filmed inland of here around the mid 1960s; Franco had wanted to create a Spanish Hollywood in Almería and dozens of famous names passed by, including Clint Eastwood, Lee Van Cleef, Elizabeth Taylor, Richard Burton, Peter O'Toole and, of course, the renowned spaghetti western director Sergio

Leone. Maybe some of the cast stayed at Pensión Americano or dined at the US-themed Chester Café on the corner. It is possible to go and see the former sets where western shows are put on with stuntmen on horseback and cancan dancing at the two most famous locations, Oasys MiniHollywood and Cinema Studios Fort Bravo Texas Hollywood. I know all this as I picked up the leaflets at the hotel in Águilas.

After seeing to the washing at the *lavandería automática* – a Spain-on-trains task to which I have yet to warm but it is always good to get it out of the way – I venture forth full of optimistic *turistico* thoughts.

These are soon dashed.

The grand-looking sixteenth-century cathedral is shut. It has just shut. It shuts at seven o'clock. By great good fortune, I learn, however, that the Moorish castle up the hill has just reopened, following a siesta period ending at seven o'clock.

It is as though the tourist authorities in Almería pass the baton of tourism from the cathedral to the castle on the hill every day precisely at seven o'clock. Maybe this manoeuvre saves on salaries on ticket office staff.

Maybe I am overthinking things.

The Alcazaba is a good solid honey-stoned castle which, like the one in Xàtiva, must have been nigh on impossible to attack successfully. The clutter of housing below is in every shade of ochre, pink and rust-red, mixed in among whitewashed cube-like structures and all tightly packed along narrow lanes, most of which look too small for vehicles other than mopeds. If ever a city could be said to look thrown together, Almería is that city. A ferry and a cruise ship occupy the harbour beneath the cloudless blue sky and Spanish connection with North Africa, just across the water, feels stronger than ever. Between Águilas and Almería something happened and that something was Andalusía. Perhaps the best known of all the *comunidades autónomas*, my final one, whose name comes from the Arabic *Al-Andalus*, stretches from here all the way to the Portuguese border.

Fountains trickle in the gardens at the top of the Alcazaba, which was once, in the eleventh century, the epicentre of a wealthy kingdom of traders with as many as 20,000 people living within the ramparts and a court to rival the one in Granada (my next stop-off down the line). A local saying goes that "when Almería was Almería, Granada was but its farm". If this is true then the castle here, before it was stripped of its art and stucco work in the seventeenth century, must have been quite a sight by the sea; the Alhambra, much of which was constructed after the Alcazaba, is after all considered by many to be Spain's greatest fortress.

Food for thought, if not for eating. Hungry, I retrace my steps, passing a faded information sign that says that part of *Lawrence of Arabia* (Peter O'Toole's visit) and *Indiana Jones and the Last Crusade* were filmed in Almería. A map shows exactly where on a *ruta del cine* (cinema route) of the city. Spain, I am increasingly noticing, has an awful lot of such *rutas*, but then again, it does have a very large number of tourists so it needs to give them things to do.

The walk down the hill takes me across the town hall square, beyond which I find I am in the neighbourhood described by Gerald Brenan in his chapter on the city entitled simply: "Almería and Its Brothels".

The plot of this chapter runs thus. Brenan meets a "scraggy" man in a gloomy diner. This man takes him to various brothels, during which he is told all about the man's addiction to vice and learns of the degraded poverty-stricken lives of the women, some of whom work on the ironically named Calle de la Esperanza (Hope Street). The "scraggy" man, named Augustin, opens his desolate heart to Brenan. He cuts a tragic wine-sodden figure, constantly trawling the backstreets of the old port in the grip of his addictions. Yet he is both lost and loquacious, living in an *abstracto* stream of often poignant and poetic soliloquies. After staying up till dawn, Brenan gets some sleep before writing down all that happened the night before; a matter of twenty pages of *South from Granada*. He realizes that he owes Augustin a debt of gratitude for revealing to him "his remarkable self", while in turn, Brenan's piece of travel writing recounting what happened is strikingly remarkable too. He captures a moment in time in this ancient labyrinthine city by the sea with vivid precision, honesty and a great deal of pathos.

I cannot find Calle de la Esperanza but I can locate Calle Esperanza and – who knows? – maybe this is where Augustin and Brenan met the madams almost a century ago now. The *calle* is a tiny alley-like street with burnt-out walls, ugly graffiti and grilled windows. There is nothing else to describe and I wonder why I bothered to go to look. But then again "book tourism" is not always "normal" and it can also take you to places you may never otherwise have gone, just as Orwell did for me back in the *trencheras* of Aragon, Lee by the Cliff of Crows in Segovia and Cervantes in Ciudad Real, not that I thought much of the *museo* there.

One way or another, literature can open doors.

I find a brilliant tapas bar on Plaza San Sebastián, where with each small *cerveza* first-rate tapas is delivered: olives and tomatoes on toast; tuna and anchovies; ham, anchovies and Heinz ketchup (known as a *Soviético* tapas and not as awful as it sounds); and finally, pork loin with hot sauce served on toast with a creamy aioli sauce. The tapas bar's "system" works like this. You place an order. The waiter yells the order to the chef. The chef yells confirmation. The waiter yells confirmation of his confirmation. Then he yells at the barman regarding the drink. The barman yells back. And the waiter, who does not feel any need to confirm the barman's confirmation, falls silent for a while. Soon both the chef and the barman are yelling at the waiter that the food and drinks are ready, and he is yelling back confirmations. Meanwhile, during my visit, two men who appear to be old buddies are yelling stories at each other by the bar. Their yelling gets steadily louder the more tapas and drinks are ordered. It is a shouting match of a tapas bar and if you happen to be reading Gerald Brenan's tales from the Alpujarra in a corner you may as well just put your book to one side and watch on with open eyes (and ears) as the cacophony rises and falls periodically. As I said, brilliant place.

All that is left is to walk to the port to see the disused railway pier – which is just as mad and suicidal-looking as its cousin in Águilas –

drink an anise at Chester Café, and listen for a while to an electronic Big Ben tune that chimes on the half hour and the hour in the hall of Pensión Americano. Someone sneezes. Steps shuffle above. A tap is turned on and water rushes down a pipe. Clicking noises begin. Clicking noises end. Big Ben chimes. A bed squeaks. A television blares. Someone coughs. It is very good value at Pensión Americano, but I may splash out a bit in Granada. I'm all for *keeping it real*... but perhaps a bit less real would be nice in one of the "tourist honeypots" of Spain that my guidebook says is the one town I must make sure I visit if I only visit one town in Spain.

A little too late for that.

However, I am enjoying the sense of anticipation; nothing wrong with guidebooks ramping it up a bit. After the Alcazaba, I am very much looking forward to laying eyes on the Alhambra.

The good, the bad and the lovely
Almería to Granada

Almería's supermarket-warehouse-style station is one of the worst in Spain, in my experience.

A television blares in the café, no one watching the show of course. There are flickering fruit machines and flies. I order and pay for a second *café largo* at the counter and wait for a while at a table, as instructed, but the *café largo* never comes and when I go up to ask again for the coffee I notice I have been overcharged by one euro, which a member of staff realizes straight away when I show the receipt and returns the euro.

But none of this really matters as outside nature is putting on a show.

Beyond the platforms the sun is rising and the sky has turned a perfect caramel colour fringed with ethereal streaks of tangerine. It is an awe-inspiring moment. Despite any minor inconveniences, taking trains round this big hot country is an absolute pleasure, especially on the early morning rides. The tracks gleam on the line. Swallows flit above. The horizon, with whatever lies in store, spreads out ahead.

Of course, at this moment I discover that a BAM replacement bus service is in operation. Yet this is just for a short distance to Huercal-Viator Station, where we all disembark and get on the train to Granada. We are about to go up. Granada, despite being just 40 miles from the coast, is at an altitude of 740 metres on the edge of the Sierra Nevada mountains, not all that far from one of Spain's best ski resorts: the Sierra Nevada Ski Station. The first part of our ride, before snaking around the peaks, involves travelling through the Desierto de Tabernas, 110 square miles of what is considered the only proper desert in Europe. This was where many of the spaghetti westerns were filmed; a semi-arid land of gullies, shrubs and steppes covered with grasses. Out there somewhere are yellow scorpions, black widow spiders and no fewer than two species of Spanish hedgehog. It is usually very hot, with an average summer temperature in the shade of plus 40ºC. The *desierto* is known as Spain's badlands and is, naturally, home to an official tourist *ruta* of the locations of Sergio Leone's films *A Fistful of Dollars*, *For a Few Dollars More* and *The Good, the Bad and the Ugly*.

We pull away at 08:26 past tumbledown houses, sunlight kissing the peaks of rose-tinted mountains ahead. A man at the end of the carriage hacks and gurgles from time to time but otherwise all is calm. And I make a friend.

Maria is conducting a survey for ADIF (*Administrador de Infraestructuras Ferroviarias*) and she is resigned to the fact that, with only six passengers on board, she is not going to get a great number of results on this ride.

"The company want to know if people would catch an AVE if there was one between Almería and Barcelona," Maria says, asking for my point of view. I explain my preference for slow trains, although I can understand why locals might want fast ones. Maria considers which box to tick on her tablet. I am her third "yes" of four interviewees.

I ask her if she likes high-speed trains. "I have never caught an AVE so I don't know what it's like," she says before asking me a few more questions about where I am from and whether I have a car.

Maria is conducting this survey for nine days as a temporary job and she sits down sociably to join me for a while. She has done other such survey jobs. "I was put on buses first, then cars at fuel stations and now they put me on trains."

She pauses as we regard the rolling arid landscape. The light has mutated from caramel to orange across the dotted shrubs and grasses of the plains. There is a glorious isolation about the scenery and I can already tell this will be one of the finest rides.

"At the fuel stations people really didn't want to talk to me," says Maria, looking out. "They didn't have the time – and they seemed afraid to talk."

With this she gathers her tablet and goes to question the final two passengers to Granada, including the hacking man. Soon afterward she returns and says: "They both said 'no'. They like it how it is." The train has a fifty-fifty split on the matter. Then she says goodbye and moves back to the middle carriage to keep an eye out for anyone boarding at stations along the way.

There is a temptation to wax lyrical about the landscapes of the Desierto de Tabernas and the Sierra Nevada. Beyond the desolate gullies and plateaus of the beautiful badlands, rose-red hills crumble upward as the train rises into rough and rocky territory. Yet as the train gains altitude, seas of fruit and olive trees envelop the plains and the scenery becomes more civilized. This does not last long as the land soon becomes dustier and drier once more as the tracks bend around abandoned villages with prickly pears and scrapyards. A panting dog observes our passage with a mixture of suspicion and bewilderment from beside a pair of old train carriages which have been converted into sheds, or perhaps dwellings of some sort. Wind turbines on red-earth ridges resemble giant thistles as the sun streams through the windows, bathing the seats in golden light. The mountains of the Sierra Nevada appear on the left, some looking as though they have patches of snow on upper slopes (perhaps my eyes are deceiving me).

Vineyards and purple and emerald crops have been planted on the edge of Guadix, where houses on an escarpment have windows cut into the cliff face as though the abodes are half house, half cave. We pass an oasis-like area of green, with forests planted for timber. We cross a fantastic viaduct, the shadow of the train silhouetted on esparto grass growing far below. And then we go up, up, up into the mountains.

Maria returns. She feels like having a chat as all passengers have been interviewed and her job is done until the train back.

She is aged twenty-one, from Almería, and is studying sociology at Granada University, where she is about to complete her final year. Her mother is a nanny, and her father is a customs officer. She is working over the summer to cover her studies; previously she has stacked shelves at a supermarket. She asks me if I know what "sociology" is and I say I do. "In Spain most people do not know," she sighs. All of the other passengers surveyed, six more, were in favour of AVE trains. So fast trains, inevitably perhaps, have won. She admits the job can make her nervous: "Sometimes when I ask the questions, I feel a bit sick."

Maria has an open friendly face, chestnut eyes, a silver nose ring and a gold handbag. She is in a talkative mood, as you may have gathered.

We discuss Spanish politics, in particular the rise of the far-right party Vox. Many had thought the far right was finished in the country with memories of Franco's fascism still fresh.

"In the natural context in Spain, people do not want an extreme right party," Maria says. "I don't think people really believe in Vox – I think it is just a reaction. My opinion is we are contrary to the extreme right wing in our souls. They try to destroy human rights. Not just for the refugees. It's for homosexual persons and with the women." She pauses to find the right words. "It is like they want to take it back to twenty years ago – no, more like forty years ago: women in the kitchen, staying at home, babies. No work – just staying at home. Make the food and look after the children. It's like in the Franco period, *La Guía de la Buena Esposa*."

This translates as *The Good Wife's Guide*, an eleven-point set of instructions as to how women should best engender harmonious relations with their other halves, dating from 1953. The guide includes tips such as polishing saucepans until they sparkle, serving newspaper-reading husbands coffee in their armchairs, avoiding both foul language (*evitar el mal lenguaje*) or nagging husbands with complaints about *problemas insignificantes*, cooking *deliciosa* food, fixing make-up to look beautiful, vacuuming, getting the kids dressed for the day, and remembering always: *Se dulce e interesante* (Be sweet and interesting). It is not, you might say, particularly "woke".

Maria leans forward and raises her eyebrows to steadily increasing heights as she relates this information.

I ask if young people are positive about the future.

She hesitates before replying. "Yes – and I think this belief has changed in the last year," she says. "It is a consequence of the economy. If I want a job, I can get a job, but younger people are willing to do jobs that older people are not."

The Spanish GDP has recently enjoyed modest growth despite two recessions in a decade and the country still being home to more than three million unemployed, the highest number in Europe. Feelings among the young in especially blighted regions, such as Extremadura, are of course another matter.

We pull into Granada Station and Maria switches subject.

"My boss," she confides, "he said to me: 'While waiting at the station for the train back, ask some people for the survey.' I said to him: 'What? I have twenty minutes! I prefer to take my coffee.'" She laughs and tucks her tablet in her gold bag.

We disembark, say farewell. Maria heads for the station café, and I make a mental note: always talk to ADIF survey people on Spanish trains. They can make very good company.

CHAPTER ELEVEN

GRANADA TO ALGECIRAS, VIA MÁLAGA AND TORREMOLINOS

"TWO PINK GINS AND A 'PARADISE'"

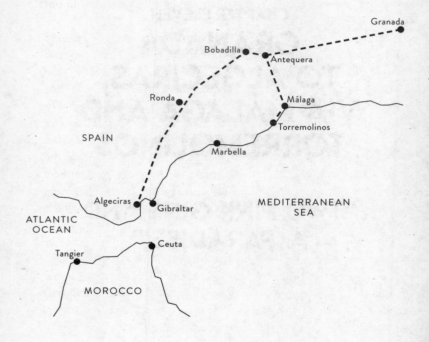

A little diversion here on English-language newspapers in southern Spain. These are something of a phenomenon and full of intrigue – and horrors. On the train from Almería I placed my collected copies of editions on the table, which have been adding quite a bulky weight to my backpack. And, in between bursts of Maria and enjoying watching the desert and the mountains unfold, gave them a good read; Gerald Brenan and his quirky goings-on put to one side for a while.

In front of me I had *Costa Blanca News: Serving the English Community Since 1971*; *The Olive Press: Your Expat Voice in Spain*; *EuroWeekly News: Voted the Best Free Newspaper in Spain 2017 and 2018*; *Round Town Times: 25,000 copies to Benidorm, Alfraz, Albir and more than any other free read!*; *The Post: Free Every Wednesday!*; *The Weekender: Your Weekend Starts Here!*; *The Holiday Guide: The Free Guide to the Costa del Sol for the Holidaymaker*; and *Sur in English* – the last being a translation of a local Spanish paper. I include the various subheads and exclamation marks to convey the atmosphere of fervent competition in the southern Spanish English-language newspaper market. All are free other than *Costa Blanca News*, which cost two euros and twenty cents.

The *Costa Blanca News* is my favourite for its enormous range of scandals: police on the lookout for burglars in Moraira who have been using drones to case apartments to see if residents are home before scaling balconies and forcing open windows; "hugger mugger" gangs of women in Benidorm arrested for approaching drunken men and either lifting their wallets or suggesting sex for payment, taking "victims" to cashpoints and noting PIN numbers before stealing cards (what the Coach and Horses barman back in Benidorm had mentioned); and a fraudster caught in Calpe after telling tourists that cashpoints are not issuing correct amounts, watching re-entered PINs and pickpocketing cards.

Meanwhile, a psychotic youth has gone on a violent, bloody rampage in Pedreguer, brought only to an end when shot in the legs by a *Guardia Civil*. A British man has fallen to his death from a balcony in Benidorm after a dispute following a drinking session. A concrete terrace of an apartment in Dénia has collapsed, very luckily missing people walking below.

Email scams about false parking fines and lottery tickets have been uncovered. Pharmacists are running out of drug supplies. An orange farmer is giving away oranges in despair due to low market prices. An aircraft arriving at Alicante-Elche Airport has somehow lost *every single piece of luggage* belonging to its 160 passengers.

All in just *a few days in sunny Spain* as reported in a single paper.

Elsewhere, from *The Weekender*: a British tourist has died after falling from a promenade at Orihuela Beach while taking a "selfie".

From *The Olive Press*: an Irish woman has been robbed while under sedation for an operation at a Costa del Sol hospital.

From *The Post*: a carer has been arrested for stealing 5,300 euros from an elderly woman.

From *EuroWeekly News*: a driver on a highway near Gandia has been caught going at 223 kilometres an hour (139 miles per hour) while under the influence of "several narcotic substances".

From *The Holiday Guide*: warnings to watch out for "thieves hanging around cash machines ready to pounce".

From *Round Town Times*: a feature highlighting how to "avoid typical scams" involving pickpockets and beach thieves.

From *Sur in English*: a prostitution network involving sexual exploitation and money laundering has been uncovered in Marbella, while "fully-loaded military-grade weaponry" including an AK-47, revolvers, silencers and grenades belonging to a Dutch drug-smuggling gang has been seized by the *Guardia Civil* in Málaga.

Read the local English-language papers and an extraordinary catalogue of nefarious activities and clandestine misdemeanours by the shores of the *Mediterráneo* is revealed. The sun may shine and the sea may sparkle, but behind the shutters and grilled windows and in the high-rise hotels *things are going on*.

It seems to be pretty wild out there, yellow scorpions and black widow spiders of the dusty big *desierto* aside.

* * *

The walk from Granada Station to Plaza Bib-Rambla, where I have booked a room, is a far cry from Almería's deserted lanes. After a couple of days' leave, I have returned to *España Turistica* proper. And I like it a lot.

For a start, the air is cooler up here at 740 metres. Then there are the distinguished university buildings – 82,000 students live in Granada – leading to medieval monasteries, elegant seventeenth-century palaces and delightful curious little antique shops, florists and second-hand bookshops. Beyond the Renaissance cathedral, the *turistica* world awaits with shops and stalls in tiny alleys and ancient souks selling leather handbags, fridge magnets, spices, teas, carpets, lanterns, summer dresses, espadrilles and tiles with Moorish patterns. Cafés with ceiling fans and watery mist sprays sell fruit smoothies and coffees for reasonable prices. The doors of tapas bars are open with inviting counters of nibbles lined up for the day's first customers. Like in Santiago de Compostela or in Montserrat, and in a totally different way in Benidorm, the sense of having entered a parallel Spain for the entertainment of outsiders is palpable.

The Spanish do tourism, in its various forms, very well indeed.

Having the Alhambra, of course, helps.

Given that Granada is my guidebook's number one Spanish town there are plenty of us holidaymakers about. But what is utterly brilliant is that, realizing that overtourism is a modern curse, local supremos wisely introduced a strict ticket system to limit the number of visitors to 6,600 each day. These tickets can be purchased online in advance and are issued in time slots covering morning, afternoon and evening sessions depending on which part of the great hilltop fortress-palace you intend to see. Such is the demand to visit Spain's number one tourist attraction that you are highly advised to buy your ticket ahead of arriving in Granada. You are also, when you look into how to buy a ticket online, informed of more than twenty "basic regulations for accessing the monument", ranging from not touching any stonework or plants to not using tripods for cameras, not lying down on benches, not bringing any pets and not taking off clothes or shoes. There are a lot of things you must not do and breaking the rules could lead to you being "sanctioned with expulsion from the Monumental complex".

Of course, I have not bought a ticket in advance.

So I go to a medieval Moorish ticket office in a building with walls and arches with beautiful Arabic carvings known as the Corral del Carbón, which began as an inn back in the fourteenth century and where the official ticket office is to be found. Here a woman in a green polo shirt points me in the direction of a green ticket machine when I ask for a ticket and when I press the buttons a notice comes up announcing that the machines will not offer tickets on the day of purchase. The ticket saleswoman, when I go back, tells me that I must in fact go online for a ticket for today. It is not possible to buy a ticket person-to-person with the ticket saleswoman. So I do this and four times in a row I reach the very last stage, having entered my passport details and other information – and proven several times that I am "not a robot" – before arriving at a faded green button saying *FINISH*. But this button will not click through no matter how many times I try. I demonstrate this to the ticket saleswoman, who tells me that this is unusual as the faded green *FINISH* button is normally a brighter shade of green and, when it is this brighter colour, you can indeed click through. She writes a number on a piece of paper and advises that I call the number to buy a ticket instead. I call this number and a recorded message says that the ticket assistants are busy and "will answer in a moment". After hearing this message eight times, I am asked to "call back another time" and the phone cuts off. I explain this to the ticket saleswoman, who tells me she does not make the rules and advises me to go up the hill to the Alhambra to try the ticket office there.

I go into the courtyard of Corral del Carbón and lean against a pillar for a moment to wipe my brow and collect my thoughts – there is little point in visiting Granada and not seeing the Alhambra. As I am leaning against the pillar, another (fiercer) ticket saleswoman with a green polo shirt tells me that I must not lean against the pillar as the Corral del Carbón is "the oldest hotel in the world".

I apologize and she replies: "You should know better."

I apologize once more, whereupon she stands silently, folding her arms, watching me.

And so I go up the hill, passing gorgeous gardens with orange trees and box hedges and arrive at a ticket office by the gate, where a long queue has formed. I join the queue. While I am waiting, I try for a final time to buy a ticket online and, by some small miracle, the green box is a brighter green and I am able to purchase a ticket there and then download it on to my phone, skip the queue, walk to the gate, have my ticket scanned from the screen of my phone and enter the Alhambra.

Yes, I am aware this is a rather long explanation of how I get into the Alhambra, and it may sound as though I am complaining, but I am not.

This is great! This is just how it should be!

Famous tourist attractions should have rules and regulations and limited numbers to keep dreadful overtourists, such as myself, at bay. OK, it was a tad frustrating, and if I was not heading off early tomorrow morning on a train to the coast the supremos would have won. I would simply have booked for the next day, if tickets were available then, or the day after that. Or just given up.

Being so damn difficult means that numbers are properly controlled, which is all right and proper and as it should be.

Inside the fortress it *is* crowded, but not badly. So pleased am I to be here that I seem to float through the gardens of roses and marigolds, listening to the trickle of water in octagonal fountains and lily ponds, smelling the sweet perfume of magnolia trees and enjoying the shaded passageways between dreamlike colonnaded courtyards with orange trees and terraces with views across the terracotta roofs of rose-bricked buildings way down below in the old town. In the distance piebald hills rise, framed by the faint grey outline of the Sierra Nevada mountains. The sultans and the kings thereafter certainly knew how to live – indeed, so impressed were they, Ferdinand II and Isabella I themselves resided hereabouts for a while after the culmination of the *Reconquista*, when the Naṣrid kingdom of Granada became the last Muslim enclave to fall in 1492. On this hill, the notorious Alhambra Decree was signed and practising Jews expelled from Spain.

Floating onward along paths smelling of lavender and lined by clever irrigation channels, I arrive at the Palacio de Carlos V, a large Renaissance-inspired palace with its columns, curved walls and a small fine art museum with a charge of one euro fifty cents for tourists who are not members of the European Union. I admire the old paintings of scheming bishops, demons, devils and feasts. Then I enter the sublime Palacio Nazaríes and continue to float across courtyards and chambers of colourful tiles and passages with alabaster decorations to a shaded terrace with a fountain mounted on stone lions in the heart of what was once the harem. The inner rooms of this *palacio*, no matter the heat of the day (it is 40ºC), seem so cool and restful. The tiled walls, alive in aquamarines, golds, purples and sea greens, have a hypnotic effect. It would be so easy, were rules to allow, to curl up with a cushion in a corner and enjoy a long impromptu siesta.

Instead, I go down the hill to a café beside my hotel in Plaza Bib-Rambla, where I am happy merely to *be* for a while.

To rest beneath a watery mist spray. To drink a glass of chilled white wine. To watch the tourists visiting the fridge magnet and knick-knack shops. To see a local lie out on a stone bench in the shade of a tree and take a nap. To appreciate that, despite all the tourists and the parallel world created for them, Granada would make a wonderful place to live now; all those centuries ago, the sultans picked a great spot.

To talk to the tourists too. I meet a couple, Bill and Rhona, on the table beside, Australians who have just completed the Camino de Santiago de Compostela, covering 360 miles by bike. It is an incredible feat. She had "a dynamic hip screw" installed six weeks before going and they are in their seventies on a trip to celebrate their fiftieth wedding anniversary. He is a retired mathematics teacher; she is "retired from all sorts of things". They both wear straw hats.

They have a sharp sense of humour.

They ask about my trip.

"Are you Michael Portillo?" asks Rhona, jokingly – as, no doubt, the ticket attendant had been back at Cìudad Real.

They tell me about getting stuck in Santiago as all the trains were booked and having to rent a car at great expense to reach Madrid (I seem to have been lucky).

They tell me about visiting friends near Alicante. "It was absolutely horrible," says Rhona. "At one of these British *enclaves*," she drags out the word *enclaves*, "we went to a British bar and the bartender wouldn't speak Spanish to us. We could have been in Tesco when we went to the local shop: beans, Marmite. That's what we thought, except the prices were astronomical. Apparently, people will pay them."

Bill: "Forty-storey apartment blocks."

Rhona: "Bodies on the beach that should have been white."

Bill: "But they were not."

Rhona, turning her eyes to teenaged girls beginning a steamy-looking coordinated dance to pop music in Plaza Bib-Rambla: "It's been really interesting watching the younger generations. What they get up to and what their parents will tolerate."

Bill, looking across: "They will tolerate a lot."

Rhona: "They are being a little bit suggestive."

Bill: "A little bit?"

They order more white wines.

Bill was born in America, in a place called Alhambra in California – one of the reasons they visited Granada. "When I showed my passport at the gate," he says, "they were quite confused."

Presenting your passport is another one of the Alhambra's rules.

We toast our great fortune at having visited one of the finest places in Spain. We enjoy the watery mist spray. They are flying to Zurich tomorrow and shortly afterward to San Francisco.

"Yes, we know we're the lucky generation," says Bill, referring to their age and wealth.

"That's why we travel so much," says Rhona.

"Invasion is a word that reminds me of war"
Granada to Torremolinos, via Málaga

At Granada Station a queue has formed for the 07:10 to Madrid-Atocha Station, although I will be changing at Antequera-Santa Ana Station for a connection to Málaga-María Zambrano Station. The first train is an AVE arriving at 08:02 at Antequera-Santa Ana. The second train, a slightly slower Avant service, will depart from Antequera-Santa Ana at 08:17 and be in Málaga by 08:45, according to the timetable, after which I intend to take train three of the day on a line with regular departures along the coast past Málaga Airport to Torremolinos Station. This is a journey of 18 minutes and will be the fiftieth train since leaving St Pancras.

Quite unbelievable when I think about it.

At first, I am not quite sure quite why I want to go to Torremolinos.

Like Benidorm, it has long suffered from a bad reputation, some even referring to the seaside resort as the "armpit of the Costa del Sol" due to overdeveloped tourism from the 1980s onward. Also like Benidorm, it is little written about. The guidebooks do not pay much attention and I cannot, for that matter, recall a single straightforward travel article about either Torremolinos or Benidorm in the British national press or in a mainstream travel magazine, ever. Is this snobbery? Perhaps.

Anyway, this is what has piqued my interest. What happens in mysterious Torremolinos?

Well, I guess I am about to find out.

Our AVE train rolls beyond bright adverts for Spain's high-speed train network at Granada Station. Soon we are sprinting past cypress trees on the edge of town. The sensation is of being on a very fast, long, thin milk float. The train gently purrs and we move westward at astonishing speed. During the time it takes to reach Antequera-Santa Ana I can report a blur of fruit orchards and olive groves, broad comfortable seats, fellow passengers with cropped gelled hair who look like businessmen, and two women of a certain age drinking G & Ts quite happily at this early hour in the buffet car, where I eat a decent ham-and-cheese toasted sandwich and drink a coffee for six euros and thirty cents.

Antequera-Santa Ana Station, like Segovia-Guiomar Station, seems to be a newly constructed handy high-speed-train pit stop with a modern box-like design slapped in the middle of a field of olive trees.

A dead pigeon that no one appears to want to move is stuck on the bottom of the windscreen of the AVE from Granada.

It is, however, a relaxing wait on the platform, listening to birdsong from live birds while the smell of herbs rises from the orange-earth olive fields slowly warming up in the morning sunshine. The Renfe Avant train arrives and in a short time, passing through much similar scenery, one long tunnel and beyond a derelict factory near Castañetas, we are in Málaga, where I walk quite a long way to see the Picasso Museum.

Pablo Picasso – or to give his full name: Pablo Diego José Francisco de Paula Juan Nepomuceno Crispín Crispiniano María Remedios de la Santísima Trinidad Ruiz Picasso – was born in Málaga in 1881. His family moved to A Coruña when he was aged nine as his father, himself an artist, had been made professor at a fine art museum in the Galician port. He returned only once to Málaga in his teens and never set foot in Spain again after Franco's victory in the Spanish Civil War – he had supported the Republicans – dying just two years before Franco, near Cannes in France. *Guernica*, one of his greatest paintings, which I regret not seeing in Madrid, has as its subject the terrifying destruction of a Basque Country town of that name by German bombers supporting the Nationalists.

In the spirit of Spanish artistic investigation begun in Figueres that has become a hobby on these train rides, I enter the cool whitewashed rooms of the small *museo*.

Comparing Picasso and Dalí and asking which is better is like doing the same about an apple and an orange. They are what they are, though I prefer Picasso's unique imaginative style, which is immediately evident in a series of portraits of wide-eyed figures with oblong faces and out-of-joint noses that offer glimpses of character yet at the same time seem to make a statement: *we're all pretty mixed up*. The images of mad fragments of humanity might appear messy, but the assuredness of the strokes speaks otherwise and the perfection of the balance and deliberate clash of colours is simply masterful. Franco described Picasso's art as "degenerate" – well, he would.

A video of Picasso painting the outline of a bull and a bowl of flowers on a piece of glass captures the ease with which he understood the "truth", if you like, of his subjects: without ado or ceremony, the striking images are formed with the ease of someone slapping paint on a garden wall. This is beside an insightful quote from an interview with the artist that says something of his method: "A picture is not thought out and settled beforehand. While it is being done it changes as one's thoughts change. And when it is finished, it still goes on changing, according to the state of mind of whoever is looking at it."

Just like going on a long train ride in Spain, you make it up as you go along… and when you look back on it all, many mental snapshots remain.

* * *

Mulling this over, I catch the two-tone tangerine commuter train to Torremolinos.

This passes the airport, a Coca-Cola plant, an IKEA and a McDonald's with, if my eyes are not deceiving me, a gym connected on one side: the Ronald Gym Club. Eat your Big Mac, then sweat it off (if I have this right). Welcome to twenty-first century life on the Costa del Sol.

Soon afterward, I disembark at a small underground station with an advert for Beefeater London Pink Gin near the ticket barriers. Beyond is a square where my first sight is of a British man wearing an LA Lakers basketball top and flip-flops walking with a child to whom he is saying: "I hope she's not whingeing by the time we get back."

With Picasso still on my mind, Torremolinos is best described here in a series of impressions. Like one of the great Spanish artist's skewed visages, Torremolinos is difficult to grab hold of, but I will try.

The first impression hits you straight away, and this is of Little Britain in Andalusía, as represented by La Casa de Sherlock Holmes pub, a Poundland shop and an Indian restaurant; what, after all, could be more British than that?

The second is of what appears to be a thriving LGBT scene in the form of LGBT flags by a bar and wrapped around a series of lamp posts.

The third is a note of defensiveness at the tourist office when I ask an assistant if locals mind so many British having invaded Torremolinos.

"*Invasion* is a word that reminds me of war," she says. "Without the British we wouldn't be here. There would be no tourist office. We are very used to the British here. Actually, Torremolinos has everything. It is perfect, less stressful than other places: very attractive to the rest of the world. This has always been the most modern place in Spain. When tourism began here, the rest of the country looked over at us."

After telling me all this, she recommends that I go to see Hotel Pez Espada, which opened in 1959 and was soon counting "the Hollywood set", including Frank Sinatra and Sophia Loren, among its guests.

I thank her for this tip-off. Then I ask whether Torremolinos has a particularly beautiful part.

"We do not have *a* beautiful part," she replies. "We have *many* beautiful parts."

She hands me a map and triumphantly points at several locations including the beach.

Fourth impression: a long hot walk down a winding lane through a charming, if extremely touristy, old town and along a hot beach with paddleboarders on the waves past a hotel with an LGBT flag, a bar with pink seating and very well-groomed male customers, to a section of beach with topless bathers by a pretty headland with a crumbling cliff. A promenade leads onward to Calle Los Peros, where I stop at Winston's pub and a British barmaid says: "We've got Tetley's on draft or John Smith" and replies: "OK, I'll get you a cold one" when I ask for a pint of Tetley's. This is served, and I drink the pint of bitter while watching England play Australia live in the Cricket World Cup in the company of a man with a tattoo of a frothy pint of beer on his leg. Perhaps he just points at it when he requires another drink.

Afterward, beyond the British Bar, where a waitress outside cheerfully but completely unhelpfully comments, "I bet you're sweatin' in them jeans" as I pass, I arrive at impression number five.

If you are looking for a symbolic starting point for mass-market tourism in Spain, this is it.

Hotel Pez Espada, now known officially as Medplaya Hotel Pez Espada, is an eight-storey building with a style that was modern in the mid nineteenth century (with a space age look mixed with a touch of art deco), a bar, a pool and almost two hundred rooms. The entrance is through a doorway of a rocket-like cylindrical tower and inside a long lobby runs between a corridor of missile-shaped columns set around a marble floor with a striking swirly pattern. At the far end by a grand piano, a series of signed black-and-white photographs of former guests evokes the period when Hotel Pez Espada must have been at the very height of fashionability and cutting-edge design. The Duke and Duchess of Windsor (1962), Sean Connery (1962), King Albert II of Belgium (1966), Sophia Loren (1971) and many others passed by at a time when Torremolinos was considered the new Côte d'Azur. Other unpictured names to come included Dirk Bogarde, Elizabeth Taylor, Ava Gardner, Raquel Welch and Ingrid Bergman.

In Frankie's Café you learn about the hotel's most notorious guest. In 1964, Frank Sinatra was involved in a bust-up here with a photographer and an aspiring Cuban actress who, it is said, set up a picture so Sinatra appeared to be embracing her. The story goes that Sinatra was enraged, pushed the actress away and had one of his entourage grab the camera, pull out the film and smash the camera on the floor. Police were called later that evening after the actress complained about his rough-handedness. Sinatra was taken to a police cell in Málaga, questioned, said to have compared those questioning him to the Gestapo, fined 25,000 pesetas soon after drawing this analogy, and escorted to the airport, whereupon his parting words were said to have been: "I will never return to this damned country."

And, just like Picasso, he kept his word.

This tale is related on an information panel by the bar – and there is an odd feeling at Hotel Pez Espada now, so long after those glamorous, and perhaps not always really so glamorous, days: fashions come, fashions go (and are sometimes very long gone).

One final impression of Torremolinos.

This time the impression comes in the form of Paul, to whom I get talking at yet another pub with the cricket on near my hotel.

Paul is on a five-week holiday to southern Spain that will include ten days in Benidorm soon. He is from Blackpool and studied engineering for a year at Sheffield University before dropping out. He works as a civil servant – no further explanation is offered on what type – and for two nights a week earns extra cash as a taxi driver: "Actually, I make more money from that". He is in his fifties and wears a yellow polo shirt and Slazenger shorts. His grey hair is cropped close, with sunglasses resting on top. He has a toothy grin and drinks "Carling top" – Carling lager with a splash of lemonade.

"I'm up to seventy-five days and counting," Paul says, matter-of-factly, referring to the length of time he has been on holiday this year. He has a couple of weeks coming up in Tenerife, where he goes twice annually, and he will be back in Torremolinos in the autumn.

"Certainly, another week here, at least a week," he says, as though teasing the matter over in his mind. "I was here last year for Christmas. I've been coming here for twenty-five years. It's more cosmopolitan than in Benidorm. You get French and Italians in Torremolinos. Benidorm's all British: the new Blackpool."

He sips his Carling top. He complains that southerners – from the south of Britain – have begun to visit Benidorm. "Tenerife got too expensive," he says, explaining that southerners who once went to Tenerife are switching to the Costa Blanca.

A mate of his in flip-flops walks past and asks: "All right, Pauly?"

He says he's all right and asks the man in flip-flops if he is all right. He is just fine too.

Then Pauly tells me how when he was younger, he would stay up till four in the morning playing pool in Torremolinos. "I'd drink myself sober," he says. "But I'd still win. I used to be in the Blackpool pool league."

He pauses as a man with slicked-back grey hair yells to the waitress: "That's two pink gins, doubles, and a 'Paradise' – you got that?"

Then a text pings on his phone for a taxi pick-up in Blackpool. He laughs and texts back that he is booked up right now. He takes another sip of his Carling top.

I ask if I can take Paul's picture and he says: "Sure, I'm not a criminal."

We watch the cricket for a while, making the odd observation about play.

It is hot. The drinks are cheap.

That's the bottom line regarding Torremolinos these days. Flights are cheap. *Cervezas* are cheap. Everything is generally cheap, cheap, cheap. The temperature is hot, hot, hot. For nine months of the year the daily high is above 20°C.

You can take seventy-five-day holidays on the proceeds of working as a part-time taxi driver with a civil service job, enjoy the heat and keep up with all the latest sports news. And it is indeed beautiful in parts: I follow all the marks made on my map by the tourist office people, following an old stream to the bullring overlooked by lovely lilac hills. I am surprised not more of us are doing it like Pauly.

Britain may have its north-south divide, and so definitely does Europe too. Why not hop off for a nice little seventy-five-day break in the sun? Just remember to take the trains and stop at a few stations along the way.

A view of the Rock
Torremolinos to Algeciras

The journey to Algeciras, a port overlooking the Bay of Gibraltar, involves retracing yesterday's trains and waiting for a connection at sleepy Bobadilla Station, where the televisions in the station café – a nice one with tables outside facing a mounted historic signal box – are showing a "sport" that is not cricket: highlights of the morning's Running of the Bulls in the San Fermín fiesta in Pamplona.

It seems a long time since I passed by there.

The ride to Algeciras is across a vivid tomato-red landscape beneath a moody purple sky. The train, a *Media Distancia* service, takes its time weaving between ravines, mountains and rivers lined by the snake-like pink bushes that I have come to enjoy so much (possibly oleander bushes, if my Google check is correct). Prickly pears grow by the tracks and little scatterings of Orwell-style *dice villages* appear now and then, as do village stations with elderly men at tables passing the time of day.

I only have three rides left in Spain and I have become so attuned to movement down the line that the ravines and the olive groves, the prickly pears and the pink river bushes, the distant mountains and the dice villages, and the empty carriage and the clatter of the tracks are all quite settling and *normal*. I can understand now how sailors need to rediscover their land legs after a long spell at sea. When I make it to Seville, some adjustments are going to need to be made.

* * *

Algeciras (population: 120,000) is a major port with connections to Morocco, including the enclaves of Melilla and Ceuta that I learned about on the asylum seekers march in Bilbao. Many historical battles have been fought here. Under their leader Ṭāriq ibn Ziyād, the Moors first crossed the Strait of Gibraltar and invaded Spain here in 711, establishing a city that led to the long period of Moorish occupation of the Iberian Peninsula that came to an end in Granada in 1492. Vikings attacked. Spanish kings attacked. The British and the Dutch attacked; the British subsequently keeping Gibraltar under the Treaty of Utrecht of 1713. During the Second World War, British occupation of the fortress-like rock of Gibraltar was crucial for its role in supplying troops in Malta and controlling the strait, which is in parts, as I have mentioned before, only 9 miles wide. After the war, Franco tried to claim Gibraltar, but the British did not want to go and in 1969 a stand-off led to the border being closed, causing a loss of jobs for many locals in Algeciras, about a half-hour's drive away. This border eventually partially reopened in 1982 and fully in 1985 ahead of Spain joining the European Community in 1986.

This is one of the most strategic spots in Europe, if not the world – hence so much interest over the years. Even now, somewhere out there is the detained supertanker said to be full of Iranian oil that was originally bound for Syria and that the officer back in A Coruña was so tight-lipped about. This is a major international event. The latest

Sur in English has a report quoting Gibraltar's chief minister, Fabian Picardo, who says: "I want to thank the brave men and women of the Royal Marines, the Royal Gibraltar Police, Her Majesty's Customs Gibraltar and the Gibraltar Port Authority for their work in securing the detention of this vessel and its cargo. Be assured that Gibraltar remains safe, secure and committed to the international, rules-based legal order."

Good to hear.

Yet while most people have heard of Gibraltar, Algeciras – where the Moors landed – is little known.

It is the most Arabic-feeling place in Spain so far, even more so than Almería. I am staying in a tiny room at Hostal Fes with iron-barred windows facing a peaceful arched courtyard with Moorish tiles and potted plants. At the end of the street, men sit at cafés drinking coffee and smoking hookah pipes, some dressed in ankle-length robes. Down narrow roads by the waterfront, the Rock of Gibraltar rises sharply across the bay and a stream of lorries enters the harbour, where sky-blue cranes hang by great heaps of ochre cargo containers and further out I think I can see the hazy outline of Africa and an Islamic nation stretching south to the sands of the Sahara.

Algeciras was one of Laurie Lee's late stop-offs, where he stayed for a fortnight enjoying the "potency and charm" of the port, home back then to a set of "international freaks drinking themselves into multilingual stupors". It brings a chuckle to imagine him busking with his fiddle by Plaza Alta, the main square, playing Schubert and "local ballads of mystical sex" to passers-by on request.

It is at Plaza Alta, while trying to picture Lee with his fiddle, that I find myself joining my second protest march in Spain. This one has a train theme.

Outside the Parish of Our Lady of La Palma church, beside a tiled fountain in a Moorish style decorated with frogs, a group of ten people has gathered and is holding aloft a banner with a picture of a train that reads: *UN SIGLO SIN TREN* (*A CENTURY WITHOUT A TRAIN*).

Each member of the group also holds up a piece of paper upon which the number 539 is printed.

A man with sunshades, a pink shirt and a fedora formally introduces himself. His name is Juan María de la Cuesta and he is their leader. "Now I shall explain to you that we are fighting as we do not have a train to carry merchandises," he says with great urgency, explaining that 539 is the number of days until a deadline which has been set, at which point, under some European Union rule or other, a cargo train should be provided to link Algeciras to the rest of Spain. Currently the track is not advanced enough (in a way that I do not understand) to take such trains. Currently the powers that be in the Spanish government are not paying enough attention to the EU rules. "Cargo trains! Everyone wants passenger trains, but cargo trains are needed too! If a cargo train goes from Algeciras, it can get to Madrid, then Zaragoza then Tarragona, then Perpignan! There is an EU obligation to do this! Tangiers is competing with us. So is Sines in Portugal, and València! We strongly need this railway! These are very important works: one million euros!"

A passer-by, seeing us in conversation, comes up and grabs my arm and points at Juan.

"This is a great man!" he says. "A great man!"

And then he departs, and Juan looks a little embarrassed.

We march around Plaza Alta. I have been given a piece of paper printed with 539 to wave too. Apparently, they have been holding this demonstration every afternoon for some time, changing the number obviously each day.

Another member of the group, having learned of my origins, steps forward.

"Mr Morrison!" he exclaims – a great deal of exclamation seems to go on in Plaza Alta. "Mr Morrison! Mr Juan Morrison!"

I explain that this is not my name. Juan María de la Cuesta steps in. He tells me that two British men, John Morrison, a Scottish engineer, and Alexander Henderson, an English financier, were responsible for the construction of the first railway between Algeciras and Bobadilla in the late 1880s. It was built so the British on the Rock could connect with the rest of Spain, but the station did not go directly to the Rock as the Spanish were touchy about the British presence; as they still are, despite the 1985 climbdown. There are, I discover, streets named after Juan Morrison and Alexander Henderson in Algeciras. The "century without a train" banner refers to their line, created by the Algeciras Gibraltar Railway Company.

We all shake hands. There is a brief round of applause as the day's demonstration is officially brought to a close.

Afterward, I may be the first tourist in the history of Algeciras to go on a spur-of-the-moment tour of the streets named after Juan Morrison and Alexander Henderson. These are not far from Plaza Alta. On Calle Juan Morrison, opposite a shop selling clothes for tall women in a good neighbourhood with yellow-ochre and peach-coloured houses, a plaque remembering the Scot says: *Delegado de la compañía de ferrocarriles en 1898* (Delegate of the railway company in 1898). On Calle Alexander Henderson I cannot find a plaque, although there is a canine beauty parlour, a homeless man asleep in a doorway and another fellow feeding innards to a cat by a wall with a view of the sea.

Britain's connections with the south of Spain predate all the high-rise hotels. The railways came first. Then a trickle of tourists. Then the planes.

Then the deluge.

CHAPTER TWELVE
ALGECIRAS TO SEVILLE, VIA RONDA

"A VERY TOURISTICAL PLACE"

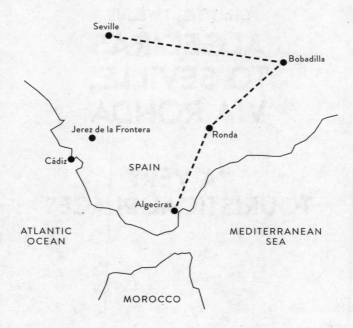

Seville

Bobadilla

Jerez de la Frontera

Ronda

Cádiz

SPAIN

Algeciras

ATLANTIC
OCEAN

MEDITERRANEAN
SEA

MOROCCO

In the morning – yes, I know travel writers are not meant to begin sentences, let alone chapters, with "in the morning" (if some former editors are to be believed), although frankly the phrase can be quite helpful – I catch the 08.43 to Ronda. First, I drink a coffee at a café at the bus station opposite the train station as the train station at Algeciras, highly unusually for Spain, has no café.

The man next to me at the bus station bar is partaking of a double whisky and looks as though he has just come off a long work shift. Perhaps he is a sailor returning from a voyage on one of the cargo ships. Or perhaps this is just what he does each day. I do not ask as he seems wrapped up in his thoughts.

I return to the train station and board *Tren 9367, con destino a* Madrid-Atocha Station, which slides into blazing sunshine along yesterday's line, courtesy of Morrison and Henderson, as I now know. We cross a bridge above a pale-grey river that I did not previously notice. The train emits a hollow, echoey sound. Then we make sedate progress beyond gullies and boulder-strewn land northward through a wide sunflower field that I cannot recall from yesterday either. Egrets step carefully across a ploughed plain in search of something, looking like confetti against the ochre soil.

We rise in altitude between granite peaks and soon arrive in Ronda.

* * *

My penultimate stop on my trains round Spain is simply *maravillosa*.

The station is a ten-minute walk down a hot street lined with orange trees to the old town, where I have booked a room at a hotel on a corner near the old bullring. This bullring (1781) is where modern bullfighting is said to have begun and it is next to an elegant park, Alameda del Tajo (Mall of the Gorge), planted with palm trees with a terrace by a cliff at the far end – and one of the finest views in the entire country.

On these rides around Spain I have selected where to go largely on the basis that *just about everywhere is interesting so you cannot really go wrong*. This has been my modus operandi, useful as the requirement for time-consuming advance research is kept to a minimum and you have plenty of surprises. While I had some notion that Ronda was special, a tourist honeypot of the highest order, renowned for its Andalusian loveliness, I had no idea just how dramatic the town's setting would be.

From the terrace by the bullring, a valley of patchwork farmland dotted with stone properties with terracotta roofs stretches out below. The cliff drops like a plumb line and bald mountains mark the horizon beneath a hazy blue sky. The feeling here is of being a long way up, which we are, at 740 metres. The air is thin and there is a magic about the location as though Ronda has been lifted by Andalusian spirits and is somehow preferred land. No wonder everyone from prehistoric times through to the Romans, the Visigoths and the Moors liked it so much here. Interestingly, having been so recently in Granada, it was to remote mountains spots such as Ronda that many Moriscos, as Moors who converted to Christianity were known, came in 1492, many secretly practising Islam. When, in 1567, Philip II – busy in so many ways – banned Arabic and ordered that house doors were left open to prevent clandestine Friday prayers, an initially successful Morisco rebellion took place in Ronda, which eventually led to their expulsion from the town. During these times, Moriscos were made to wear blue crescents on their headgear, a persecution-by-clothing similar to Hitler's yellow stars.

Much of which I learn on one of my final acts of Spanish tourism on this journey.

After seeing the fine balconied bullring where Goya captured many scenes, including those in Zaragoza, and where the cloaks and swords of current bullfighting were introduced, I join a city walking tour.

This is led by Jaime. We – some Americans, a couple from Singapore and I – meet by the tourist office by the bullring.

"If you want to stop to pick up a beer just shout. OK? The police don't mind. They're not going to say nothing," says Jaime, all designer stubble and gelled hair, breaking the ice.

We follow and are shown a statue of Pedro Romero, an eighteenth-century bullfighter.

"He was the bullfighter who changed the rules. He was friends with Goya. He killed five thousand [bulls]. Before him, people would put up wood barriers on the square and people would get drunk and everyone would participate, dogs would run around. It was really, really 'orrible. 'Orrible!" says Jaime, repeating what we soon learn is his catchword. "I'm not a fan but it is my culture so it's very OK, this bullfighting. Only official bullfighters participate, and it is important that the bulls don't suffer. The people of Spain don't want the blood. They are very, very intelligent animals. You can only fight them once. If more than once they will go for legs. They know how to do it. They go at forty-five kilometres an hour [twenty-eight miles per hour] – like a horse. Very sharp horns. I assure you it is very, very real fighting."

We walk along a clifftop to a spectacular bridge across the gorge, the Puente Nuevo. "Ronda is a very safe town. No problems. No villains," he says. "There used to be people who came up from Málaga but they are not from this country. Be a little careful around the bridge. This is very touristical – Ronda is a very touristical place. There are some wonderful places in Ronda but also there are some very 'orrible places. 'Orrible!"

The Americans ask if a bullfight will be on today and Jaime says that the bullfights here are only held in September, an event known as Feria Goyesca or by some as Feria de Pedro Romero. "The bullring only has four thousand five hundred seats, so it is not profitable for fighting," he says. "Matadors want two hundred thousand euros – the big names. Now they win more money from the tourists."

By this he means that the bullring owners "win more money" than they would by holding extra bullfights. The September festival, however, is one of the most prestigious in Spain, attracting the great and the good aplenty. "De Niro, Cristiano Ronaldo, Madonna, Antonio Banderas," he says. Bullfighting in Ronda is part of the social circuit, like the Henley Regatta or Wimbledon in the UK. "People come to see how pretty you are," Jaime says – not necessarily to watch the action in the ring.

We walk down a terrace into the gorge, looking back up at the bridge, with the Río Guadalevín glistening below, where Jaime used to swim as a child. The first bridge here collapsed in 1741 soon after opening, resulting in fifty deaths – a terrifying way to die; the distance to the base is 120 metres. During the Civil War some soldiers met a sticky end at the Puente Nuevo, as described in Hemingway's *For Whom the Bell Tolls*. Somewhere in the middle of the arches at the top is a former prison cell – a terrifying place to wait to die terrifyingly, no doubt.

Jaime tells us about an old Arabian clifftop palace and how slaves had to carry boulders up two hundred steps for its construction: "Incredible, 'orrible, 'orrible work!"

We walk up a hill above the remains of some ancient Arabian baths and Jaime describes completing part of the Camino de Santiago de Compostela last year. "Every day it was 'orrible!" he says. "Thirty thousand people out each day. 'Orrible! 'Orrible! But very good. Like a drug."

He paces up the hill. We reach the top of the hill, near the bridge, and Jaime, the smooth operator that he is, drops us at the Centro de Interpretación del Vino de Ronda. The Americans, the Singaporeans and I spend five euros each extra for a wine tasting and the tourists mingle.

I meet Monica, a traffic engineer from Texas.

"I gotta figure out ways to alleviate congestion," she says of her job. "The highways are at capacity."

We talk about highway jams in San Antonio for a while. The situation on the roads of southern Texas would appear to be at breaking point.

Monica and I are drinking *vinos* made from Tempranillo and Cabernet Sauvignon grapes, which you pour yourself from taps in barrels. This *centro de interpretación* is more like a *barra libre* (free bar), once you've paid your five euros.

There is also sherry, which Monica has not tried. This is also *libre*. We move on to the sherry.

"All I knew about sherry was what I saw on *Frasier*," she says, referring to the American comedy sitcom in which two brothers sharing an apartment in Seattle enjoy a tipple from a decanter in almost every episode. In the US, sherry is regarded by some as rather English and "intellectual".

Monica knocks back her glass. She likes it.

"Hey, Jenny," she cries over to her aunt. "Have you tried this stuff?"

Jenny joins us, tries sherry, and likes sherry too. We all pour ourselves more sherries.

We talk about Brexit. "What's that all about?" Monica asks.

We talk about Donald Trump. "What's that all about?" I ask.

We talk about how Jenny met her husband at work in a previous job. Her husband works in the US Navy. Frank joins us and tries sherry for the first time and likes sherry. Everyone, it is agreed, likes the sherry. Jenny tells me how she opened an olive oil import business after going on a holiday in Greece a few years back but is now looking to sell and start something new. "Sherry perhaps?" I ask.

"Maybe," she replies, refilling her glass.

Monica's cousin asks me about cricket: "You gotta stick and a ball, right?" I tell him yes.

"And the guy with the stick's gotta hit it?"

That's the long and the short of it, I reply.

We talk about the orange trees by the roads in Ronda. "You can't eat them – the oranges," says the cousin. "Too sour. Only used for marmalade."

This is good information. I've been all the way round Spain wondering why people just don't pick the public oranges for snacks.

We finish our sherries. We have a group photograph taken by the sherry barrels. Then the Americans head off to take a minibus to Seville – they have booked the bus and the driver for a fortnight in Spain. No trains for them.

What nice Americans, nevertheless.

Watching them go, enjoying a "sherry buzz", I reflect on tourism in Spain: let's face it, this is what most people come to Spain to do. This is what Spain now *does* – an awful lot of it. No point in ignoring such an important aspect of what makes the country tick. You see interesting historical and *touristical* sights in a hot climate, you get to try unusual foreign food and drink, you may meet sociable people, and it can be a whole lot of fun. To understand modern Spain, you've got to appreciate this entertainment business, the sheer scale of it... and how it is not going away anytime fast.

All that is left *touristically* on my last night in Spain is to go to a flamenco show. This I do on Plaza del Socorro in the distinguished setting of the Casino de Ronda.

A handful of other flamenco-goers are sitting in rows of red seats capable of taking many more in a courtyard surrounded by arches and walls hung with mirrors and gilded paintings. On a small stage, a small middle-aged woman in a red dress decorated with flowers, her hair pulled back tightly in a ponytail and adorned with pink and red hair ties, claps her hands slowly to the accompaniment of an intensely intricate guitar solo performed by a bald man in black sitting on a simple chair. Next to him another man in black with a polka-dot tie and twitchy features has just completed an intensely intricate love song. The woman looks to one side as though considering a matter of great importance as she slowly claps and the guitar speeds up and the guitarist taps his feet and the singer next to him does the same, clapping too and closing his eyes as though lost in the rhythm.

And just when all of this is building up into a perfect storm of intense intricacy, the small woman slams her heels on the stage precisely and fiercely as though telling the neighbours downstairs to keep it down for God's sake. Then she moves with almost impossible agility and speed while tapping and slamming her feet as the singer takes up once again, his eyes still closed, and the guitarist relents and speeds up and relents and speeds up. All the while the dancer slams and shuffles and taps and suddenly stops, only to repeat it all again, her arms held elegantly aloft and her face at one moment fierce and in the next dignified and in the next hurt and betrayed. An hour flies by and the handful of tourists and I step out into Plaza del Socorro after shaking the hands of the dancer, singer and guitarist, dazed and feeling like changed people.

Spain can do this to you.

Trains of thought
Ronda to Seville

Out on Alameda del Tajo, I sit on a stone step above the patchwork landscape watching a kestrel balancing in the breeze by the clifftop. It is almost motionless, as though showing off its sheer perfection in the last bronzed light of the day.

Looking back after so many trains in Spain, as I am now on the final night, I try to find words to express why I have fallen for Spain so much.

Because this is what has happened.

Escaping across the Pyrenees has been a pure relief. Somewhere along the line through the mountains, another world opened up. Northern Europe turned into southern Europe and a spider's web of railways awaited with intriguing little towns, sleepy villages and centuries-old cities all brimful with tales of yore: bloodthirsty kings, conniving queens, conquests of peoples, long bitter struggles, half-forgotten scandals, artistic triumphs, heroic moments, political set-tos, mishaps, fables, legends and, of course, trains, trains, trains.

Let trains lead the way and let Spain reveal itself as seen from the trackside. No invention has so shaped the physical layout of the planet – where railways go, life is to be found. So in Spain, as it is elsewhere. There are fast trains, there are slow trains, there are medium-paced trains. In no need to speed about, I took as many slow ones as possible.

The impulse was to step away from the hyperactive conveyor belt of twenty-first century existence. The rapid-fire information. The compulsion to act according to small electronic messages. The pop-up alerts. The subscription deals. The scramble to "perform" on a billion little stages. The headless scurry "forward". The dance to the digital devil.

The result is, I hope, a series of offbeat glimpses of Spain from its railways that somehow combine to form a larger picture, albeit fragmented, of one of the most interesting countries in Europe at a very interesting time.

This was never intended to be the complete story of Spain. Many others, Jan Morris et al., have done that. This is just *a story*; one travel story told from the tracks.

Spain is what it is, a large European country pulling in many directions: calls for Catalonian independence; the rise of the far right; stalemate at the top; anger about overtourism; confusion about the future. There are pockets of poverty, as in parts of Extremadura. There are pockets of wealth, as in parts of Santander. There are pockets within pockets – and then there is the wider scenario of Europe's wealthy north by comparison with its troubled south.

Spain is colourful, loud, prone to festivities, fond of bloody bullrings, passionate about football and overrun in parts by tourists. It is by turns ebullient, loud, sleepy, bureaucratic, inscrutable, carefree, joyful, expansive and hopeful too.

On the tracks on a long train journey, like a dinner at a tapas bar, you get many tastes. You also understand the sense of possibilities in this big sparsely populated land that seems to be expressed by its growth in railways in recent times: the modern railway mania, if you like, for new lines.

Along the way, I have let curiosity pull me one way or another.

Having travelled down more than 3,000 miles of tracks on fifty-two Spanish rides, the feeling that railways are important to Spain pervades, strongly. The trains came late, in the form of the little line north from Barcelona to Mataró, but soon they were all over, helping to cement the modern nation that has survived despite a civil war, the rise and fall of fascism and the bubbling, irremovable presence of Basque and Catalonian separatism.

Now, since the first high-speed train from Madrid to Seville in the early 1990s, trains in Spain have become a matter of national pride. Lines are being laid here, there and just about everywhere. Part-time employees, like Maria in Almería, case the country gauging public opinion. Asked "Would you like a nice new quick train line?", the answer tends naturally to be *sí*. There is plenty of dusty empty land. This is not the Chilterns or north London, as with HS2 back home. The Not In My Back Yard brigade is absent, just about, on the Iberian Peninsula. ¡*Todo vapor!* (Full steam ahead!)

Yes, the journey has been chaotic at times, consulting timetables in the blink of an eye and rolling onward soon after; and what is slow about that, you might ask? But there is a rhythm to the routine and a simple pleasure that comes from dipping your toe in a place and moving on without getting bogged down.

Requirements? 1) Don't doze off. 2) Disembark at the correct station. 3) Take a look around.

Jump on, jump off. Investigate. Repeat. People complain of a "shrinking world", yet big adventures are to be had close to home on trains. And Spain seems to be made for long lazy journeys down winding lines.

I could at this moment, I suppose, beat a big green drum about how much more eco-friendly trains are than planes – as I mentioned at the start. But plenty of others are doing that and *of course* trains are greener than planes. If you are feeling any deep-seated Swedish *flygskam* (flight shame) then you could do far worse than go to Spain and take a few trains.

The scenery is beautiful, shifting delightfully from region to region, the people are (usually) welcoming, the food and drink is excellent, the music is easy on the ear, there are some marvellous sights, and it is normally very hot. There you have it. Ordinary observations, perhaps, but there is joy to be taken in ordinary *touristical* pursuits as well as in the everyday concerns of the Spanish Slow Train Life: the pleasant station cafés; the uplifting station architecture (I think immediately of

València and Bilbao); the fellow passengers passing the time of day; the necessity to book *hostals* (often quickly, on the hoof); the requirement to find somewhere to eat at often odd times; to get a little lost or a little frustrated; to work out the timetables; to accept the odd replacement bus; to shoot the breeze with Spanish ticket assistants – among the best, if not the very best, as I have said, in the world.

Add to this: Dalí's mad art, botanical gardens, railway museums, ancient hilltop monasteries, the works of Goya, civil war trenches, *pintxos* bars, bullrings, wild coastlines, ancient ports, pilgrimage cathedrals, Moorish fortresses, the splendid capital, a wild west, Roman ruins, mercury mines, tales of Don Quixote, palaces, artistic colonies, world-class marinas, industrial uprisings, crazy *costas*, deserts, mountains, oases, more fortresses, more palaces, the paintings of Picasso, fine old hotels, Moorish architecture, views of Africa and *touristical* highlights in general... galore.

Mix with the rattle, the clatter, the whistle, the judder, the honk, the toot, the hoot, the hum, the hiss and the heat of the tracks.

Mix also with encounters along the line, not just with railway staff, as delightful as so very many proved to be: the barmen, the barwomen, the station café owners, the hoteliers, the *hostal* owners, the bull runners, the asylum campaigners, the nuns, the bagpipers, the pilgrims, the naval officers, the tourist officers, the guides, the train lovers, the backpackers, the dropouts, the fiesta organizers, the mechanics, the teachers, the engineers, the psychology professors, the taxi drivers, the buskers, the brigadiers, the bookshop owners, the expats, the drag artists, the cargo train campaigners, the flamenco dancers and musicians (right at the end). As rich as the sights and the experience and the sense of movement may be, it is the people that so often make a trip.

Sprinkle some curiosity and a willingness to let it all go *incorrecto* from time to time.

And you have the essence of a long train journey in this magnificent country.

* * *

In the morning, I eat *desayuno* at Café Hemingway, consider purchasing a souvenir porcelain bull, watch Japanese tourists taking selfies by Puente Nuevo and catch the train via Bobadilla to Seville.

One of Spain's finest (and hottest) cities awaits. A brilliant ancient Alcázar is to be explored. A splendid cathedral containing the tomb of Christopher Columbus, no less, to be savoured. Little lanes chock-a-block with some of the country's best tapas bars to be leisurely investigated. More flamenco shows to be enjoyed! More *mercados* overflowing with hams, cheeses and wines to visit! More quiet plazas hidden away from the tourist crowds in which to while away a lazy morning with a *café largo* or two after the judder of the line. Spanish slow rides have delivered me to the city of Figaro, Carmen and Don Juan. What a perfect nation for taking to the tracks!

Muchas gracias, España.

I like you and your trains very much.

AFTERWORD

At St Pancras International at the beginning of this journey around Spain – 30 months ago now – the various alarming news stories of the day had me pondering "the sheer scale of the general mayhem of the average year of the early twenty-first century". The instinct then had been to slip away and escape, to take to the tracks and potter slowly around Spain one step removed from the hurly-burly.

It was an easy journey to make. Just find your way to the cool, shadowy haven of the Eurostar platforms below the high-arched roof of St Pancras and roll south. It was this sense of immediate freedom, of adventure on your doorstep that train travel allows, that this book hoped to capture.

Looking back, of course, it seems a much simpler time – the "hurly-burly" child's play compared to what was about to come. In December 2019, five months after returning, a disease began to spread in the little-visited industrial city of Wuhan in China, a place that Chinese bullet trains had taken me while writing another train book, *Ticket to Ride: Around the World on 49 Unusual Train Journeys*. I had not liked it much back then on a pollution-clogged stopover during which a guide had said: "Wuhan has the worst air. When I was young, five years old, I could see blue sky and clouds." *Not anymore*, he meant by implication, and it was indeed awful that day, an ominous brown haze looming above its endless smokestacks and dreary tower blocks. If a world pandemic was going to emerge from anywhere, Wuhan seemed a likely spot.

There has been plenty of water under the bridge since then, as we all know only too well, with lockdowns, easing of restrictions, more lockdowns, Delta variants, Omicron variants, travel bans and the requirement of pricey tests to move about abroad (with who quite knows who pocketing large sums of cash, thank you very much). Yet, as I re-write this Afterword for the paperback edition, it is suitably the day after the British government scrapped almost all travel restrictions. Grant Shapps, the transport secretary, has declared that "Britain is open for business" and that 2022 is the year in which costly and fiddly rules on going abroad will be "firmly placed in the past".

Hurrah for that! Back to normal! Back to the possibility of jumping on a train and going just about anywhere you like one day soon with no Covid tests or fuss. Yet it's not all plain sailing quite yet. Again as I write, France requires fully vaccinated visitors to have proof of a negative PCR Covid test before entering, although Spain is allowing all such travellers to come freely. Meanwhile, unvaccinated travellers face ten-day quarantines in France and outright bans in Spain.

Just like everywhere, Spain has been hit hard by the disease with more than nine million cases to date and 92,000 deaths. Every area of life has been affected, especially tourism, recently referred to as "a motor of the Spanish economy" by the Spanish news agency EFE. This important industry unsurprisingly collapsed during the pandemic with income dropping from 12.4 per cent of Gross Domestic Product in 2019 to 5.5 per cent in the depths of the lockdowns, says EFE. Already, however, as Covid appears to wane and symptoms become milder, latest figures show monthly visitor numbers from abroad at three quarters of those in 2019.

To put things in perspective, Spain was the second most visited country in the world before the pandemic, behind France (with Britain topping arrivals figures). No wonder Spain's tourism minister Reyes Maroto seemed so pleased at news of the recent bounce-back in numbers, heralding the "recovery of international tourism" to great fanfare. Holidaymaking, as mentioned in the chapter on Benidorm, is now so embedded in the country, such a big deal, that what counts as *Spanish culture* in many parts, especially the sunniest coastlines, is how overseas visitors are entertained, courted and made to feel comfortable. *Tourism*, in other words.

The point of this book, aside from extolling the gentle joys of slow train travel in our usually (way too) fast-paced world, however, was to step away from Spain's regular haunts, letting its lesser-used regional trains open-up another vision of the complex country, seen from the tracks. Sure, plenty of famous (and occasionally infamous) spots made the route – Benidorm, Torremolinos, Santiago de Compostela, Pamplona, Madrid – but many a pleasure was to be had in the places in-between down the long, dusty, clattering tracks.

Yet as the pandemic plays out and visitors return to Spain, most of those coming back will do so by one means: planes. During the week of the busy upcoming half-term holidays in the UK, a staggering 1,330 flights will depart to Spain from Britain alone. The number of Eurostar trains from London to Paris a day right now? A mere nine, down from 19 pre-Covid – and it has been a torrid time for Eurostar, which almost went bust during the pandemic, saved only by big cash injections from shareholders while both the British and French governments turned their backs as they busily propped up airlines. This was, according to Mark Smith, founder of the first-rate train travel website seat61.com, an "appalling" act of "negligence".

He's right. But it is not all doom and gloom for trains versus planes when it comes to getting about in Europe. The message of the recent COP26 United Nations Climate Change Conference in Glasgow that urgent action must be taken to reduce global warming has undoubtedly increased the focus on train travel, and even given the (six times) greener way of getting about a dash of fashionability, with many now considering travel on a burgeoning number of sleeper services in Europe. "People are thinking: 'I shouldn't fly, I should take a train,'", says Smith. "That is making people think of trains for longer distances than they would [previously] have done."

Bravo! Or, perhaps more suitably here: *Olé!* Capturing the trains-over-planes mood, Greta Thunberg, the teenage Swedish environmental campaigner, said succinctly in a recent interview: "I don't need to fly to Thailand to be happy."

So maybe it's time to take a train to Spain instead… then catch a lot of slow trains round the wonderful country. See where the lines take you, sit back and enjoy the slow rides.

25 January 2022, Mortlake, London

NOTE: Shortly before this book went to press, Spain had some train news. Despite the coronavirus gloom, an announcement was made by French and Spanish authorities to re-open an old cross-border Pyrenean line that operated between 1928 and 1970. This 58-mile line from Pau in France through the Somport Tunnel to Canfranc in Aragon was closed after a horrific crash in March 1970 when a French freight train careered out of control at 100 kilometres an hour (62 miles an hour) into a wrought-iron bridge, destroying the structure; luckily no one died as the drivers managed to step off when the total brake failure was established. The plan now is to restore the extraordinarily vast station at Canfranc – nicknamed the "Titanic of the Mountains" when it opened, complete with 365 windows, 200-metre platforms and giant sheds allowing freight to be switched from standard gauge trains to Iberian gauge trains (the station and adjoining hotel are about ten times the size of St Pancras). Meanwhile, European Union cash is said to be in place to fix bridges and tracks. Of course, it does seem as though the coronavirus might throw a spanner in the works, but who knows? Maybe it will happen, maybe not. If it does, I intend to be on the first train across.

ACKNOWLEDGEMENTS

Many thanks to all those I met along the way who made my journey so enjoyable – many of whom advised me where to go, making the trip what it is, especially the Spanish station staff and conductors. Extra thanks, as ever, go to my parents Robert Chesshyre and Christine Doyle, as well as to Meg Chesshyre, Kate Chesshyre, Edward Chesshyre, Danny Kelly, Ben Clatworthy, Jamie Fox and Julia Brookes for their encouragement. Kasia Piotrowska put up with my tapas-fuelled updates and steered me through the writing. Also, many thanks to: Mark Palmer, travel editor of the *Daily Mail*; Hattie Sime, deputy travel editor of the *Daily Mail*; and Hugo Brown of the *Daily Mail*'s lively *Escape* travel section; as well as to Sarah Hartley, travel editor of *The Mail on Sunday*, who has offered great support, as has Glen Mutel of *National Geographic Traveller* and Liz Edwards of *The Times* and *The Sunday Times*. Thanks also to Helena Caletta and the staff of the Open Book in Richmond and to Stanfords maps and travel bookshop in Covent Garden. Claire Plimmer, editorial director at Summersdale, made this book possible and Sophie Martin, Chris Turton and Hannah Adams have been wonderfully supportive overseeing the book's production, while Debbie Chapman's input before going and during editing has been invaluable, as has Madeleine Stevens's sharp eye in the final edit. Dean Chant's tireless enthusiasm has been much appreciated for getting the word out. Many thanks to Hamish Braid for the excellent maps.

TRAINS TAKEN

1. Hammersmith to King's Cross – London Underground, 24 minutes, 6 miles
2. St Pancras International to Paris Gare du Nord – Eurostar, 2 hours and 17 minutes, 290 miles
3. Paris Gare du Nord to Paris Gare d'Austerlitz – Paris Métro, 13 minutes, 3 miles
4. Paris Gare d'Austerlitz to Toulouse – SNCF, 7 hours and 53 minutes, 413 miles
5. Toulouse to Figueres – Renfe/SNCF, 2 hours and 16 minutes, 145 miles
6. Figueres to Blanes – Rodalies de Catalunya, 1 hour and 25 minutes, 49 miles
7. Blanes to Barcelona – Rodalies de Catalunya, 1 hour and 27 minutes, 40 miles
8. Barcelona to Vilanova i la Geltrú – Rodalies de Catalunya, 1 hour and 8 minutes, 32 miles
9. Vilanova i la Geltrú to Bellvitge, Barcelona – Transports Metropolitans de Barcelona, 54 minutes, 27 miles
10. Bellvitge, Barcelona to Monistrol de Montserrat – Transports Metropolitans de Barcelona, 1 hour, 28 miles
11. Monistrol de Montserrat to Montserrat – Cremallera i Funiculars de Montserrat, 15 minutes, 3 miles
12. Montserrat to Monistrol de Montserrat – Cremallera i Funiculars de Montserrat, 15 minutes, 3 miles
13. Monistrol de Montserrat to Manresa – Transports Metropolitans de Barcelona, 37 minutes, 13 miles
14. Manresa to Lleida – Renfe, 1 hour and 57 minutes, 71 miles

15. Lleida to Zaragoza – Renfe, 43 minutes, 89 miles
16. Zaragoza to Huesca – Renfe, 51 minutes, 46 miles
17. Huesca to Zaragoza – Renfe, 1 hour and 10 minutes, 46 miles
18. Zaragoza to Pamplona – Renfe, 1 hour and 47 minutes, 109 miles
19. Pamplona to San Sebastián – Renfe, 1 hour and 44 minutes, 55 miles
20. San Sebastián to Bilbao – Euskotren, 2 hours and 10 minutes, 67 miles
21. Bilbao to Santander – Renfe Feve, 3 hours and 1 minute, 67 miles
22. Santander to Oviedo – Renfe Feve, 5 hours, 120 miles
23. Oviedo to Ferrol – Renfe Feve, 6 hours and 14 minutes, 157 miles
24. Ferrol to A Coruña – Renfe, 1 hour and 24 minutes, 30 miles
25. A Coruña to Santiago de Compostela – Renfe, 40 minutes, 40 miles
26. Santiago de Compostela to Ourense – Renfe, 38 minutes, 63 miles
27. Ourense to Zamora – Renfe, 3 hours and 12 minutes, 158 miles
28. Zamora to Segovia – Renfe, 1 hour and 2 minutes, 103 miles
29. Segovia to Madrid-Chamartín – Renfe, 1 hour and 53 minutes, 54 miles
30. Madrid-Chamartín to Tribunal – Metro, 13 minutes, 4 miles
31. Madrid-Atocha to Badajoz – Renfe, 5 hours and 18 minutes, 250 miles
32. Badajoz to Mérida – Renfe, 45 minutes, 39 miles
33. Mérida to Almadén – Renfe, 2 hours and 36 minutes, 135 miles
34. Mining Park of Almadén, 2 minutes, 400 metres
35. Almadén to Ciudad Real – Renfe, 2 hours, 61 miles
36. Ciudad Real to Alcázar de San Juan – Renfe, 1 hour and 6 minutes, 53 miles
37. Alcázar de San Juan to Aranjuez – Renfe, 47 minutes, 56 miles
38. Aranjuez to Cuenca – Renfe, 2 hours and 14 minutes, 91 miles
39. Cuenca to València – Renfe, 3 hours and 37 minutes, 127 miles
40. València to Alcoy – Renfe, 1 hour and 52 minutes, 65 miles
41. Alcoy to Xàtiva – Renfe, 1 hour and 14 minutes, 32 miles

42. Xàtiva to Alicante – Renfe, 59 minutes, 63 miles
43. Alicante to Benidorm – TRAM Metropolità d'Alacant, 1 hour and 19 minutes, 28 miles
44. Benidorm to Alicante – TRAM Metropolità d'Alacant, 1 hour and 16 minutes, 28 miles
45. Alicante to Murcia – Renfe, 1 hour and 19 minutes, 74 miles
46. Murcia to Águilas – Renfe, 1 hour and 55 minutes, 62 miles
47. Almería to Granada – Renfe, 2 hours 52 minutes, 100 miles
48. Granada to Antequera-Santa Ana – Renfe, 52 minutes, 63 miles
49. Antequera-Santa Ana to Málaga – Renfe, 28 minutes, 30 miles
50. Málaga to Torremolinos – Renfe, 18 minutes, 9 miles
51. Torremolinos to Málaga – Renfe, 18 minutes, 9 miles
52. Málaga to Bobadilla – Renfe, 52 minutes, 36 miles
53. Bobadilla to Algeciras – Renfe, 2 hours and 38 minutes, 104 miles
54. Algeciras to Ronda – Renfe, 1 hour and 25 minutes, 63 miles
55. Ronda to Bobadilla – Renfe, 53 minutes, 41 miles
56. Bobadilla to Seville – Renfe, 2 hours and 29 minutes, 86 miles

Total distance: 3,944 miles

Total distance in Spain: 3,137 miles

Total time spent on trains: 95 hours and 20 minutes (almost exactly four days: four times twenty-four hours)

Please note: distances and times are approximate.

No hospitality was taken for this book.

In some instances, names of those encountered during the train journeys for this book have been altered.

BIBLIOGRAPHY

Brenan, Gerald *South from Granada* (1957, Hamish Hamilton)

Cervantes Saavedra, Miguel de *Don Quixote* (translated by Rutherford, John; 2000, Penguin Books; first published by Juan de la Cuesta, 1604–5 and 1615)

Gardner, Nicky and Kries, Susanne *Europe by Rail: The Definitive Guide* (2017, Hidden Europe Publications)

Gilot, Françoise *Life with Picasso* (1990, Virago Press)

Hemingway, Ernest *Fiesta: The Sun Also Rises* (1927, Jonathan Cape)

Hemingway, Ernest *For Whom the Bell Tolls* (1941, Jonathan Cape)

Houellebecq, Michel *Lanzarote* (translated by Wynne, Frank; 2000, Vintage Books)

Howse, Christopher *The Train in Spain: Ten Great Journeys through the Interior* (2013, Bloomsbury)

Lee, Laurie *As I Walked Out One Midsummer Morning* (1969, André Deutsch)

Lewis, Norman *Voices of the Old Sea* (1984, Hamish Hamilton)

Morris, Jan *Spain* (1964, Faber & Faber)

Nooteboom, Cees *Roads to Santiago* (translated by Rilke, Ina; 2014, Vintage Books)

Orwell, George *Homage to Catalonia* (1938, Secker & Warburg)

Tremlett, Giles *Ghosts of Spain: Travels through a Country's Hidden Past* (2006, Faber & Faber)

Walker, Ted *In Spain* (1987, Secker & Warburg)

Have you enjoyed this book?

If so, why not write a review on your favourite website?

If you're interested in finding out more about our books, find us on Facebook at **Summersdale Publishers**, on Twitter at **@Summersdale** and on Instagram at **@summersdalebooks** and get in touch. We'd love to hear from you!

Thanks very much for buying this Summersdale book.

www.summersdale.com